POET IN SPAIN

Poet in Spain

FEDERICO GARCÍA LORCA

New Translations by

SARAH ARVIO

ALFRED · A · KNOPF

New York, 2017

THIS IS A BORZOI BOOK
PUBLISHED BY ALFRED A. KNOPF

Library of Congress Cataloging-in-Publication Data
Names: García Lorca, Federico, 1898–1936 author. | Arvio, Sarah, 1954–
translator. | García Lorca, Federico, 1898–1936. Poems. Selections.
English. | García Lorca, Federico, 1898–1936. Poems. Selections.
Title: Poet in Spain / by Federico García Lorca ;
new translations by Sarah Arvio.
Description: First edition. | New York : Alfred A. Knopf, 2017. |
Includes bibliographical references and index. | Description based
on print version record and CIP data provided by publisher;
resource not viewed.
Identifiers: LCCN 2016059642 (print) | LCCN 2017021123 (ebook) |
ISBN 9781524733117 (hardcover) | ISBN 9781524733124 (ebook)
Subjects: LCSH: García Lorca, Federico, 1898–1936—Translations
into English.
Classification: LCC PQ6613.A763 (ebook) | LCC PQ6613.A763 A2 2017
(print) | DDC 861/.62—dc23
LC record available at https://lccn.loc.gov/2016059642

Jacket image: Federico García Lorca by Daniel Vázquez Díaz
© 2017 Artists Rights Society (ARS), New York / VEGAP, Madrid.
Print: Universal History Archive / UIG / Bridgeman Images
Jacket design by Carol Devine Carson

Manufactured in the United States of America
First Edition

In memoriam

MARK STRAND

my lifelong friend and mentor

Contents

Poems

from Poem of the Cante Jondo

Three Cities · Tres ciudades

Gypsy Ballads

The Tamarit Diwan

Gacelas · Gacelas

Casidas · Casidas

Lament for Ignacio Sánchez Mejías

Dark Love Sonnets

Fragment of a dark love sonnet

Love poem to a young man

Blood Wedding

LAST SCENE · CUADRO ÚLTIMO

White room with arches and thick walls. · Habitación blanca con arcos y gruesos muros. 475

Introduction

FEDERICO GARCÍA LORCA was held to be a brilliant and extraordinary soul—a creative genius. He was beloved wherever he went, and he charmed and moved all with his gaiety, his songs, his poems and his plays. He was also somber, moody, worried. He suffered terribly. He had great fears—he was afraid of death. He had an unusual love of life, and this may have been why he so feared death. A profound feminist, humanist and socialist, he was also homosexual. His assassination—while still a young man at the height of his creative powers—became a literary cause célèbre.

The reason the world cares what happened to him is that he wrote—for us—something original, profoundly beautiful, lyrical and essential. His works have been translated all over the world. His plays are staged, his poems set to song, his lectures and letters read and read again. He memorably defined the concept of duende: "All that has black sounds has duende," he wrote, quoting the cantaor Manuel Torre. He went on, "The angel and the muse come from elsewhere . . . but the duende must be waked in the last rooms of the blood. You must toss out the angel and kick out the muse . . . the true struggle is with the duende." He was describing that implike indwelling spirit whose presence makes all the difference between artless art and true art. The word is an elision of *duen de casa*: master of the house. The usual expression is *tener duende*—to "have duende"—and this is indeed what Lorca had.

There are many moods in his poems: whispering, shouting, cajoling, pleading, loving, laughing, crying, wailing, dancing. But I hear two voices and see two landscapes.

There are the moonlit earthbound Spanish poems about love and death, and full of irony, whimsy, plain talk and exalted lyricism. And the land is of course Spain—the poplars, rivers, low hills and high sierra. They are full of the joy of expression; even the most painful image is exalting because the poet, as he speaks it, exults in his imaginative powers.

There are the New York poems: avant-garde, abstractionist, often surreal, and influenced by Lorca's love for Salvador Dalí, both as a man—a beloved—and as an artist. Their backdrop is skyscrapers, skies, the Hudson River. These are poems of alienation, protest, anger, intention; they are strident, they are full of raw and electric urban energy, and they have no irony. They are pained and darkly self-deprecating.* When he wrote these poems, he was also rebelling against Dalí's criticism of his madly successful Gypsy Ballads as folkloric and traditional. Luis Buñuel strongly agreed.

To my ear, these voices are so different they could almost be the voices of two different poets. Or, let's say they are at least as different from each other as any of Pessoa's heteronyms. Poet in New York has often been considered his masterpiece. American poets, in particular, have adored it. In my choice of poems for this book, I have wanted to give the Spanish voice, uninterrupted, a chance to contend for that position: "Poet in Spain."

Lorca hoped his readers would understand that his work—all his work—was new. He rankled against being called the "gypsy poet." As a poet of styles and forms, not only did he write in forms but he commented on these forms by using them. In this sense, he was postmodern. He studied traditional forms as a foundation for his work; he deepened and refined them, and also made them wilder and edgier. The Spanish poems, too, are full of surrealism—a wild, innate, local surrealism.

> Big San Cristóbal naked
> covered in skyblue tongues
> watches the girl playing
> a sweet absent flute
>
> Girl let me lift your skirt
> so I can see you down there
> Open in my ancient fingers
> the blue rose of your womb
>
> *Preciosa and the Wind*

* What I call the New York voice emerged a while before his arrival in that city, and continued for a time after he left—as expressed in the Odes and The Public, among several other radically avant-garde works. A year or so after returning to Spain, he went back to his Spanish voice.

I return again and again to a thought expressed by Federico's sister Isabel in her memoir. She describes his enactment of the mass—for the family's beloved housekeeper, Dolores, a Catholic believer—as simultaneously "parody" and "sympathy." He was both spoofing and believing. It seems to me that in all of the poet's literary enactments, he is both inside, sympathizing, and also looking in from outside, parodying. This may be a clue to his power of enchantment.

THE STORY of Lorca's life and death has been told and retold; there are wonderful biographies. And yet, the biography keeps shifting. His love life and the circumstances of his death have been the occasion for poems, novels, plays, music, dance and opera—not to mention the legal briefs, investigations and countless newspaper articles. Lorca is constantly in the Spanish news; he is a subject in himself, like the presidency or the economy or the weather. He may be a national obsession, an entire nation searching its soul. The country that killed its greatest poet must find out whom he loved and how he died and where his body lies. And the rest of the world listens in, relaying the stories from news service to news service.

There was a big adoring family. His father, Federico García Rodríguez, was a prosperous farmer, his mother, Vicenta Lorca, a well-read schoolteacher—the extended family included cooks, maids and farmhands. They lived, successively, in two paradisal villages on the Vega of Granada, and then two houses in town near the confluence of the rivers Darro and Genil. Later there was also a country house set in a lovely *huerta*—an orchard garden—called the Huerta de San Vicente. Federico was born in 1898 and had three younger siblings, his brother, Francisco, and his sisters, Concha and Isabel; they all, in their ways, carried on his legacy after his death.[*]

As a child, he fell in love with puppet theater, and from then on created his own dramas and spectacles, constructing sets, dressing up his friends and siblings to play parts. He did not do well in school; he seems

[*] The death of a baby brother, named Luis, may have given rise to his fascination with the death of young boys; see the fragment from Suites: "[And his eyes were]."

to have been unable to apply his mind to what didn't attract him. And yet, he became deeply knowledgeable about literature and art. He played the piano; he knew all the musical forms and had a vast repertoire—he could entertain for hour on hour. He was an enchanting raconteur. He also made many drawings—playful, pert, surprising, sometimes sad.

In his university years, Lorca lived at the now-famous Residencia de Estudiantes in Madrid, where he formed friendships with Dalí and Buñuel. There, and in years to come, he befriended the artists and intellectuals of the day: Rafael Alberti, Vicente Aleixandre, Jorge Guillén, Juan Ramón Jiménez, Antonio Machado, Luis Cernuda, Miguel Hernández, Pedro Salinas, to name the best known.

He wrote and wrote; he worked hard; and yet, since he had no profession, his father supported him—even covering the costs of his early editions. He was gratified when the Ballads sold thousands of copies, making him Spain's best-selling poet of all time. He was also crushed by Dalí's and Buñuel's rejection of this celebrated work on aesthetic grounds. He had hoped to join them in Paris but he changed his mind. He also learned, at around the same time, that the two of them had made a short film called *Un chien andalou* (An Andalusian Dog). He knew that they were making fun of him—that *he* was the dog—though Buñuel denied it. Hoping to escape from his suffering, in 1929 he traveled to New York on a ship, accompanying the renowned professor and liberal thinker Fernando de los Ríos, who was also a friend of his father's. He stopped in Cuba on the way home; the journey had lasted a year.

Not long after his return, he founded and directed La Barraca, a university theater that traveled around Spain, bringing the classics to the countryside and cities. He lived in Madrid on the calle Alcalá. He fell in love with the theater's manager, Rafael Rodríguez Rapún; this man seems to have been the love of his life.

Still a young man, Lorca was celebrated for his plays not only in Spain but also in Argentina, Uruguay, Mexico. He traveled to Buenos Aires and Montevideo, where great audiences cheered him. The plays made real money; he became independent of his father at last.

And then he was assassinated—at age thirty-eight, in Granada, during the late summer of 1936. He was whisked away by members of the fascist Falange that only days before had launched its offensive against the left-leaning Republican* government, marking the start of the Spanish Civil War. His death broke the hearts of his family and friends and shocked the world. Concha's husband, Manuel, his brother-in-law—the young new socialist mayor of Granada—was killed too, only a day or so before.

When asked about the poet's disappearance, General Franco declared that these were "natural accidents of war." During the fascist regime, which lasted forty years, it was unwise to utter Lorca's name in public. His works were first banned and later censored. Homosexuality was also severely criminalized.

Decades later, a man attested that he had buried Lorca in a gulch near an olive grove alongside three others, a teacher and two anarchist bullfighters. They had been shot just before dawn. This olive grove was not far from the Fuente Grande of Viznar—the Great Fountain, which was shaped like a teardrop and known as the Fountain of Tears. Another witness revealed that one of the killers had shouted "*rojo maricón*"—commie fag—as he pointed his gun at the poet and fired.

After long debate and litigation, the shared grave was dug up, and there was nothing there. Not a rag or a bone, not even a bullet shell—said the director of excavations. The ground had never been disturbed. Another burial site was identified: this, too, was dug up, and nothing.

In response to a letter of inquiry from a French writer, in 1965, almost thirty years after the poet's death, a police report was written. It never reached France and was not leaked to the Spanish press until 2015. The only known official documentation of the role of the government in the death of the poet, the report blatantly states that Lorca was killed because he was a Freemason,† a socialist and a homosexual. It mentions only one other victim, locating the place of execution as "two kilometers from the Fountain."

Other motives, including envy of his fame and his family's wealth, have been mooted. Recently, one writer suggested that some of the men who carried out the assassination were members of rival—and politically conservative—families on the Vega.

---

* Meaning "antimonarchist": not to be confused with the American political party.
† It also reveals that his masonic name was Homero—Homer.

One notices, reading the work, how often Lorca mentions death—and his own death. He seems to have had an uncanny—almost otherworldly—prescience about his destiny.

The distinguished art historian Juan Ramírez de Lucas died in 2010, leaving behind a letter and a love poem from Lorca.* Half Lorca's age at the time of their friendship, he had kept the affair hidden for over seventy years. A debate struck up: *who* was the beloved of the Dark Love Sonnets, Juan or Rafael?

These famous sonnets had been "lost" for almost fifty years. Lorca had read them to Pablo Neruda while soaking in a bathtub. After his death, Neruda asked around about them—hailing their greatness; no one seemed to know where they were.

AS A YOUNG MAN in his early twenties, Lorca and his friend the composer Manuel de Falla roamed the countryside, listening to gypsy cantaores and learning *cante*—their songs. Lorca and Falla were especially intrigued by authentic forms of cante jondo, a culture of song they feared would soon be lost. Together they organized a festival—the Concurso del Cante Jondo—inviting singers, some of whom came on foot through the fields to the Alhambra, in Granada. Preparing for the festival, Lorca gave his first public lecture. In it he proposed that cante jondo (deep song) was an old form of music that the gypsies had brought from India, and that it had merged with primitive forms of music already present in Spain, and later with the music and songs of Al-Andalus.

So cante jondo was a form of flamenco: the deepest. And, owing to its narrow melodic range and repetitive use of the same note, it gives the impression of *prosa cantada*: "sung prose"—that "breaks" the "metrical rhythm."

He also wrote his own Poem of the Cante Jondo. The four central poems of the sequence are named for forms of song: the spare, undu-

---

* Dashed off on the back of a bill from the Academia Orad—the school Juan was attending.

lant wail of the *saeta*, sung during Holy Week; the languid, piercing *soleá;* the arrhythmic trills of the somber and plaintive *petenera;* the raw and sorrowful lament of the *siguiriya*, commencing with a cry. All are improvisations, like American jazz. Lorca's Poem of the Cante Jondo might be seen as an improvisation *on,* rather than within, these rhythms. The poems don't scan—they don't reiterate the rhythms of flamenco in a way that's singable as that form; rather they reflect or suggest them.

Can we say that these poems are sung prose with broken rhythm? They have prose and singing, and the rhythm is continually broken— set in motion, and then broken. Is this different from a description of free verse? Some of these poems have edgy enjambments, *breaking* the line dramatically.

In Lorca's poem, the *siguiriya*, the *soleá* and the *petenera* are personified; each is both the song form and also a woman. All three forms—in fact, nearly all flamenco *palos*—can be sung solo, accompanied by one or several guitars, or a chorus of voices, or riffs of quick clapping and hand tapping; they can also be danced to the hard thrum of heels. The *saeta* is both the song form and an arrow. It is always sung solo—by one man or one woman who stops still in a crowd and opens the throat. "Flamenco Vignettes" is a paean to the cantaores of the *cafés cantantes* (singing cafés), and to the café life of lamps and mirrors; the poem "Conjury" evokes a Tarot card reading. "Three Cities" evokes the cities where they sang.

Cantaores now often sing Lorca's poems—a wonderful kind of poetic justice.

LORCA WROTE in sequences throughout his writing life. His first sequence was Suites, which he began before Poem of the Cante Jondo and returned to later on. These were short poems assembled in groups. Short lines, too—some lines were just one or two words. Lightly staccato rhythms. Haiku was then stylish, and Lorca was reaching for a contemplative, casual sound. These poems evoke the natural world— which is haiku-like. But Lorca's temperament is so different from that of the haiku makers. In the poems from Suites I like best, Lorca moves quickly into strong and sensual feeling. And yet, I sense that he would like the "three ideas about natural things at the core of Buddhist mysticism" evoked by Robert Hass in his opus on haiku: "that they are transient, that they are contingent, and that they suffer."

For a while Lorca spoke of publishing his suites; he arranged and rearranged them. Then, setting them aside again, he wrote Songs—and he plundered the suites for poems to fit into those new sequences. Now, when his works are produced as a whole, some poems appear in both Suites and Songs, and some are called "other poems from Suites" or "discarded poems from Suites"—letting us know that the manuscript was deconstructed and reassembled in different ways. Several of my favorites are from these categories: "other" and "discarded." The striking image, the deft lyricism, the repeating words and sounds, the rhythms moving toward chant, the fascination with death and desire—all these are aspects of the work to come. In Songs, too, I read the future. I'm thinking about "Andaluzas," which seem to be sketches for the Ballads; one is in octosyllabic ballad meter:

¿Quién mira dentro la torre	Who looks in the ornate
enjaeʒada, de Sevilla?	tower of Seville?
Cinco voces contestaban	Five voices answered
redondas como sortijas.	as round as rings

[My girl went to the sea]

Lorca was on his way to becoming a master of prosody. As early as Suites and Songs, he slipped easily between patterned and free verse.*
He was the ballet dancer doing modern: his body knew all the classical moves, and he could choose to use them or depart from them. He could write in rhythm or with casual flatness. His free verse may be something like the broken rhythm of cante jondo: a rhythm that starts and stops and starts again. His choice of formal strategy was never casual, or the

---

* In my section titled "Poems," "Delirium" and "[On the green sky]" are in hexasyllables, "Western Sky" in heptasyllables, and "Half Moon" in octosyllables, to cite some examples. Eventually, Lorca wrote naturally and easily in hexasyllables (6), heptasyllables (7), octosyllables (8), hendecasyllables (11), dodecasyllables (12) and alejandrinos—a fourteen-syllable form based on the twelve-syllable French alexandrine.

form may have inspired the content: Poem of the Cante Jondo is spoken flamenco, as Lorca suggested: the dance and landscape of gypsy life, with a wail echoing in the hills; the Gypsy Ballads are folk narratives, however wild and surreal; in the Persian/Arabic–inspired Tamarit Diwan, the gacelas and casidas are about erotic love, loss, death, grief, fatality; the Dark Love Sonnets are ravagingly felt poems of tormented love.

HE COMPOSED the Ballads in the Spanish tradition, calling his book the *Primer romancero gitano.* The title in English has never reflected the word *primer*—first. The "First Book of Gypsy Ballads": meaning that never before had there been a book of ballads devoted to gypsies—despite their many songs.

These passionate narratives are exquisite, daring and strange. They made Lorca famous; they also made him many enemies. The first line of the "Dreamwalking Ballad," *"Verde que te quiero verde"* ("Green I want you green"), is probably the most adored line of poetry in Spanish. If someone says the word "green," someone else chimes in, "I want you green." The opening line of "The Cheating Wife," *"Y que yo me la llevé al río,"* with its heavy beats on *yo* and *río* ("And I took her to the river"), is also one of those catching lines that people repeat to each other, taking pleasure in the rhythm.

Some of these ballads are narrated in a single voice; sometimes the narrator addresses the character; often the voice of the narration mingles with the voice of the character: creating a weave or texture of voices, heard, overheard, reading like a lament or an echo.

> Black sorrow wells up
> in the lands of the olive
> under the rustling leaves
> Soledad how you sorrow
> Such terrible sorrow
> You shed lemon-rind tears
> sour waiting sour mouth
> In sorrow I scurry
> through my house like a fiend

. . . .

I'm blackened by sorrow
my skin and my clothes

Ballad of the Black Sorrow

In Spanish, although the verse forms are syllabic, they also have rhythmic patterns—unlike our modern syllabic verse, which is intentionally arrhythmic. The form of the *romance*—the ballad—is a sixteen-syllable phrase broken into a couplet of two lines of eight, with the phrase sometimes reaching through a second couplet. The three stresses in each line form a dactylic-trochaic pattern, often with two stronger stresses—so that the music seems to swing across the line from side to side.*

There are gypsies in these ballads who don't match our notion that gypsies wear rags and travel in caravans. The gypsy nun embroiders and drinks lemon tea; Soledad has a kitchen and a bedroom; the marked man lies awake in Roman sheets. The gypsies of Andalusia belonged to a refined, ancient culture—the culture of the cante jondo. Some were wealthy aristocrats; some were poor. Notice the elegant shoes, "red as currants," worn by Antoñito el Camborio. In Granada, the gypsies lived in the cave houses of Sacromonte and in the Albaicín. However rich or poor, they were spurned and marginalized by the dominant Andalusian culture.

In "Ballad of the Spanish Civil Guard," Lorca describes the crushing oppression of the gypsies of Jerez de la Frontera, a town in southwestern Andalusia.

Hunched in the night
where they go they command
silence of dark rubber
and fear of fine sand

* Only one ballad departs from this pattern: "Burla of Don Pedro on Horseback." The form is experimental: an opening stanza (in hexasyllables), then three stanzas called "lagoons" (in free verse), interleaved by two called "segues" (in heptasyllables). The mood is different, too—more jauntily and artfully humorous than the other ballads, while at the same time describing a tragedy.

They go where they will
hiding in their heads
a blurred astronomy
of abstract guns

. . . .

. . . .

Up the steep streets
climb the evil capes
with scissors twirling
behind them as they come

The civil guardsmen are ever-present in the ballads: they guard the consul's house; they walk on with the judges after Juan Antonio de Montilla has been killed in a brawl; they pound at the door as the green girl leans on her railing, longing for her beloved; they've got Antoñito by the elbows and are marching him away . . .

Each of the three ballads of the gypsy archangels, Miguel, Rafael and Gabriel, is an homage to an Andalusian city: Granada, Cordoba and Seville. "San Miguel" presents the portrait of a fancy gay cleric, having a "tantrum / of nightingales and plumes."

San Miguel dressed in lace
in his tower chamber
shows his pretty thighs
smoothed by the lamps

. . . .

He sings in the windows
Ephebe of three thousand nights
reeking of cologne
and far from the flowers

In "San Rafael," boys on a riverbank ask the fish lovely lyrical questions. These boys undressing by the river—Tobias's students—could be the same boys in Thomas Eakins's *Swimming*, a homoerotic

American painting. "Merlins of the waist" provocatively describes the slim-waisted magic of young men.

> Inscrutable boys
> undress by the river
> students of Tobias
> and Merlins of the waist
> They bother the fish
> with ironic questions—
> do you want wine-flowers
> or half-moon leaps?

I'm also reminded of the young boys "wounded by water" who later inhabit The Tamarit Diwan.

"San Gabriel" suggests that Gabriel, who carries the lilies, is the father of the Christ child, whose mother is named Annunciation.

> San Gabriel: here I am
> with three nails of joy
> Your fire opens jasmines
> in my gleaming face
>
> .   .   .   .
>
> To Annunciation's surprise
> a child sings at her breast
> Three green-almond bullets
> quaver in his voice

In addition to this threesome of archangels, there's a female saint, Olalla (our Eulalia), who is associated with another Andalusian city, Mérida. She is tortured, maimed, mangled; her hands are cut off; her breasts are carried on a tray; her sex "quivers like a bird / caught in the brambles." The final three words read as chant: "Holy Holy Holy." The intense exaggeration of her martyrdom suggests ridicule. This saint is a woman whose sexual life is maimed.

"The Cheating Wife" is a celebration of adultery. She lies with her lover in a hole in the mud.

Not nard or snails
have such tender skin
nor does glass in moonlight
shine with such a glow

In "Ballad of the Black Sorrow," Soledad Montoya drags her long braids from room to room, in a minipanorama of frustrated sexual hunger and sorrow.

Ay my linen blouses
Ay my poppy thighs
Wash your body Soledad
with the water of larks

The tale of Tamar and Amnon, borrowed from the Old Testament, is an incestuous rape, and yet sublimely erotic.

Let me alone brother
your kisses on my back
are wasps and light winds
in two swarms of flutes

I sometimes wonder how closely these beloved ballads were read; they are full of radical iconoclasm: homosexual, feminist, anti-State, anti-religion. The descriptions of human desire, oppression and suffering are cloaked in a language so lovely that you hardly notice the social criticism, the compassion for oppressed people, the belief in sexual liberty. Note the poet's profound, almost joyful cynicism toward the traditions and taboos of Spanish society.

DURING THE EXHILARATING early months of La Barraca—this was 1931—Lorca wrote the play Blood Wedding, basing it on a story he had read in a newspaper: a girl, just married, flees her wedding with a former lover, and the husband and lover kill each other. This earthy Andalusian tragedy is the first in a trilogy of tragedies about—most of all about—the subjugation and disempowerment of

Spanish women by their families and husbands. The real-life events had occurred in rural Almería; site of the Alcazaba, a Moorish fort. Despite its modernist structure and lyrical intensity, the play may seem quaint and traditional—something like American local color. And yet, it strikes me that the chatteldom of women—their treatment as sexual property, a condition imposed through violence—is even now a fact of life in some parts of the world. A more recent newspaper story tells us that the woman who inspired the character of the bride lived the rest of her life in seclusion.

The play moves between spoken dialogue and song or chant or poem; the dialogue, too, often resembles poetry. The lines of poetry are full of foreboding, giving us something singable but not tellable. (And isn't this almost a definition of the poem?) Remarkably, each of these songs has a different prosodic structure, reminding us that the play Blood Wedding is also a great tragic poem.

Formal Spanish verse is divided into *arte mayor* (greater art) and *arte menor* (lesser art). Syllable counts of eight or less are *arte menor;* nine or more are *arte mayor.* The longer the line, the slower and more solemn. Humor, even dark humor, irony and song are often handled as *arte menor.* In Blood Wedding, the lullaby is in a verse form called the *romancillo*—little ballad—which is hexasyllabic. The short line with its three stresses gives a quick, cradling rhythm. But this lullaby is strangely troubling—not lulling:

> *Nana, niño, nana*   Lullaby—little boy—
> *del caballo grande*   of the great horse
> *que no quiso el agua.*   that didn't want water
>
>   *Act One, Scene Two*

It also turns out to be a newer, darker variant of a Granadan lullaby that Lorca quoted in a talk he gave about Spanish lullabies:

> *A la nana, nana, nana*   Lullaby lullaby
> *a la nanita de aquel*   lullaby of the boy
> *que llevó el caballo al agua*   who led his horse to water
> *y lo dejó sin beber.*   and didn't let him drink

The "wedding song" is in short mixed meters, repeating hypnotically: "may the bride awake" . . . "may she awake" . . . "with the green bouquet" . . . Moon speaks her terrible "moon song" in octosyllables, with four stresses. This isn't the singsong meter of the ballads; the rhythm is flatter and the tone darker.

> *La luna deja un cuchillo* The moon leaves a knife
> *abandonado en el aire,* waiting on the wind—
> *que siendo acecho de plomo* its leaden blade wants
> *quiere ser dolor de sangre.* to be the ache of blood.
>
> *Act Three, Scene One*

The Beggar answers Moon in slow, sober hendecasyllables.

> *Esa luna se va, y ellos se acercan.*
> *De aquí no pasan. El rumor del río*
> *apagará con el rumor de troncos*
> *el desgarrado vuelo de los gritos.*
>
> The moon goes and they come.
> Beyond here they will not pass.
> The murmuring river and the rustling trees
> will muffle the torn flight of screams.
>
> *Act Three, Scene One*

When Leonardo and the bride flee through the woods, again the desperate whispered disagreement is in quicker three-stress octosyllables.

> *Y cuando te vi de lejos* When I saw you from afar
> *me eché en los ojos arena.* I threw sand in my eyes.
> *Pero montaba a caballo* But I climbed on my horse
> *y el caballo iba a tu puerta.* and it went to your door.
>
> *Act Three, Scene One*

When the girls wind wool into skeins, they sing in a light patter of hexasyllables.

Heridas de cera,	Wounds of wax,
dolor de arrayán.	pain of myrtle.
Dormir la mañana,	Sleep in the morning,
de noche velar.	stay up all night.

Act Three, Last Scene

The mother-in-law's final "knife song" reads like flamenco jazz: with the refrain *"con un cuchillo, / con un cuchillito"* ("with a knife, / with a little knife").

THE LAST YEARS of Lorca's life were stunningly fecund. Around the time of Blood Wedding, he also began to write The Tamarit Diwan. Tamarit is the name of the *huerta* beside his family's own Huerta de San Vicente. A "diwan" (or "divan") is a collection of poems in Persian or Arabic, by one author—another kind of garden. But, since these poems are all about love and non-love, Lorca was *also* evoking the soft Persian couch by that name. I've chosen "diwan"—because it evokes first the book and then the couch, rather than the other way around.

The Diwan is also composed in many different measures: some poems are in free verse, some formal. Pained, intense, playful and full of longing, the moods seem to follow the line lengths.* Some of the Diwan's intrigue and fascination—its moody, fluctuating passion— arises from this pattern changing.

Lorca called the poems "gacelas" and "casidas," after the old forms.†
He had read the ghazals of the Persian poet Hafiz of Shiraz. In his paper

---

* The gacelas "Of Sudden Love" and "Of the Powerful Presence," for instance, are in plaintive hendeca- and dodecasyllables, and "Of Tormented Love" in octosyllabic couplets that carry the weight of their sixteen syllables. You can appreciate the much lighter feel of "Of Love with One Hundred Years," which is hexasyllabic with a refrain that drops one syllable each time it appears.

† *Gacela* and *casida* are Spanish spellings of the "ghazal" and the "qasida." An Arabic *ghazal* was a lyrical love text—in poetry *or* prose. The Arabic *qasida* was a long tripart poem on any theme, with an opening passage that praised the beloved, called the *nasib*. Later the *nasib*, splitting off from the rest of the *qasida*, became the short love poem called a *ghazal*. The Persian ghazal makes the Arab ghazal more intricate.

for the Concurso del Cante Jondo he called them *jondísimo*: meaning "very cante jondo!" and also "very deep!" He was enchanted, as well, by a book called *Poemas arábigoandaluces**—fresh, deep, imagistic works by Arabic poets of Al-Andalus, with their surprising depictions of homoerotic love. From these poems, Lorca borrowed the mood, the exquisite image, the bare emotionalism, and the love theme.

In secretive and interesting ways, Lorca adapted formal aspects of Arabic, Persian and Andalusian Arabic poetries. In an Arabic ghazal, all lines are divided in two by a caesura. In the first line, the final syllables of the two half lines rhyme, and the same rhyme repeats at the end of every line that follows. Internal rhymes also pick up and repeat. In Lorca's gacela "Of the Memory of Love," every line ends with an *o* rhyme. In the gacela "Of Sudden Love," a single varying rhyme repeats, both inside the lines and at the ends of lines: *vientre, dientes, frente, mientras, nieve, simientes,* leading up to the three-times-spoken *siempre*—and ending the poem with *muerte*.†

In a Persian ghazal, the end *phrases* of the first two half lines rhyme, creating a phrase-rhyme that weaves through the rest of the poem. There is also a form in Andalusian Arabic poetry called the *moaxaja*,‡ meaning "sash" or "belt"—in which the sash stanzas re-create the rhythms and rhymes of a saucy, colloquial love lament that serves as the final stanza.§ All through the Diwan, there are echoes—vestiges of these rhyming strategies. Words and phrases repeat and vary. Often, it is the opening line that repeats:

> Night does not want to come
> so that you will not come
> and I can't go
>
> But I will go
> · · · ·

* Rendered in Spanish by Emilio García Gómez, a dear friend of Lorca's who became a renowned scholar and translator of Arabic poetry.
† Groin, teeth, brow, [while], snow, seed, forever, ever, ever, death.
‡ García Gómez's Spanish transliteration of the Arabic term "muwashshah."
§ The *jarcha*—"kharja"—written in Mozarabic.

But you will come

.   .   .   .

Day does not want to come
so that you will not come
and I can't go

But I will go

.   .   .   .

But you will come

.   .   .   .

Of Tormented Love

—as though iterations of a not quite forgotten formal text.

Peter Cole tells us that the Arabic word *ghaᵹal* derives from the verb *ghaᵹala*, meaning "to spin," and—an instance of "linguistic slippage"—in traditional Arabic poetry, the word *ghaᵹal* assumed the associations of the gazelle. Most poignantly for Lorca, the gazelle and similar creatures—deer, hart, doe, and so on—were homoerotic images in the arabicized poetry of Spain: the masculine beloved. In Spanish, the word for the poem is *gaᵹal* or *gacela*—and the animal we call a gazelle is also called *gacela*. That same animal called *gacela* is also a beautiful woman—or let's say any beautiful beloved.

One of these creatures appears in the gacela "Of Love That Won't Be Seen":

Only to hear
the bell of the Vela
I tore up my Cartagena garden

Granada was a pink doe
among the weathervanes

Only to hear
the bell of the Vela

I burned in your body
not knowing whose it was

Lorca's gacelas are love lyrics—poems of intense homosexual desire:
difficult longing, racked desire, desolation.

No one understood the fragrance
dark magnolia of your groin
No one knew you martyred
love's hummingbird in your teeth

Of Sudden Love

One commentator suggested that this hummingbird (an exotic
American bird, not native to Spain) was a tongue in a girl's lips. It now
seems clear that this is a phallus in a man's. Lorca was expressing, in
hermetic language, his desire for men and disinterest in women. And
death as the game of erotic love, or erotic love as the game of death.
But also, the lover's rejection, and the taboo against homosexual love.
The love urge is mingled with the idea of death:

your body shunning me forever
in my mouth the blood of your veins
your mouth with no light for my death

Of Sudden Love

In the gacela "Of Wonderful Love," the beloved is called "a love
reed, a wet jasmine." For Lorca, reeds and jasmine flowers are akin to
erotic love. There are no grammatical indicators in the gacelas to show
the sex of the addressee—no gender-inflected adjectives. The beloved
is simply addressed as *tú* (the familiar you). He has also sublimated his
love for men into the figure of the boy—the dead boy, the boy wounded
by water—who is surely both the poet and the object of desire.

Lorca's casidas are about love, loss, passion, death—and again, the
boy wounded by water. But they are *not quite* love poems, with the pos-
sible exception of "Of the Hand That Can Never Be," in which all
desire for love, and for care, is subsumed in the caring (and absent)

hand that will help guide the poet through his death. This casida also shows us the dove that will later appear in "Gongoresque Sonnet in Which the Poet Sends His Love a Dove."

All the poems in the Diwan that mention females are tucked into the casidas. One speaks directly to the beloved: "Of the Woman Lying Down." It begins "*Verte desnuda . . .*"—"Seeing you naked . . ." The adjective is feminine: *desnuda*. Her naked body—the woman's—is called a "land with no reeds," and a "horizon with no future." In other words, *not* a wished-for beloved. The "love reed" is missing. There is no future in this, the poet is saying. The love for men and the rejection of the female body have been skillfully hidden.

ONE OF FEDERICO'S GREAT FRIENDS was the bullfighter Ignacio Sánchez Mejías—fatally gored in the ring in 1934, only two years before the poet's death. He was also a pilot, a modernist playwright, an adventurer, and a patron and friend of poets. How surprising that this man could have been a torero and also a patron of poets. And yet, the bullfight was considered both a sport and an art form of beauty and daring, as we learned from Hemingway, who was frequenting Spanish bullrings a few years before Ignacio's death.

The bullfighter's mistress was the flamboyant, dark-eyed flamenco singer known as La Argentinita. Federico had collected and arranged Spanish folk songs, and she sang his arrangements while he played the piano; a recording exists. To her Lorca dedicated his elegy—Lament for Ignacio Sánchez Mejías—and he gave her the manuscript. In Spanish the poem is called "*Llanto . . . ,*" which translates as "lament" or "elegy" but is also an everyday word for crying or sobbing. Unlike the Ballads and the Diwan, which depict stylized and figurative deaths, Lament is a heartbroken elegy for a loved friend.

Here, line lengths are mixed within parts of the poem. "The Goring and the Death" is in sober eleven-syllable lines interspersed with the reverberating nine-syllable lines of the refrain:

Eran las cinco de la tarde [refrain]	At five o'clock
¡Ay qué terribles cinco de la tarde!	Ay what terrible fives
¡Eran las cinco en todos los relojes!	it was five on all the clocks
¡Eran las cinco en sombra de la tarde!	In the afternoon shadows

Lament, Part 1

The bullring had already appeared in the Picassoesque casida "Of Dreaming in the Night Air," which offers surreal dislocations, jasmine flowers, and the bull as a "bloody dawn braying."

Part 2, "The Spilled Blood," uses an eight-syllable ballad line with a six-syllable refrain: "*¡Que no quiero verla!*" (I don't want to look); the alternating lines giving it a kind of hurried and breathless panic.

¡Que no quiero verla!	I don't want to look
Dile a la luna que venga,	Tell the moon to come
que no quiero ver la sangre	I don't want to behold
de Ignacio sobre la arena.	Ignacio's blood in the ring
. . . .	. . . .
¡Que no quiero verla!	I don't want to look
Que mi recuerdo se quema.	My memory is burning
¡Avisad a los jazmines	Tell the jasmine flowers
con su blancura pequeña!	so small and so white

Lament, Part 2

Part 3, "The Body Lies Here," uses the majestic, slow-paced fourteen-syllable *alejandrinos,* and part 4, "The Soul Is Gone," a combination of hendecasyllables and *alejandrinos,* to express grief and to pay tribute to a lost friend.

LORCA'S LAST POETIC SEQUENCE was Dark Love Sonnets, for many years thought to be irretrievably lost. The matter of why these sonnets did not reach the reading public is shrouded in history, and the displacements of war and tyranny. With certainty, we know only that they weren't published until long after the poet's death—as I said, almost fifty years. In an epilogue to the first Spanish edition of the "complete works,"* Vicente Aleixandre mourned their absence:

> He read me his *Dark Love Sonnets* . . . a pure, fiery monument to love, whose raw materials are the poet's flesh and heart and soul being ravaged. I was so amazed, all I could do was stare. I said, "Federico, your heart has loved and suffered so much!" He gazed back at me and smiled like a child . . . If these poems are *not* lost, this glory of Spanish poetry, this pleasure for generations to come . . . if the originals might be safe somewhere . . .

There are words and lines in these lushly stark poems that give away the harsh political and emotional context in which the love affair *and* the poems unfolded. References to death, danger and loss are rife.

> I want to kill the only witness
> to the assassination of my flowers
>
> *The Poet Speaks the Truth*

There is a sense of poignant and necessary secrecy:

> Ay secret cry of dark love—
>
> *[Ay secret cry of dark love—]*

A sense of the overwhelmingness of an intense love:

> this ache of one idea
> this torment of sky and world and hour
>
> *Wounds of Love*

* Lorca was not published in Francoist Spain until 1954, in a censored edition authorized, paradoxically, by Franco—in response to growing interest in the poet worldwide.

The sensation of being watched:

> People leap in the gardens
> looking for your body and my death
>> *Love Sleeps in the Poet's Chest*

The fear of persecution:

> Law that shakes the flesh and a star
> by now has entered my aching heart
>> *Love Sleeps in the Poet's Chest*

And again the same in the soul-stirring line,

> Ay dog at heart—hunted cry—
>> *[Ay secret cry of dark love—]*

—which says so much as well about love between men.

"The Poet Speaks with Love on the Telephone" amusingly evokes the notion of distance from the beloved. The voice is "muffled" and "distant": the fuzzy sound given by an early model of the telephone. A hotel phone, surely: you can still see these wood-lined booths in old European hotels. But the "distant" voice also reminds Lorca of the doe, that figure of the masculine beloved from the homoerotic poetics of Al-Andalus—beautifully counterpointing ancient and new:

> distant sweet and muffled voice

> Distant as the dark wounded doe
> sweet like a sob in a snowfall
> distant and sweet and in the marrow

The Spanish sonnet is Petrarchan—a form beloved in Spain since the Golden Age. Hendecasyllabic with five stresses, it matches our sonnet line of five feet. While emulating Quevedo, Góngora and Lope de Vega, Lorca wrote sonnets that are edgily—and sexily—personal in ways theirs aren't. Chatting with friends about his new work, he also invoked the sonnets of Shakespeare. He would have known of the English poet's amorous obsession with a younger man, and with the question of mortality. What has no precedent is the intensity, immediacy, sexual passion and fear that motivate these sonnets.

I have the sense that Lorca progresses, through the course of his short but prolific writing life, from playacting to real life. So that by the time he writes his Dark Love Sonnets, in the last year of his life, he has let the mask drop and bared his heart and being. But the mask didn't drop, did it, since the mask *is* the literary form.

There is only one male-designated addressee in the sonnets, revealed by the last word in the second line of "Love Sleeps in the Poet's Chest," whose title in Spanish is *"El amor duerme en el pecho del poeta"*:

> *Tú nunca entenderás lo que te quiero*
> *porque duermes en mí y estás dormido.*

> You'll never know how I love you
> because you sleep in me and are asleep

Dormido (asleep) is a masculine adjective that modifies "tú." And yet, it occurs to me that this "tú" may not be the particular *you* of a beloved, but rather *love* as *el amor*, *love* as Eros—announced in the title. When Dark Love Sonnets was published at last, this passage was taken as proof of Lorca's homosexuality; it may have been another subterfuge.

LORCA WAS A POET of flowers, colors, images—an image maker, finding brilliant and precise visual associations. The spikes of agave on the hillside are the claws of a cat. The wings of an angel are the blades of a knife. Two men entangled in a love embrace—the poet and his lover—are a *doble lira*, a double lyre, two lyres. Looking at images of the lyre, I see that, yes, it resembles the legs of a man. And at the same time makes music: lyrical music, lyricism.

The dove sent to the beloved is a *doble lirio*, a double lily: and you can see that the wings folded against the sides of the dove are like these two lilies, tucked close. The *lirio de Judea* (Judea lily)—may also be a tiny black Yehud coin from Persia on which two or three strokes, representing the stalk, petals and stamen of a lily, resemble a crucifix. Could Lorca, who was so intrigued by art and culture, have seen one of these rare coins?

As the moon scythes the water in "Half Moon," I see that the moon and the scythe have the same shape. And here is a visual game that becomes a synesthetic game, the two moons turning into two cymbals:

> Under the water
> the words carry on
> On the top of the water
> a round moon
> swims
> rousing the envy
> of the other
> high-up moon!—
> A boy on the shore
> looks at the moons
> —Play the cymbals!—
> he says to the night
>
> *Burla of Don Pedro on Horseback*

The wonderful homonym *cymbals/symbols* is an accident in English; the Spanish word for cymbals—*platillos*—doesn't offer that pun.

Red, green, purple, yellow: all these colors have a strong presence in Lorca's work. There is a bit of blue here and there: blue telegrams, the blue rose of Preciosa's womb, the immortal blue handkerchief of sky and death. Blue is rare. Orange appears only as the fruit. There are many blacks and some grays. But white is the color that seems to mean the most—quietly, this non-color or all-color color. White creates mood; black punctuates. White inhabits Lorca's poetic mind more than any other color. He creates an ambience of whiteness:

> and this sadness of white thread
> for sewing a hanky
>
> *This Is True*

I'm hunting bright stars

. . . .

The whole white night
in a bundle!

Woodcutter

The gypsy Christ's eyes are also white. White dresses, white lutes,
white hair, white shadows on La Petenera's purple sky. A white sheet.
Does white express longing, absence, death—and also erotic love?

There are many flowers, and most of them—by far the most—are
white. Nard, *nardo,* is a fleshy, creamy white flower on a long stalk, with
a penetrating fragrance, resembling a lily.* There are also many white
lilies, called either *lirio* or *azucena* by Lorca. The word *lirio,* lily, has a
lush beauty; *lirio* is also like *lira,* lyre. *Azucenas* are the white lilies that
Rafael brings to the Virgin. Lorca would have known, and felt, the lily
as a flower associated with religion, love and death.

Often, the white flower is near other white things, and they enhance
each other.

Whether a pale lily of whitewash
or a dove lashed to my heart

Of the Hand That Can Never Be

In the white infinite
of snow nard and salt

Juan Ramón Jiménez

There are also black lilies and red lilies. The black lily—*lirio negro*—
has a surprising dark power. A girl is compared to a red lily—*lirio rojo.*
There are *clavellinas,* serendipitously called "maiden pinks" in English.

The roses in Lorca's poems, though, are rarely white. They are the

---

* *Nardo* is *Polianthes tuberosa,* tuberose, from the family of the agaves. Some
translators have called it "spikenard," a medicinal flowering plant from the Hima-
layas. I have used "nard" or "white nard"—more evocative of the beautiful
flower.

dark roses blooming on the gypsy's shirt: blood roses. Or the blue rose of Preciosa's womb. The carnations are never white: they resonate with Antoñito's blood-drenched tie and his currant-red shoes.

All poets use color, and color carries resonance and association, altering and enhancing the atmosphere of a line or a stanza. But Lorca's colors are somehow denser or richer: as though he were writing with the palette of the Fauves or of Der Blaue Reiter. In "[That blond from Albacete]"—the love poem that Lorca's young friend Juan left behind in his papers—a green sunrise enhances the boy's wheaten hair. The poem then builds on these colors, offering yellow jasmine and the golden evening.

In Blood Wedding, Lorca describes the color scheme of his stage sets as though he were painting. He chose color to match or counterpoint the emotion of what was about to occur. The first room is yellow, the second pink, another in "gray whites and cold blues." Even decorations, costumes and props are color-designated. In the last scene, the room is white with "no shadows," and girls wearing blue dresses wind a skein of red yarn. The colors become starker as the tragedy deepens.

IT WAS A GREAT pleasure to work through these poems. I had tried translating Lorca once before, when I was young—it was slow going; I looked up many words in dictionaries; the results were unsatisfying, and stilted, and I gave up.

Now, after working as a translator for many years, and reading and writing a lot of poems, I tried again; this time, I wrote quickly, by ear: I listened for rhythms, and wrote down the lines in those same rhythms. The first draft was for tone, rhythm, and the movement and sound of the lines. I noticed patterns and stuck to them. Then I went back and worked over the meaning; there were words to study and reconsider, nuances to sort out, misunderstandings to revise.

Training my ear had to do with freeing something inside myself, a lyrical duende that allowed word sounds to move through me freely. There's also the matter of catching a gist when the sense of the line is unrepeatable or unreplaceable—when the words, translated one by one, don't make poetry. This calls for letting the mind roam until it finds a lyrically matching line.

Each time I finished a set, I read the poems aloud to Rigel García, a native Spanish speaker. He commented on them; he sometimes said I had not gotten the rhythm right, or had missed a meaning or dropped a line or a word; this was a crucial phase in the creation of these poems. He was a careful listener, reading the text in Spanish while I read aloud to him in English. We agreed to reject easy fixes and to avoid interpreting: to avoid making a complex poetic passage easier to understand in English than it might be in Spanish. Here and there, he had an idea for a word or phrase in English that I happily seized. More often, his insightful thinking turned me toward a new solution.

I've used almost no punctuation; this was my style of composition. I felt that punctuating, as I worked, hindered the flow of the language. When I was done it was too late to go back; the poems had their own integrity and didn't need commas and periods. So I let them stand. I was fascinated to see, studying the manuscripts, that Lorca often wrote his drafts with little or no punctuation: a stray period, a comma in the middle of a line, an exclamation mark. He added on punctuation later; manuscripts unpublished at the time of his death were punctuated by an editor.

I didn't imitate or replicate Lorca's prosodic strategies directly. I tried to *reflect* the poems—to catch their essence. Poetry is repetitive, by nature; repetitions create the patterns that give the language its beauty. So a formal or a free verse text can be made into poetry by enhancing consonance, assonance, internal rhyme, word repetitions, and rhythms—or even by reproducing the tone, another kind of pattern.

An occasional exoticism aside, Lorca wrote in the equivalent of our plain talk. He was rarely fancy; a recherché word like *japonizar* (to "japanize") in the poem "[Narcissus]" is an exception. He used everyday words, sometimes for intense and sublime effect. I have tried to follow his lead. This has meant avoiding Latinates; I've noticed that the plain-talk words in English are the monosyllabic words deriving from Anglo-Saxon.

When Romance-language poems are translated into English, the line looks and sounds shorter: since many English words are monosyllabic, English sentences have fewer syllables. I discovered that trying to match the syllabic count of the original by "padding" the English line with more syllables weakens the poetry. I came to expect that a line of eight syllables in Spanish—such as, for instance, in ballad meter—will round down to five or six in English, to give an example. This is an observation, not a formula. I noticed, translating the ballads, that I had created a two-stress line that sometimes stretched to three. I've understood my approach as accentual: hearing a stress count over a varying number of syllables. I'm analyzing with hindsight; I worked naturally, without counting, and gradually saw that I was working within identifiable rhythmic structures.

On another point, the ballad narrative shifts from present to past to future, adding to the unsettling, dream-wrought ambience. At first, I was tempted to fix those shifts, as though they were errors. I learned from W. S. Merwin, however, that time-shifting is a convention of the traditional Spanish ballads; in his translations, he avoided altering the tenses, and I've done the same.

For the sonnets, I tried not to push the lines into a fixed pattern, so as to keep the force and fluidity of the original. And I now see that my lines are variable, most often falling into eight or nine syllables with four- or five-stress lines. Although English and Spanish Petrarchan sonnets are structurally the same, this does *not* mean that a Spanish sonnet translates into an English sonnet—because, again, the Spanish tends to round down into fewer syllables.

I HAD THE PRIVILEGE of putting on a pair of white gloves and examining the manuscripts in the archive of the Fundación Federico García Lorca, in Madrid. I was struck, first of all, by their aliveness—their conveying of life. Most are on loose pages that are half the size of our usual pages, scribbled rapidly in blunt pencil—which must have been occasionally sharpened with a pencil knife—or sometimes in ink. Pale brown, pale blue, pale red almost pink, black so pale it is gray—a lot of water in the ink—with a very slim nib. And sometimes the writing is so small and so delicate that it can barely be read. Revisions are also sometimes in blunt, hurried pencil—these are the revisions that happened at the time of writing. Later revisions are almost always in ink. Titles changed or added later are in ink.

On the recto or verso, there is sometimes a small drawing, or several drawings—a face, a torso. Sometimes he writes a stanza and then turns the page upside down and writes another.

The paper is like what we call "recycled paper." It is thin and slightly gray, and the gray has begun to yellow. He did not write his drafts on fine bond.

So much can be understood about his writing method from looking. First of all, the rapid composition, headlong. Lorca wrote fast, as though trying to keep up with the speed of his thoughts. In the draft of "Dreamwalking Ballad," he has left a gap the space of four lines, with a little dot for each missing line. In the published poem, four verses fill those four empty lines. He knew that something else belonged there, musically, and he left room for it. Revisions have the same musical pattern as what they replace. If he scratched out a sound unit, he replaced it with another of the same sound pattern, but with different words and images.

He changes two lines, "*Pero qué tarde has venido*" (But how late you've come) and farther on, "*Pero yo no sé quién soy*" (But I don't know who I am) to the refrain "*Pero yo ya no soy yo*"—musically wonderful, with the stress falling on "*yo*," "*no*" and "*yo*" ("But I'm no longer me").

Sometimes he steps back from an overblown image. In the draft, this same stanza ends "Let me climb let me / to the green terrace / I want to paint her / with my red blood." In the published poem, it closes with "Let me climb let me / to the green terrace / Railing of moonlight / and the rushing water." Lorca holds back, to stronger effect. The blood has already appeared as dark roses on the wounded man's white shirt.

He also struck an arresting image—two stanzas—from "The Soleá" in Poem of the Cante Jondo. Now that I've read the passage, I can't forget it. Maybe he was wrong—this once.

> And feels that her desire
> has coiled around her neck
> like a red snake
>
> Startling she stands
> and goes to the grate—
> a wild cry rakes the sky

He replaced the two stanzas with one stanza:

> She thinks a tender sigh
> and a cry will vanish
> in the rush of the wind

I notice that both these struck images link a woman with the color red.

The most moving of all the manuscripts I saw is a draft of Dark Love Sonnets—the only draft in the poet's hand known to exist. The same thin, grayish paper: this time the letterhead of the Hotel Victoria, in Valencia; there are three sheets of long paper, which, folded, make a folio of four pages each. Three sonnets appear on the first and second of the three folios; on the third, there are four sonnets. All were rapidly written with a blunt pencil in the same hand—as though he had not paused from beginning to end. Several titles are added later, in black ink, again tiny, and with a fine nib. These are ten, and there's one more, bringing the sequence to eleven—"Sonnet of the Garland of Roses"—a clean copy transcribed by hand in pale black-brown ink on a large sheet of good white paper; this sonnet is placed first in the sequence, and thought to have been the first written.

Several of the poems are composed upside down—against the letterhead. The first side of the first folio has addresses written on it, in a different, larger hand. We know only that Lorca was in Valencia in November 1935, at around the time of their writing, with the actress Margarita Xirgu—his friend and theatrical ally. He was deeply in love; he wrote these ten superb sonnets to his absent beloved—Rafael—in a hotel room; my sense is that he wrote them without a pause, perhaps in one day or one weekend. The published text exactly matches the rough draft; no corrected text has been found.* The sonnets are impeccable, including a precise rhyme scheme—unusual for Lorca. The precision

---

* Neruda and others have said that Lorca was at work on the sonnets in spring and summer of 1936, in the months before his death; he toted them around in his pockets. Which means that a quite different version may have emerged. I find it hard to imagine what he could have done to enhance or correct these wonderful poems.

is astonishing, if these were written fast. Another possibility is that he composed the poems in his mind—as some poets do—before picking up the pencil.

The "Gongoresque Sonnet in Which the Poet Sends His Love a Dove" is a touch more mannered and ornate than the others. Lorca first wrote out the title "Gongoresque Sonnet in Which Federico Sends His Love a Dove." He then struck his own name and wrote "the Poet" above it—a revealing leap from anecdotal to universal.

Among the manuscripts is a pithy fragment that begins "Oh hotel bed oh this sweet bed." The page gives us the two quatrains of the octave. Though in a slightly different hand, and on Lorca's usual rough-draft paper, it matches the dark love sonnets in subject, style, meter and mood. No one knows, however, when or where it was written.

LORCA DIED in the fullness of life and love—and in the heady tumble of a literary life. Inconceivable is what he might have written had he lived to a great age. He was an utter perfectionist of language, and at the same time careless about his manuscripts. He often spoke of publishing; he was both ambitious and reluctant. He sent off his poems in sloppy handwriting to editors who asked for them, and then was vexed when the publications were thick with mistakes. A friend jokingly called him "pre-Gutenbergesque." He was also too busy writing poems and producing plays to bother.

He had published his set of travel vignettes, Impressions and Landscapes (1918), when barely twenty, and Book of Poems (1921) only three years later; he polished and polished his Poem of the Cante Jondo, which he wrote that same year for the Concurso, publishing it in 1931, ten years after its writing. In the meantime he had published his Songs in 1927, and Gypsy Ballads in 1928, before leaving for New York. He consented to the publication of a small set of the suites,[*] combined with a few other poems; it came out the winter before his assassination, with the title First Songs (1936).

* The full Suites, pieced together from various assemblages, was not published until 1983.

. . .

Several great works were unpublished at the time of his death. The Tamarit Diwan—with its charged but veiled references to homoerotic love—had been partly set in type in 1934. By then, Lorca was not as secretive about his preference for men. But the political mood was turning away from the open-spirited Republican cause—and fear of public disclosure may have been the reason he asked for the return of the manuscript and galleys. They were never returned; his sister Concha retrieved the pages after his death, and the family—she and her children, and her parents, Federico and Vicenta—took them to New York when they went into exile. Francisco and Isabel were already there, having shipped out together from Belgium, where he had served in the diplomatic corps for the now-defeated Republic.

None of the dark love sonnets had seen print. Lorca had asked his lover Rafael—the subject and addressee of the sonnets—to prepare a typescript. But Rafael died a year after Lorca was killed, and his home in Madrid was destroyed by a bomb; it is unlikely that a revised manuscript survived. Witnesses in the Republican camp said that Rafael had exposed himself to enemy fire; the date, August 19, was the one-year anniversary of Federico's death.

Before departing for New York, Federico's father collected all the manuscripts he could find and handed them over to a banker who had been friends with both the poet and his brother, Francisco. The banker stowed them in a vault in the Banco Urquijo—on calle Alcalá in Madrid, the very street where the poet had lived.

Sometime later a cousin made the rounds of the family's homes, gathering up objects of sentimental value—mementos, artworks, photographs—and packing them into suitcases. After traveling shipboard to New York, she handed them over to the García Lorca family, by then settled on Riverside Drive. There were surely manuscripts, too: at some point Francisco had, at his desk in New York, the three pencil-scribbled folios containing ten of the sonnets; or he may have had many more pages. We know that soon after reaching New York he published *Diván del Tamarit* in a Spanish-language literary review; this was the text that Concha had rescued. The selection included several unpublished pieces; among them a fair copy of the sonnet "The Poet Asks His Love to Write to Him,"[*] which had reached Francisco folded into a letter during the Civil War. What we don't know is why he published nothing else for many years.[†]

Following the death of their father—who had sworn never again to set foot in Spain—Isabel and Concha returned to Madrid with their mother. This was 1949, and Spain was in the grip of Francoist fascism. Francisco stayed behind, not returning until the late 1960s with his wife and his youngest daughter, Laura, bringing the papers that had lain in his desk for all those years.

It was Francisco who opened the vault at Banco Urquijo and launched the long process of sorting: there were hundreds of pages. Isabel helped out; as did Concha's son, Manolo,[‡] who recounts that he went to the bank every morning and picked up a pile of papers; in the evening he took them back to the bank. Caution was still necessary. A small group of scholars assembled, from Spain, France and Ireland.[§]

With the death of General Franco in 1975, Spanish fascism at last began to founder. Sadly, Francisco survived him by only a few months. Not long after, Isabel set up a foundation in the poet's honor, covering the cost with the sale of paintings that Dalí had given to Federico; the contents of the vault on calle Alcalá were the start of an archive. Serendipitously, the archive found a home in the Residencia de Estudiantes where Lorca, Dalí and Buñuel had formed their extraordinary friendship. Manolo visited Federico's friends and asked if they had poems, letters or drawings, passing the hat. The poet had been profligate in generosity, dedicating poems to friends and handing over the pages they were written on. The archive and opus grew.

Today the complete works make up four thick volumes: Poetry, Plays, Prose, and Early Writings.

[*] Called "Sonnet of the Letter" in a variant version.

[†] In 1955, he brought out an edition of Lorca's poems in English that included many of the finest poet-translators of the day, W. S. Merwin and Robert Bly among them.

[‡] Manuel Fernández-Montesinos, whose father had been the young Granadan mayor killed shortly before Federico. Manolo was five years old when members of the Civil Guard stormed into the Huerta looking for Federico.

[§] Ian Gibson, André Belamich and several others.

In December 1983, a small unsigned edition of Dark Love Sonnets, pocked with mistranscriptions and beautifully bound in red cloth, arrived in 250 Spanish mailboxes: a Christmas gift. It was postmarked Granada, with no return address. The Spanish literary community was thrilled and shocked. Where had these sonnets been? And who had published them?* Some people were indignant: why had these splendid and masterful love poems been kept from Lorca's readership for almost fifty years? It was suggested that the family had wanted to hide the fact of Lorca's intimate life—his homosexuality.

Soon after, the García Lorca family responded by issuing a "clean and legitimate text" in the widely read Madrid newspaper *ABC*.† In his postface, Manolo explained that a careful philological study of the full works of Lorca was under way; the sonnets would eventually have been published. But this pirated edition had forced their hand. He also acknowledged that it was surely one of the group of scholars who had leaked the text.

About five years later, an American scholar‡ published a provocative and influential essay about the reaction of the Spanish public to the publication of the lost Dark Love Sonnets. Many years afterward—in 2015—this same scholar revealed that an eminent French editor§ (and, in fact, a member of the group of scholars) had passed the sonnets—to *him*. And that *he*, in turn, and in total secrecy, had sent the text on to be printed in Spain. He had written the essay about the public's reaction with no mention of his own role in this elegant sleight of hand.

---

* "Sonnet of the Sweet Lament" made its way into the "complete works" as they appeared, first in Argentina and much later in Spain. In variant versions, this sonnet and the one published by Francisco, along with three others, popped up in a paperback edited by Hernández, as late as 1981. So five of the eleven sonnets had been seen; it was the whole set together that had so much astonishing power.

† The publisher, Luis María Anson, recalled that Neruda had urged him to find these sonnets and publish them.

‡ Daniel Eisenberg, a hispanist and literary activist against censorship and in defense of gay men—with a special interest in Lorca.

§ André Belamich, who had published *"Les sonnets de l'amour obscur"* in France in 1981. Significantly, the sonnets appeared in French *before* their publication in Spain. It seems that the mistranscriptions in the leaked Spanish text are related to a reading of the French translation.

Were the sonnets withheld? Three or four years after the poet's murder, a heartbroken father placed a huge cache of his papers in a bank vault, went into exile with his family, and died there. Three decades later, the poet's brother, returning home with his own cache of pages, opened the vault with the help of his sister and nephew. A group of scholars began to sort out pages for the first full edition, transcribing the handwritten scrawls. The work was painstaking and slow. Among the piles of manuscripts was a folder that contained the three folded sheets of hotel letterhead holding the ten pencil-written sonnets and, separately, one loose sheet of good bond paper holding the eleventh.

Francisco may have been hesitant about accepting or revealing his brother's homosexuality. He may have had trouble, there in New York, parsing out the pale pencil scrawls on those three thin folios. On his return to Spain, he would wisely have been unwilling to publish this sequence of radically passionate homosexual poems in a country where homosexuality had been brutally suppressed for decades.* Isabel and Manolo, taking over as custodians of the papers after his death, may have shared these feelings and thoughts. But nor had the family published anything else—in Spain. It might also be well to recall that the poet's name had been unutterable in public for decades. Manolo tells us in his memoir that the first Spanish homage to Federico García Lorca—a series of events celebrating his birthday—was held under strict military control and surveillance, each occasion limited to a maximum of thirty minutes. This was 1976.

No title was ever found written. Neruda and Aleixandre both remembered that Federico had called his sonnet sequence *"Los sonetos del amor oscuro."* When it appeared in *ABC* with the title *"Sonetos de amor"* (Love Sonnets) there was an outcry: what had happened to the word *oscuro*: dark? It was understood that "dark" meant something like "illicit" or "secret."

Someone said that all love was dark love—not only homosexual love—and that all amorous love sought secrecy and shadow.

Someone else argued that the love described in the poems was universal—meaning that it was *not only* homosexual love. These assertions are both true and also not true. In 1984, when the sonnets were

* Homosexuality was decriminalized in Spain in 1979.

published, the gay liberation movement was cresting in many parts of the world.

> You'll never know how I love you
> because you sleep in me and are asleep
> Weeping I hide you—haunted
> by a voice of penetrating steel
>
> Law that shakes the flesh and a star
> by now has entered my aching heart
> and disturbing words have bitten
> the wings of your stern self
>
> People leap in the gardens
> looking for your body and my death
> on horses of light with green manes
>
> But stay asleep—O my life—
> Hear the violins sing my shattered blood
> Do you see them watching us
>
> *Love Sleeps in the Poet's Chest*

Federico García Lorca had been revising these sonnets in the last days of his life, while in hiding. He was found; he was walked away into the dark morning and shot.

Poems

Claro de reloj

Me senté
en un claro del tiempo.
Era un remanso
de silencio,
de un blanco
silencio,
anillo formidable
donde los luceros
chocaban con los doce flotantes
números negros.

Cautiva

Por las ramas
indecisas
iba una doncella
que era la vida.
Por las ramas
indecisas.
Con un espejito
reflejaba el día
que era un resplandor
de su frente limpia.
Por las ramas
indecisas.
Sobre las tinieblas
andaba perdida,
llorando rocío,
del tiempo cautiva.
Por las ramas
indecisas.

Space in the Clock

I sat
in a space in time
It was a place
of silence
of white silence
a marvelous circle
where the stars
struck the twelve floating
black numbers

Caught

Among the wavering
branches
went a girl
who was life
Among the wavering
branches
With a little mirror
she caught the day
which shone
on her smooth forehead
Among the wavering
branches
she wandered lost
in the dark
Dew
streamed from her eyes
Caught by time
among the wavering
branches—

Puesta de canción
(Adolfo en 1921)

Después de todo

(la luna
abre su cola
de oro)

. . . Nada . . .

(la luna
cierra su cola
de plata.)

Lejos
una estrella
hiere al pavo real
del cielo.

Quinta página
Amanece

La cresta del día
asoma.
Cresta blanca
de un gallo de oro.

La cresta de mi risa
asoma.
Cresta de oro
de un gallo de sombra.

Songset

(Adolfo in 1921)

After all that

the moon spreads
its golden tail

. . . Nothing . . .

the moon folds
its silver tail

Far away
a star
wounds the peacock
of the sky

Fifth Page

Dawn

The crest of the day
rises
White crest
of a golden rooster

The crest of my laughter
rises
Golden crest
of a rooster of shadow

Total

La mano de la brisa
acaricia la cara del espacio
una vez
y otra vez.
Las estrellas entornan
sus párpados azules
una vez
y otra vez.

La selva de los relojes

Entré en la selva
de los relojes.

Frondas de tic-tac,
racimos de campanas
y bajo la hora múltiple,
constelaciones de péndulos.

Los lirios negros
de las horas muertas,
los lirios negros
de las horas niñas.
¡Todo igual!
¿Y el oro del amor?

Hay una hora tan sólo.
¡Una hora tan sólo!
¡La hora fría!

All

The hand of the wind
strokes the face of space
again
and again
The stars droop
their blue eyelids
again
and again

Forest of Clocks

I went into the forest
of clocks

Leaves of tick tock
clusters of bells
and under the multiple hour
constellations of pendulums

The black lilies
of the dead hours
and the black lilies
of the young hours
All are the same!
And the gold of love?

There is only one hour
Only one hour
The cold hour

Curva

Con un lirio en la mano
te dejo.
¡Amor de mi noche!
Y viudita de mi astro
te encuentro.

Domador de sombrías
mariposas,
sigo por mi camino.
Al cabo de mil años
me verás.
¡Amor de mi noche!
Por la vereda azul,
domador de sombrías
estrellas,
seguiré mi camino.
Hasta que el Universo
quepa en mi corazón.

Poniente

Sobre el cielo exquisito,
más allá del violado,
hay nubes desgarradas
como camelias grises,
y un deseo de alas
sobre las crestas frías.

Un ocaso teñido
de sombra como éste
dará una noche inmensa
sin brisa ni caminos.

Curve

I leave you with a lily
in your hand
Love of my night!
Little widow of my star
I have found you

Tamer of dark
butterflies
I go on my way
In a thousand years
you will see me again
Love of my night!
On the blue path
tamer of dark
stars
I will go on my way
Until the universe
fits in my heart

Western Sky

On an exquisite sky
beyond the violet
there are torn clouds
like gray camellias
And a longing for wings
over the cold crests

A sunset like this
tinged with shadows
announces a vast night
with no wind and no roads

Meditación primera y última

El Tiempo
tiene color de noche.
De una noche quieta.
Sobre lunas enormes,
la Eternidad
está fija en las doce.
Y el Tiempo se ha dormido
para siempre en su torre.
Nos engañan
todos los relojes.
El Tiempo tiene ya
horizontes.

[Una . . . dos . . . y tres]

Una . . . dos . . . y tres.
Sonó la hora en la selva.
El silencio
se llenó de burbujas
y un péndulo de oro
llevaba y traía
mi cara por el aire.
¡Sonó la hora en la selva!
Los relojes de bolsillo,
como bandadas de moscas,
iban y venían.

En mi corazón sonaba
el reloj sobredorado
de mi abuelita.

First and Last Meditation

Time
is the color of night
of a quiet night
On the great moons
Eternity
is stuck at twelve o'clock
And Time fell asleep
forever
in its tower
All the clocks
trick us
Time at last
has horizons.

[One . . . two . . . and three]

One . . . two . . . and three
The hour chimed in the forest
The silence
filled up with bubbles
and the golden pendulum
swung my face
back and forth through the air
The hour chimed in the forest!
Pocket watches
came and went
like flocks of flies

My grandmother's
gilded watch
was ticking in my heart

La hora esfinge

En tu jardín se abren
las estrellas malditas.
Nacemos bajo tus cuernos
y morimos.
¡Hora fría!
Pones un techo de piedra
a las mariposas líricas
y, sentada en el azul,
cortas alas
y límites.

Pan

¡Ved qué locura!
Los cuernos de Pan
se han vuelto alas
y como una mariposa
enorme
vuela por su selva
de fuego.
¡Ved qué locura!

Sphinx Hour

The cursed stars
bloom in your garden
We are born under your horns
and we die
Cold hour
You build a stone roof
over the lyrical butterflies
and sitting in the blue
you cut
wings
and limits.

The sphinx butterfly—*mariposa esfinge*—
is our death's head hawk moth. S.A.

Pan

How wild!
Pan's horns
have turned into wings
and like a great
butterfly
he flies over the forest
of fire
How wild!

Leñador

En el crepúsculo
yo caminaba.
"¿Dónde vas?", me decían.
"A cazar estrellas claras."
Y cuando las colinas
dormían, regresaba
con todas las estrellas
en la espalda.
¡Todo el haz
de la noche blanca!

Cazador

¡Alto pinar!
Cuatro palomas por el aire van.

Cuatro palomas
vuelan y tornan.
Llevan heridas
sus cuatro sombras.

¡Bajo pinar!
Cuatro palomas en la tierra están.

Woodcutter

I was out walking
at dusk
Where are you going
they said
I'm hunting bright stars
And when the hills fell asleep
I came back
with all the stars
on my back
The whole white night
in a bundle!

Hunter

High grove of pines
Four doves fly through the air

Four doves
fly and veer
drawing behind them
their four wounded shadows

Low grove of pines
Four doves on the ground

Cortaron tres árboles

a Ernesto Halffter

Eran tres.

(Vino el día con sus hachas.)

Eran dos.

(Alas rastreras de plata.)

Era uno.

Era ninguno.

(Se quedó desnuda el agua.)

Árboles

1919

¡Árboles!
¿Habéis sido flechas
Caídas del azul?
¿Qué terribles guerreros os lanzaron?
¿Han sido las estrellas?

Vuestras músicas vienen del alma de los pájaros,
De los ojos de Dios,
De la pasión perfecta.
¡Árboles!
¿Conocerán vuestras raíces toscas
Mi corazón en tierra?

They Cut Down Three Trees

for Ernesto Halffter

There were three.

(Day came with its axes.)

There were two.

(Silver wings touching the ground.)

There was one.

There were none.

(The water was naked.)

Trees

1919

Were you once arrows
falling from the sky
What terrible warriors shot you
Were they the stars

Your music comes from the souls of the birds
from the eyes of God
from the perfect passion
Trees
Have your rough roots found
my heart in the dirt

Caprichos

SOL

¡Sol!
¿Quién te llamó
sol?

A nadie le extrañaría,
digo yo,
ver en el cielo tres letras
en vez de tu cara
de oro.

PIRUETA

Si muriera el alfabeto
morirían todas las cosas.
Las palabras
son las alas.

La vida entera
depende
de cuatro letras.

[ÁRBOL]

Árbol.
La *ele* te da las hojas.

Luna.
La *u* te da el color.

Amor.
La *eme* te da los besos.

Capriccios

SUN

Sun—
who called you 'sun'

No one would be surprised
I think
to see three letters in the sky
instead of
your golden face

PIROUETTE

If the alphabet died
all things would be dead
Words
are wings

All of life
depends
on four letters

[TREE]

Tree
The *r* gives you leaves

Moon
The *oo* gives you color

Amor
The *m* gives you kisses

de Tres crepúsculos

a Conchita, mi hermana

I

La tarde está
arrepentida
porque sueña
con el mediodía.
(Árboles rojos y nubes
sobre las colinas.)
La tarde soltó su verde
cabellera lírica
y tiembla dulcemente
. . . le fastidia
ser tarde habiendo sido
mediodía.

II

¡Ahora empieza la tarde!
¿Por qué? ¿Por qué?
. . . Ahora mismo
he visto al día inclinarse
como un lirio.
La flor de la mañana
dobla el tallo
. . . ahora mismo . . .
La raíz de la tarde
surge de lo sombrío.

from Three Sunsets

for Conchita, my sister

I

The evening is
full of regret
because it's dreaming
of noon
(Red trees and clouds
on the hills)
The evening has shaken out
its lyrical
green hair
and now trembles sweetly
. . . it isn't happy
to be evening
having once been
noon

II

The evening starts now
why why
. . . Right now
I saw the day droop
like a lily
The flower of the morning
bends its stalk
. . . Right now
the root of the evening
soars up from the dark

Murió al amanecer

Noche de cuatro lunas
y un solo árbol,
con una sola sombra
y un solo pájaro.

Busco en mi carne las
huellas de tus labios.
El manantial besa al viento
sin tocarlo.

Llevo el No que me diste,
en la palma de la mano,
como un limón de cera
casi blanco.

Noche de cuatro lunas
y un solo árbol.
En la punta de una aguja,
está mi amor ¡girando!

He Died at Daybreak

Night of four moons
and only one tree
with only one shadow
and only one bird

I search my skin for
the mark of your lips
The water kisses the wind
without touching it

I have the No you gave me
in the palm of my hand
like a wax lemon
almost white

Night of four moons
and only one tree
On the point of a needle
my love spins—

Serenata
Homenaje a Lope de Vega

Por las orillas del río
se está la noche mojando
y en los pechos de Lolita
se mueren de amor los ramos.

Se mueren de amor los ramos.

La noche canta desnuda
sobre los puentes de marzo.
Lolita lava su cuerpo
con agua salobre y nardos.

Se mueren de amor los ramos.

La noche de anís y plata
relumbra por los tejados.
Plata de arroyos y espejos.
Anís de tus muslos blancos.

Se mueren de amor los ramos.

Serenade
Homage to Lope de Vega

Down on the riverbanks
the night is getting wet
and in Lolita's breasts
the branches die for love

The branches die for love

The night sings naked
on the March bridges
Lolita washes her body
with white nard and brine

The branches die for love

The anise and silver night
shines on the roofs
Silver of creeks and mirrors
Anise of your white thighs

The branches die for love

Madrigalillo

Cuatro granados
tiene tu huerto.

(Toma mi corazón
nuevo.)

Cuatro cipreses
tendrá tu huerto.

(Toma mi corazón
viejo.)

Sol y luna.
Luego . . .
¡ni corazón,
ni huerto!

Little Madrigal

Your orchard
has four pomegranate trees

(Take my new heart)

Your orchard
will have four cypresses

(Take my old heart)

Sun and moon
and then—
no heart
and no orchard

Huerto de marzo

Mi manzano,
tiene ya sombra y pájaros.

¡Qué brinco da mi sueño
de la luna al viento!

Mi manzano,
da a lo verde sus brazos.

¡Desde marzo, cómo veo
la frente blanca de enero!

Mi manzano . . .
(viento bajo).

Mi manzano . . .
(cielo alto).

March Orchard

My apple tree
already has a shadow and some birds

How my dream leaps
from the moon to the wind!

My apple tree
gives its arms to the green

In March
how does the white face of January
look to me—

My apple tree
(low wind)

My apple tree
(high sky)

Canción de noviembre y abril

El cielo nublado
pone mis ojos blancos.

Yo, para darles vida,
les acerco una flor
amarilla.

No consigo turbarlos.
Siguen yertos y blancos.

(Entre mis hombros vuela
mi alma dorada y plena.)

El cielo de abril
pone mis ojos de añil.

Yo, para darles alma,
les acerco una rosa
blanca.

No consigo infundir
lo blanco en el añil.

(Entre mis hombros vuela
mi alma impasible y ciega.)

Song of November and April

The cloudy sky
turns my eyes white

To bring them to life
I show them a yellow flower

I can't stir them up
they're white and stiff

Between my shoulders
flies my full golden soul

The April sky
turns my eyes indigo

To give them a soul
I show them a white rose

I can't seem to instill
white into indigo

Between my shoulders flies
my blind unfeeling soul

[¿Agua, dónde vas?]

Agua, ¿dónde vas?

Riyendo voy por el río
a las orillas del mar.

Mar, ¿adónde vas?

Río arriba voy buscando
fuente para descansar.

Chopo, y tú, ¿qué harás?

No quiero decirte nada.
Yo . . . ¡temblar!

¿Qué deseo, qué no deseo,
por el río y por la mar?

(Cuatro pájaros sin rumbo
en el alto chopo están.)

Media luna

La luna va por el agua.
¿Cómo está el cielo tranquilo?
Va segando lentamente
el temblor viejo del río
mientras que una rana joven
la toma por espejito.

[Water where do you go]

Water where do you go

—Down the river I go laughing
to the shores of the sea

Sea where do you go

—Up the river I go looking
for a place I can rest

Poplar what will you do

—I won't say a thing
I'm trembling

What do I wish what don't I wish
on the river and on the sea

Four birds with nowhere to go
in the tall poplar

Half Moon

The moon slides across the water
How can the sky be so calm?
Slowly the moon scythes
the river's old tremble
The young frog uses her
as a little mirror

[Narciso]

Narciso.
Tu olor.
Y el fondo del río.

Quiero quedarme a tu vera.
Flor del amor.
Narciso.

Por tus blancos ojos cruzan
ondas y peces dormidos.
Pájaros y mariposas
japonizan en los míos.

Tú diminuto y yo grande.
Flor del amor.
Narciso.

Las ranas, ¡qué listas son!
Pero no dejan tranquilo
el espejo en que se miran
tu delirio y mi delirio.

Narciso.
Mi dolor.
Y mi dolor mismo.

[Narcissus]

Narcissus
your scent
and the riverbottom

I want to stay on your riverbank
flower-of-love
narcissus

Through your white eyes swim
waves and sleeping fish
Birds and butterflies
japanize in mine

You small and me tall
flower-of-love
narcissus

The frogs are so quick
but they keep ruffling
the mirror where the eyes
of your delirium
and my delirium meet

Narcissus
my pain
my very same pain

Delirio

Disuelta la tarde
y en silencio el campo.

Los abejarucos
vuelan suspirando.

Los fondos deliran
azules y blancos.

El paisaje tiene
abiertos sus brazos.

¡Ay, Señor, Señor,
esto es demasiado!

Delirium

The day blurs
in the silent fields

Bee-eaters
sigh as they fly

The blue and white
distance
is delirious

The land has its arms
thrown wide

Ay lord lord
All this is too much

[Y sus ojos tuvieron]

. . . .

y sus ojos tuvieron
profundidad de siglos
mientras se le irisaba
la gran perla del pico.
Adiós, pájaro verde.
Ya estarás en el Limbo.
Visita de mi parte
a mi hermano Luisillo
en la pradera
con los mamoncillos.
¡Adiós, pájaro verde,
tan grande y tan chico!
¡Admirable quimera
del limón y el narciso!

[And his eyes were]

. . . .

And his eyes were
as deep as centuries
and the big pearl
of his beak was a rainbow
Goodbye
   green bird
By now you're in Limbo
Pay a visit for me
to little Luis
my brother
in the great meadow
of the suckling babes
Goodbye
   green bird
So big and so little
Wonderful chimera
of lemon and narcissus!

Limonar

Limonar.
Momento
de mi sueño.

Limonar.
Nido
de senos
amarillos.

Limonar.
Senos donde maman
las brisas del mar.

Limonar.
Naranjal desfallecido,
naranjal moribundo,
naranjal sin sangre.

Limonar.
Tú viste mi amor roto
por el hacha de un gesto.

Limonar,
mi amor niño, mi amor
sin báculo y sin rosa.

Limonar.

Lemon Grove

Lemon grove
moment
in a dream

Lemon grove
nest
of yellow breasts

Lemon grove
breasts where sea breezes
suckle

Lemon grove
orange grove dying and then dead
orange grove with no blood

Lemon grove
you saw my love slashed
by the axe of a glance

Lemon grove
my babyboy love
my love
with no solace and no rose

Lemon grove

[Sobre el cielo verde]

Sobre el cielo verde,
un lucero verde
¿qué ha de hacer, amor,
¡ay! sino perderse?

Las torres fundidas
con la niebla fría,
¿cómo han de mirarnos
con sus ventanitas?

Cien luceros verdes
sobre un cielo verde,
no ven a cien torres
blancas, en la nieve.

Y esta angustia mía
para hacerla viva,
he de decorarla
con rojas sonrisas.

[On the green sky]

On the green sky
one green star
what can it do—love—
—ay—but be lost—

The towers blur
in the cold fog
From the tiny windows
how can we be seen—

One hundred green stars
on a green sky
can't see a hundred
white towers in the snow

And to make my anguish
come alive
I have to decorate it
with red smiles

Horizonte

Sobre la verde bruma
se cae un sol sin rayos.

La ribera sombría
sueña al par que la barca
y la esquila inevitable
traba la melancolía

En mi alma de ayer
suena un tamborcillo
de plata.

Sirena

¡Qué claro está el horizonte!
¿Y esta tristeza?

(Si irá corriendo
conforme regresas.)

¡Cómo brilla el horizonte!
¿Y esta tristeza?

(Ven a mis brazos.
¿No ves
cómo se aleja?)

¡Oh qué llama de horizonte!
¿Y esta tristeza?

(Arde conmigo
y con ella.)

Horizon

On the green mist
a rayless sun shines

The shadowy shore
dreams along with the boat
and the inevitable bell
deepens the sadness

In my old soul
a small silver drum
beats

Siren

The horizon is radiant
and why the sadness

It will all rush away
when you return

The horizon gleams
and why the sadness

Come into my arms—
don't you see it rush away?

A flame on the horizon
and why the sadness

It's blazing in me
and in her

[Por encontrar un beso tuyo]

Por encontrar un beso tuyo,
¿qué daría yo?
¡Un beso errante de tu boca
muerta para el amor!

(Tierra de sombra
come mi boca.)

Por contemplar tus ojos negros,
¿qué daría yo?
¡Auroras de carbunclos irisados
abiertas frente a Dios!

(Las estrellas los cegaron
una mañana de mayo.)

Y por besar tus muslos castos,
¿qué daría yo?

(Cristal de rosa primitiva,
sedimento de sol.)

[To find a kiss of yours]

To find a kiss of yours
what would I give
A kiss that strayed from your lips
dead to love

My lips taste
the dirt of shadows

To gaze at your dark eyes
what would I give
Dawns of rainbow garnet
fanning open before God

The stars blinded them
one morning in May

And to kiss your pure thighs
what would I give
Raw rose crystal
sediment of the sun

Primer aniversario

La niña va por mi frente.
¡Oh, qué antiguo sentimiento!

¿De qué me sirve, pregunto,
la tinta, el papel y el verso?

Carne tuya me parece,
rojo lirio, junco fresco.

Morena de luna llena.
¿Qué quieres de mi deseo?

Segundo aniversario

La luna clava en el mar
un largo cuerno de luz.

Unicornio gris y verde,
estremecido pero extático.

El cielo flota sobre el aire
como una inmensa flor de loto.

(¡Oh, tú sola paseando
la última estancia de la noche!)

First Anniversary

The girl passes across my forehead
oh what an ancient feeling

What use to me I ask
are ink and paper and poems

To me your skin resembles
red lilies and fresh reeds

Dark-eyed girl of the full moon
What do you want from my desire

Second Anniversary

The moon gores the sea
with a long horn of light

Gray and green unicorn
shaking but ecstatic

The sky floats on the air
like a giant lotus flower

Oh you alone wandering
in the last room of the night

Malestar y noche

Abejaruco.
En tus árboles oscuros.
Noche de cielo balbuciente
y aire tartamudo.

Tres borrachos eternizan
sus gestos de vino y luto.
Los astros de plomo giran
sobre un pie.
        Abejaruco.
En tus árboles oscuros.

Dolor de sien oprimida
con guirnalda de minutos.
¿Y tu silencio? Los tres
borrachos cantan desnudos.
Pespunte de seda virgen
tu canción.
        Abejaruco.
Uco uco uco uco.
        Abejaruco.

Suffering and Night

Bee-eater
in your dark woods
Night of stammering sky
and stuttering wind

Three drunks eternalize
their antics of wine and grief
The leaden stars whirl
around a foot
                    Bee-eater
in your dark woods

Pain of an oppressed forehead
wearing a garland of minutes
And your silence—? The three
drunks sing naked
backstitching
    your song
    in virgin silk
                    Bee-eater
Eater eater eater
                    Bee-eater

Canción de la muerte pequeña

Prado mortal de lunas
y sangre bajo tierra.
Prado de sangre vieja.

Luz de ayer y mañana.
Cielo mortal de hierba.
Luz y noche de arena.

Me encontré con la Muerte.
Prado mortal de tierra.
Una muerte pequeña.

El perro en el tejado.
Sola mi mano izquierda
atravesaba montes sin fin
de flores secas.

Catedral de ceniza.
Luz y noche de arena.
Una muerte pequeña.

Una muerte y yo un hombre.
Un hombre solo, y ella
una muerte pequeña.

Prado mortal de lunas.
La nieve gime y tiembla
por detrás de la puerta.

Un hombre, ¿y qué? Lo dicho.
Un hombre solo y ella.
Prado, amor, luz y arena.

Song of the Little Death

Field of moons
with blood beneath the ground
field of old blood

Past light future light
sky of grass
light and night of sand

I met Death
field of dirt
a little death

The dog on the roof
my left hand all alone
crossed the endless hills
of dried flowers

Cathedral of ash
light and night of sand
a little death

A death—and me as a man—
a man alone
and a little death

Field of moons
the snow moans and trembles
behind the door

A man and what—all that was said—
a man alone and his death
field love light and sand

[El campo segado]

El campo segado
y la luna disuelta.

Por el aire van los sueños
de las semillas.

Espiga azul
y amapola blanca.

Mi alma,
una sola flor
delirante.

El campo segado
y la luna disuelta.

[The mown field]

The mown field
and a hazy moon

Through the air drift
the dreams of seeds

Spike of blue wheat
and white poppy

My soul
one delirious
flower

The mown field
and a hazy moon

Solitario
Zujaira

Sobre el pianísimo
del oro . . .
mi chopo
solo.

Sin un pájaro
armónico.

Sobre el pianísimo
del oro . . .

El río a sus pies
corre grave y hondo
bajo el pianísimo
del oro

Y yo con la tarde
sobre mis hombros
como un corderito
muerto por el lobo
bajo el pianísimo
del oro.

Alone
Zujaira

On the slow
gold

my poplar
all alone

not even
a singing bird

on the slow
gold

The river
below
runs deep
and solemn

under the slow
gold

and me
with the evening
on my shoulders
like a little lamb
killed by the wolf

under the slow
gold

Desde aquí

Decid a mis amigos
que he muerto.

El agua canta siempre
bajo el temblor del bosque.

Decid a mis amigos
que he muerto.
(¡Cómo ondulan los chopos
la gasa del sonido!)

Decid que me he quedado
con los ojos abiertos
y que cubría mi cara
el inmortal pañuelo
del azul.

¡Ah!
y que me fui sin pan a
mi lucero.

From Here

Tell my friends
I have died

Water always sings
under the trembling woods

Tell my friends
I have died

How the poplars
sway the silken sound—

Tell them my eyes
stayed open

that the immortal
blue handkerchief
covered my face

And ah!

that I went to my star
without bread

Omega
Poema para muertos

Las hierbas.

Yo me cortaré la mano derecha.
Espera.

Las hierbas.

Tengo un guante de mercurio y otro de seda.
Espera.

¡Las hierbas!

No solloces. Silencio. Que no nos sientan.
Espera.

¡Las hierbas!

Se cayeron las estatuas
al abrirse la gran puerta.

¡¡Las hierbaaas!!

Omega
Poem for the Dead

The grass

I will cut my right hand
Wait

The grass

I have a glove made of mercury
and another of silk
Wait

The grass—

Don't cry Silence Let them not hear us
Wait

The grass—

The statues fell down
when the great door opened

The gra-a-a-a-ss—

Poema de la feria

Bajo el sol de la tuba
pasa la Feria
suspirando a los viejos
pegasos cautivos.

La Feria
es una rueda.
Una rueda de luces
sobre la noche.

Los círculos concéntricos
del tiovivo llegan,
ondulando la atmósfera
hasta la luna

Y hay un niño que pierden
todos los poetas.
Y una caja de música
sobre la brisa.

Poem of the Fair

Under the tuba sun
there's a Fair
sighing to the old
captive Pegasuses

The Fair
is a wheel
A wheel of lights
in the night

The carousel's
concentric circles
ripple the air
as far as the moon

There's the child
that all the poets lose
There's a music box
playing in the wind

Otro sueño

1919

¡Una golondrina vuela
Hacia muy lejos! . . .

Hay floraciones de rocío
Sobre mi sueño,
Y mi corazón da vueltas,
Lleno de tedio,
Como un tiovivo en que la Muerte
Pasea a sus hijuelos.
¡Quisiera en estos árboles
Atar al tiempo
Con un cable de noche negra,
Y pintar luego
Con mi sangre las riberas
Pálidas de mis recuerdos!
¿Cuántos hijos tiene la Muerte?
¡Todos están en mi pecho!

¡Una golondrina viene
De muy lejos!

Another Dream

1919

A swallow goes flying
far away—

Dew blooms
in my dream
And my tired heart spins
like a carousel where Death's
children ride
I want to tie up time
in these trees
with a rope of black night
And later I will paint
the pale riverbanks of my memories
with my blood
How many children does Death have?
All are in my heart

A swallow comes flying
from far away—

Cancioncilla del niño que no nació

¡Me habéis dejado sobre una flor
de oscuros sollozos de agua!

El llanto que aprendí
se pondrá viejecito
arrastrando su cola
de suspiros y lágrimas.

Sin brazos, ¿cómo empujo
la puerta de la Luz?
Sirvieron a otro niño
de remos en su barca.

Yo dormía tranquilo.
¿Quien taladró mi sueño?
Mi madre tiene ya
la cabellera blanca.

¡Me habéis dejado sobre una flor
de oscuros sollozos de agua!

Little Song of the Boy Who Wasn't Born

You left me on a flower's
dark sobs of water

The cry that I learned
will grow old
dragging its tail
of sighs and tears

Without arms
how do I push open
the door of Light?

They served as oars
in another boy's boat

I was sleeping peacefully—
who pierced my dream?
Now my mother's
hair is white

You left me on a flower's
dark sobs of water

Dos lunas de tarde

1

a Laurita, amiga de mi hermana

La luna está muerta, muerta;
pero resucita en la primavera.

Cuando en la frente de los chopos
se rice el viento del Sur.

Cuando den nuestros corazones
su cosecha de suspiros.

Cuando se pongan los tejados
sus sombreritos de yerba.

La luna está muerta, muerta;
pero resucita en la primavera.

2

a Isabelita, mi hermana

La tarde canta
una *berceuse* a las naranjas.

Mi hermanita canta:
La tierra es una naranja.

La luna llorando dice:
Yo quiero ser una naranja.

No puede ser, hija mía,
aunque te pongas rosada.
Ni siquiera limoncito.
¡Qué lástima!

Two Evening Moons

I

for Laurita, my sister's friend

The moon is dead dead
—it will come back to life in the spring

when a south wind
ruffles the brow of the poplars

when our hearts yield
their harvest of sighs

when the roofs wear
their little grass hats

The moon is dead dead
—it will come back to life in the spring

2

for Isabelita, my sister

The evening sings a lullaby
to the oranges

My little sister sings
'the earth is an orange'

The moon weeping says
'I want to be an orange'

You can't be—my dear—
even if you turn pink
or a little bit lemon
How sad!

Nocturnos de la ventana

a la memoria de José de Ciria y Escalante. Poeta

1

Alta va la luna.
Bajo corre el viento.

(Mis largas miradas,
exploran el cielo.)

Luna sobre el agua.
Luna bajo el viento.

(Mis cortas miradas
exploran el suelo.)

Las voces de dos niñas
venían. Sin esfuerzo,
de la luna del agua,
me fui a la del cielo.

2

Un brazo de la noche
entra por mi ventana.

Un gran brazo moreno
con pulseras de agua.

Sobre un cristal azul
jugaba al río mi alma.

Los instantes heridos
por el reloj . . . pasaban.

Window Nocturnes

to the memory of José de Ciria y Escalante, Poet

1

High goes the moon
Low flows the wind

(My long gazes
searching the sky)

Moon on the water
Moon under the wind

(My short gazes
searching the ground)

Hearing the shouts
of two little girls
I flew—without trying—
from the moon of the water
to the moon of the sky

2

An arm of the night
comes through my window

A burly dark arm
wearing water bracelets

On the glassy blue
my soul played the river

The moments wounded
by the clock—went by—

3

Asomo la cabeza
por mi ventana, y veo
cómo quiere cortarla
la cuchilla del viento.

En esta guillotina
invisible, yo he puesto
las cabezas sin ojos
de todos mis deseos.

Y un olor de limón
llenó el instante inmenso,
mientras se convertía
en flor de gasa el viento.

4

Al estanque se le ha muerto
hoy una niña de agua.
Está fuera del estanque,
sobre el suelo amortajada.

De la cabeza a sus muslos
un pez la cruza, llamándola.
El viento le dice "niña"
mas no puede despertarla.

El estanque tiene suelta
su caballera de algas
y al aire sus grises tetas
estremecidas de ranas.

3

When I stick my head
out the window I see
how the blade of the wind
wants to cut it off

In this unseen
guillotine I have laid
the eyeless heads
of all my desires

And the smell of lemon
filled the vast moment
while the wind turned
into a silky flower

4

Today the pond
drowned a little girl
She lies beside it
shrouded on the ground

From her head to her thighs
a fish swims—crying out—
The wind says *little girl*
but she can't be waked

The pond keeps her weedy
hair hanging loose
In the air her gray teats
are quivering frogs

"Dios te salve" rezaremos
a Nuestra Señora de Agua
por la niña del estanque
muerta bajo las manzanas.

Yo luego pondré a su lado
dos pequeñas calabazas
para que se tenga a flote,
¡ay! sobre la mar salada.

Residencia de Estudiantes, 1923

God save you Let us pray
to Our Lady of the Water
for the little pond girl
dead beneath the apples

Later I will lay
two little pumpkins beside her
so that she can float
—ay!—on the salty sea

Residencia de Estudiantes, 1923

Tres retratos con sombra

Verlaine

La canción,
que nunca diré,
se ha dormido en mis labios.
La canción,
que nunca diré.

Sobre las madreselvas
había una luciérnaga,
y la luna picaba
con un rayo en el agua.

Entonces yo soñé,
la canción,
que nunca diré.

Canción llena de labios
y de cauces lejanos.

Canción llena de horas
perdidas en la sombra.

Canción de estrella viva
sobre un perpetuo día.

Three Portraits with Shadow

Verlaine

The song
I will never say
has fallen asleep on my lips
The song
I will never say

On the honeysuckle
there was a firefly
and the moon spiked
the water with a ray

And so I dreamed
the song
I will never say

Song full of lips
and distant riverbeds

Song full of hours
lost in the shadow

Song of a living star
in a perpetual day

BACO

Verde rumor intacto.
La higuera me tiende sus brazos.

Como una pantera, su sombra,
acecha mi lírica sombra.

La luna cuenta los perros.
Se equivoca y empieza de nuevo.

Ayer, mañana, negro y verde,
rondas mi cerco de laureles.

¿Quién te querría como yo,
se me cambiaras el corazón?

. . . Y la higuera me grita y avanza
terrible y multiplicada.

BACCHUS

Pristine green roar
The fig tree reaches out its arms

Its shadow like a panther
stalks my lyrical shadow

The moon counts the dogs
and miscounts and starts again

Yesterday tomorrow
black and green
you roam around my laurel trees

If you changed my heart
who would love you as I do

The fig tree yells at me
and takes a step—
fearsome and multiple

Juan Ramón Jiménez

En el blanco infinito,
nieve, nardo y salina,
perdió su fantasía.

El color blanco, anda,
sobre una muda alfombra
de plumas de paloma.

Sin ojos ni ademán,
inmóvil sufre un sueño.
Pero tiembla por dentro.

En el blanco infinito,
¡qué pura y larga herida
dejó su fantasía!

En el blanco infinito.
Nieve. Nardo. Salina.

VENUS
Así te vi

La joven muerta
en la concha de la cama,
desnuda de flor y brisa
surgía en la luz perenne.

Quedaba el mundo,
lirio de algodón y sombra,
asomado a los cristales
viendo el tránsito infinito.

La joven muerta,
surcaba el amor por dentro.
Entre la espuma de las sábanas
se perdía su cabellera.

Juan Ramón Jiménez

In the white infinite
of snow nard and salt
he lost his fantasy

The color white wanders
over a soundless carpet
of dove feathers

No eyes no expression
he does not stir as he dreams
but he trembles inside

In the white infinite
his fantasy left behind
a long pure wound

In the white infinite
of snow nard and salt

> VENUS
> *I saw you like this*

> The young dead girl rose
> from the shell of the bed
> nude of flowers and breezes
> in the everlasting light

> The world stayed on—
> lily of cotton and shadow
> looking out the window
> and watching her infinite transit

> The young dead girl
> cut a wake through the love inside her
> and shed her long hair
> in the foam of the sheets

Debussy

Mi sombra va silenciosa
por el agua de la acequia.

Por mi sombra están las ranas
privadas de las estrellas.

La sombra manda a mi cuerpo
reflejos de cosas quietas.

Mi sombra va como inmenso
cínife color violeta.

Cien grillos quieren dorar
la luz de la cañavera,

Una luz nace en mi pecho,
reflejado, de la acequia.

NARCISO

Niño.
¡Que te vas a caer al río!

En lo hondo hay una rosa
y en la rosa hay otro río.

¡Mira aquel pájaro! ¡Mira
aquel pájaro amarillo!

Se me han caído los ojos
dentro del agua.

¡Dios mío!
¡Que se resbala! ¡Muchacho!

. . . y en la rosa estoy yo mismo.

Cuando se perdió en el agua,
comprendí. Pero no explico.

Debussy

My shadow passes soundlessly
over the water of the ditch

Under my shadow the frogs
have no stars

The shadow sends my body
the gleam of quiet things

My shadow moves like a huge
violet-colored mosquito

A hundred crickets want to gild
the light in the reeds

Light leaps on my chest—
a gleam from the ditch

NARCISSUS

Boy
you'll fall in the river—

       In the deep pool there's a rose
       and in the rose another river

Look at that bird
look at that yellow bird

       My eyes fell
       into the water

Lord
he's falling—boy—

       and I am in the rose

When he was lost in the water
I understood But I can't explain

Andaluzas

a Miguel Pizarro (en la irregularidad
simétrica del Japón)

Canción de jinete
1860

En la luna negra
de los bandoleros,
cantan las espuelas.

Caballito negro.
¿Dónde llevas tu jinete muerto?

. . . Las duras espuelas
del bandido inmóvil
que perdió las riendas.

Caballito frío.
¡Qué perfume de flor de cuchillo!

En la luna negra,
sangraba el costado
de Sierra Morena.

Caballito negro.
¿Dónde llevas tu jinete muerto?

La noche espolea
sus negros ijares
clavándose estrellas.

Andaluzas

*for Miguel Pizarro (with the symmetrical
irregularity of the Japanese)*

Horseman's Song

1860

Under the bandits'
black moon
the spurs sing

Little black horse
where are you bearing
your dead rider

. . . The hard spurs
of the motionless bandit
who let go of his reins

Cold little horse
Ay scent of a knife-flower

Under the black moon
bled the flank
of the Sierra Morena

Little black horse
where are you bearing
your dead rider

The night spurs
the black flanks
nailing up the stars

Caballito frío.
¡Qué perfume de flor de cuchillo!

En la luna negra,
¡un grito! y el cuerno
largo de la hoguera.

Caballito negro.
¿Dónde llevas tu jinete muerto?

Adelina de paseo

La mar no tiene naranjas,
ni Sevilla tiene amor.
Morena, qué luz de fuego.
Préstame tu quitasol.

Me pondrá la cara verde
—zumo de lima y limón—.
Tus palabras—pececillos—
nadarán alrededor.

La mar no tiene naranjas.
Ay amor.
¡Ni Sevilla tiene amor!

Cold little horse
Ay scent of a knife-flower

Under the black moon
a shout and the long
horn of the bonfire

Little black horse
Where are you bearing
your dead rider

Adelina Out Walking

The sea has no oranges
Seville has no love
girl with dark hair
the gleam of a fire

Lend me your parasol
my face will turn green
—zest of lemon and lime—
and your words—little fishes—
will swim all around

Ay love
the sea has no oranges
Seville has no love

[Zarzamora con el tronco gris]

Zarzamora con el tronco gris,
dame un racimo para mí.

Sangre y espinas. Acercaté.
Si tú me quieres, yo te querré.

Deja tu fruto de verde y sombra
sobre mi lengua, zarzamora.

Qué largo abrazo te daría
en la penumbra de mis espinas.

Zarzamora, ¿dónde vas?
A buscar amores que tú no me das.

[Blackberry bush with gray bark]

Blackberry bush with gray bark
give me a cluster for me

Blood and thorns Come near
If you love me I love you

Blackberry—touch my tongue
with your pith of shadow and green

The long embrace I would give you
in the shade of my thorns

Blackberry where are you going?
To find the love you won't give

[Mi niña se fue a la mar]

Mi niña se fue a la mar,
a contar olas y chinas,
pero se encontró, de pronto,
con el río de Sevilla.

Entre adelfas y campanas
cinco barcos se mecían,
con los remos en el agua
y las velas en la brisa.

¿Quién mira dentro la torre
enjaezada, de Sevilla?
Cinco voces contestaban
redondas como sortijas.

El cielo monta gallardo
al río, de orilla a orilla.
En el aire sonrosado,
cinco anillos se mecían.

[My girl went to the sea]

My girl went to the sea
to count pebbles and waves
but on the way she met
the river of Seville

Amid bells and oleander
five boats swayed
with oars in the water
and sails in the wind

Who looks in the ornate
tower of Seville?
Five voices answered
as round as rings

The gallant sky climbs
over the river—bank to bank—
In the blushing air
swayed the five rings

Tarde

¿Estaba mi Lucía con los pies en el arroyo?

Tres álamos inmensos
y una estrella.

El silencio mordido
por las ranas, semeja
una gasa pintada
con lunaritos verdes.

En el río,
un árbol seco,
ha florecido en círculos
concéntricos.

Y he soñado sobre las aguas,
a la morenita de Granada.

Canción de jinete

Córdoba
Lejana y sola.

Jaca negra, luna grande,
y aceitunas de mi alforja.
Aunque sepa los caminos
yo nunca llegaré a Córdoba.

Por el llano, por el viento,
jaca negra, luna roja.

Evening

Did my Lucía have her feet in the creek?

Three great poplars
and a star

The silence nibbled
by the frogs is like
gauze painted
with little green dots

In the river
a dry tree
has flowered in concentric
circles

Leaning over the water
I dreamed
of the little dark-eyed girl
from Granada

Horseman's Song

Cordoba
far away and alone

Black mare great moon
and olives in my pouch
Though I know the roads
I will never reach Cordoba

Over the plains in the wind
black mare   red moon

La muerte me está mirando
desde las torres de Córdoba.

¡Ay qué camino tan largo!
¡Ay mi jaca valerosa!
¡Ay que la muerte me espera,
antes de llegar a Córdoba!

Córdoba.
Lejana y sola.

Es verdad

¡Ay qué trabajo me cuesta
quererte como te quiero!

Por tu amor me duele el aire,
el corazón
y el sombrero.

¿Quién me compraría a mí,
este cintillo que tengo
y esta tristeza de hilo
blanco, para hacer pañuelos?

¡Ay qué trabajo me cuesta
quererte como te quiero!

Death is watching me
from the Cordoba towers

Ay what a long way
Ay my valiant mare
Ay the death that awaits me
before I reach Cordoba

Cordoba
far away and alone

This Is True

Ay how hard it is
to love you as I do—

For your love the air hurts
and my heart
and my hat

Who would buy
my hatband from me
and this sadness of white thread
for sewing a hanky

Ay how hard it is
to love you as I do—

[Arbolé arbolé]

Arbolé arbolé
seco y verdé.

La niña del bello rostro
está cogiendo aceituna.
El viento, galán de torres,
la prende por la cintura.

Pasaron cuatro jinetes,
sobre jacas andaluzas
con trajes de azul y verdé,
con largas capas oscuras.

"Vente a Córdoba, muchacha."
La niña no los escucha.

Pasaron tres torerillos
delgaditos de cintura,
con trajes color naranja
y espadas de plata antigua.

"Vente a Sevilla, muchacha."
La niña no los escucha.

Cuando la tarde se puso
morada, con luz difusa,
pasó un joven que llevaba
rosas y mirtos de luna.

"Vente a Granada, muchacha."
Y la niña no lo escucha.

La niña de bello rostro
sigue cogiendo aceituna,

[Tree oh tree tree]

Tree oh tree tree
dry and so green

The girl with the sweet face
is gathering olives
The wind—lover of towers—
takes her by the waist

Four horsemen rode by
on Andalusian horses
in blue and green suits
and long dark capes

Come to Cordoba girl
The girl won't listen

Three toreros went by
with narrow waists
wearing orange suits
and swords of old silver

Come to Seville girl
The girl won't listen

When the evening became
a soft purple glow
a young man went by
with moon myrtle and roses

Come to Granada girl
But the girl won't listen

The girl with the sweet face
goes on gathering olives

con el brazo gris del viento
ceñido por la cintura.

Arbolé, arbolé
seco y verdé.

[Galán]

Galán,
galancillo.
En tu casa queman tomillo.

Ni que vayas, ni que vengas,
con llave cierro la puerta.

Con llave de plata fina.
Atada con una cinta.

En la cinta hay un letrero:
Mi corazón está lejos.

No des vueltas en mi calle.
¡Déjasela toda al aire!

Galán,
galancillo.
En tu casa queman tomillo.

The gray arm of the wind
tight around her waist

Tree oh tree tree
dry and so green

[Lover]

Lover—
lover boy
they burn thyme in your house

Whether you come or you go
I'll lock the door with a key

A key of fine silver
tied to a ribbon

On the ribbon a note
'my heart is far away'

Don't walk down my street
Leave it to the wind!

Lover—
lover boy
they burn thyme in your house

from Poem of the Cante Jondo

Poema de la siguiriya gitana

a Carlos Morla Vicuña

Paisaje

El campo
de olivos
se abre y se cierra
como un abanico.
Sobre el olivar
hay un cielo hundido
y una lluvia oscura
de luceros fríos.
Tiembla junco y penumbra
a la orilla del río.
Se riza el aire gris.
Los olivos
están cargados
de gritos.
Una bandada
de pájaros cautivos,
que mueven sus larguísimas
colas en lo sombrío.

Poem of the Gypsy Siguiriya

for Carlos Morla Vicuña

Landscape

An olive
orchard
spreads and folds
like a fan
Over the olive trees
a sunken sky
and a dark rain
of cold stars
On the riverbank
reed and shadow tremble
The gray air curls
The olive trees
are fraught
with cries—
A flock
of caught birds
swinging their long long
tails in the dark

La guitarra

Empieza el llanto
de la guitarra.
Se rompen las copas
de la madrugada.
Empieza el llanto
de la guitarra.
Es inútil
callarla.
Es imposible
callarla.
Llora monótona
como llora el agua,
como llora el viento
sobre la nevada.
Es imposible
callarla.
Llora por cosas
lejanas.
Arena del Sur caliente
que pide camelias blancas.
Llora flecha sin blanco,
la tarde sin mañana,
y el primero pájaro muerto
sobre la rama.
¡Oh guitarra!
Corazón malherido
por cinco espadas.

The Guitar

The guitar begins
to sob
The goblets of dawn
shatter
The guitar begins
to sob
There's no way to hush it
It can't be hushed
It sobs monotonously
the way water sobs
the way wind sobs
over the fallen snow
It can't be hushed
It sobs for distant things
hot sands of the south
asking for white camellias
It sobs
arrow with no target
afternoon with no morning
and the first dead bird
on the branch
O guitar!
heart slashed
by five swords

El grito

La elipse de un grito,
va de monte
a monte.

Desde los olivos,
será un arco iris negro
sobre la noche azul.

¡Ay!

Como un arco de viola,
el grito ha hecho vibrar
largas cuerdas del viento.

¡Ay!

(Las gentes de las cuevas
asoman sus velones.)

¡Ay!

El silencio

Oye, hijo mío, el silencio.
Es un silencio ondulado,
un silencio,
donde resbalan valles y ecos
y que inclina las frentes
hacia el suelo.

The Cry

The arc of a cry
goes from hill
to hill

Up from the olive trees
black rainbow
in the blue night

    Ay!

Like the bow of a viola
the cry has struck
the long chords of the wind

    Ay!

(The folks in the caves
lean out with their lanterns)

    Ay!

The Hush

Listen to the hush—my boy—
the undulant hush
where valleys and echoes drift
The hush
that tilts heads
toward the ground

El paso de la siguiriya

Entre mariposas negras,
va una muchacha morena
junto a una blanca serpiente
de niebla.

Tierra de luz,
cielo de tierra.

Va encadenada al temblor
de un ritmo que nunca llega;
tiene el corazón de plata
y un puñal en la diestra.

¿Adónde vas, siguiriya,
con un ritmo sin cabeza?
¿Qué luna recogerá
tu dolor de cal y adelfa?

Tierra de luz,
cielo de tierra.

Después de pasar

Los niños miran
un punto lejano.

Los candiles se apagan.
Unas muchachas ciegas
preguntan a la luna,
y por el aire ascienden
espirales de llanto.

Las montañas miran
un punto lejano.

The Siguiriya Goes By

Among the black butterflies
goes a girl with dark hair
beside a snake of white mist

Land of the light
sky of the land

She goes tied to the tremor
of a rhythm that won't arrive
She has a heart made of silver—
in her right hand a knife

Where are you going—siguiriya—
to a rhythm that has no head
What moon will rake up
your sorrow of oleander and whitewash

Land of the light
sky of the land

After She Goes By

Children are staring
at a distant spot

The oil lamps sputter out
Some blind girls
ask questions of the moon
and through the air rise
whorls of lament

The mountains are staring
at a distant spot

Y después

Los laberintos
que crea el tiempo,
se desvanecen.

(Sólo queda
el desierto.)

El corazón,
fuente del deseo,
se desvanece.

(Sólo queda
el desierto.)

La ilusión de la aurora
y los besos,
se desvanecen.

Sólo queda
el desierto.
Un ondulado
desierto.

And After That

The mazes
made by time
disappear

(Only the desert
stays)

The heart
source of desire
disappears

(Only the desert
stays)

The illusion
of dawn and kisses
disappears

(Only the desert
stays—
the undulant
desert)

Poema de la soleá

Tierra seca,
tierra quieta
de noches
inmensas.

(Viento en el olivar,
viento en la sierra.)

Tierra
vieja
del candil
y la pena.
Tierra
de las hondas cisternas.
Tierra
de la muerte sin ojos
y la flechas.

(Viento por los caminos.
Brisa en las alamedas.)

Poem of the Soleá

for Jorge Zalamea

Dry land
quiet land
of vast nights

(Wind in the olive trees
wind in the mountains)

Old
land
of oil lamps
and sorrow
Land
of deep wells
Land
of death with no eyes
and of arrows

(Wind on the paths
wind in the poplars)

Pueblo

Sobre el monte pelado
un calvario.
Agua clara
y olivos centenarios.
Por las callejas
hombres embozados,
y en las torres
veletas girando.
Eternamente
girando.
¡Oh pueblo perdido,
en la Andalucía del llanto!

Puñal

El puñal,
entra en el corazón,
como la reja del arado
en el yermo.

> *No.*
> *No me lo claves.*
> *No.*

El puñal,
como un rayo de sol,
incendia las terribles
hondanadas.

> *No.*
> *No me lo claves.*
> *No.*

Andalusia

On the bare hill
three crosses
Clear water
and ancient olive trees
In the alleys
men shrouded
to the eyes
On the towers
weathervanes whirl—
whirling forever
Oh lost people
Andalusia of tears

Knife

The knife
plows the heart
the way the blade of the plow
strikes the barren field

     No
Do not stick it in me
     No

The knife
burns like a ray of sun
in the terrible
gullies

     No
Do not stick it in me
     No

Encrucijada

Viento del este;
un farol
y el puñal
en el corazón.
La calle
tiene un temblor
de cuerda
en tensión,
un temblor
de enorme moscardón.
Por todas partes
yo
veo el puñal
en el corazón.

Crossroads

An east wind
a streetlamp
and the knife
in his heart
The street
trembles
like a taut
rope
or a huge horsefly
Everywhere I look
I see
the knife
in his heart

¡Ay!

El grito deja en el viento
una sombra de ciprés.

(Dejadme en este campo
llorando.)

Todo se ha roto en el mundo.
No queda más que el silencio.

(Dejadme en este campo
llorando.)

El horizonte sin luz
está mordido de hogueras.

(Ya os he dicho que me dejéis
en este campo
llorando.)

Ay!

On the wind
a shout lays the shadow
of a cypress

(Leave me in this field
crying)

The whole world is broken
Only silence is left

(Leave me in this field
crying)

The dark horizon
is bitten by bonfires

(I told you to leave me
in this field
crying)

Sorpresa

Muerto se quedó en la calle
con un puñal en el pecho.
No lo conocía nadie.
¡Cómo temblaba el farol!
Madre.
¡Cómo temblaba el farolito
de la calle!
Era madrugada. Nadie
pudo asomarse a sus ojos
abiertos al duro aire.
Que muerto se quedó en la calle
que con un puñal en el pecho
y que no lo conocía nadie.

La soleá

Vestida con mantos negros
piensa que el mundo es chiquito
y el corazón es inmenso.

Vestida con mantos negros.

Piensa que el suspiro tierno
y el grito, desaparecen
en la corriente del viento.

Vestida con mantos negros.

Se dejó el balcón abierto
y al alba por el balcón
desembocó todo el cielo.

¡Ay yayayayay,
que vestida con mantos negros!

Surprise

He lay dead in the street
with the knife in his heart
No one knew him
How the streetlamp trembled
Mama—
How the little lamp trembled
in the street
It was dawn No one
could look in his eyes
open wide in the hard air
I said he lay dead in the street
with the knife in his chest
and that no one knew him

The Soleá

Dressed in black robes
she thinks the world is small
and the heart is vast

Dressed in black robes

She thinks a tender sigh
and a cry will vanish
in the rush of the wind

Dressed in black robes

No one shut the balcony
and at dawn
all the sky
poured through it

Ay ay ay!
Dressed in black robes

Cueva

De la cueva salen
largos sollozos.

(Lo cárdeno
sobre lo rojo.)

El gitano evoca
países remotos.

(Torres altas y hombres
misteriosos.)

En la voz entrecortada
van sus ojos.

(Lo negro
sobre lo rojo.)

Y la cueva encalada
tiembla en el oro.

(Lo blanco
sobre lo rojo.)

Cave

From the cave rise
long sobs

(purple on red)

The gypsy dreams
of distant lands

Tall towers and
strange men

His eyes move
with his halting voice

(black on red)

The whitewashed cave
trembles
in the gold

(white on red)

Encuentro

Ni tú ni yo estamos
en disposición
de encontrarnos.
Tú . . . por lo que ya sabes.
¡Yo la he querido tanto!
Sigue esa veredita.
En las manos,
tengo los agujeros
de los clavos.
¿No ves cómo me estoy
desangrando?
No mires nunca atrás,
vete despacio
y reza como yo
a San Cayetano,
que ni tú ni yo estamos
en disposición
de encontrarnos.

Meeting

We can't meet
you and I
And you know the reason
I have loved her so much!
Go on down that path
There are holes
in my hands
from the nails
Don't you see me
bleeding
Don't ever look back
go on slowly
and pray as I do
to San Cayetano
for you and I
can't meet

Alba

Campanas de Córdoba
en la madrugada.
Campanas de amanecer
en Granada.
Os sienten todas las muchachas
que lloran a la tierna
soleá enlutada.
Las muchachas
de Andalucía la alta
y la baja.
Las niñas de España,
de pie menudo
y temblorosas faldas,
que han llenado de luces
las encrucijadas.
¡Oh, campanas de Córdoba
en la madrugada,
y oh, campanas de amanecer
en Granada!

Dawn

Bells of Cordoba
in the deep hours
Bells of the dawn
in Granada—
heard by all those girls
weeping to the tender
mournful soleá
Girls from High
and Low
Andalusia
Girls from Spain
with slight feet
and tremulous skirts
who have strewn the crossroads
with lights
O bells of Cordoba
in the deep hours
O bells of the dawn
in Granada—

Poema de la saeta

a Francisco Iglesias

Arqueros

Los arqueros oscuros
a Sevilla se acercan.

Guadalquivir abierto.

Anchos sombreros grises,
largas capas lentas.

¡Ay, Guadalquivir!

Vienen de los remotos
países de la pena.

Guadalquivir abierto.

Y van a un laberinto.
Amor, cristal y piedra.

¡Ay, Guadalquivir!

Poem of the Saeta

Archers

The dark archers
approach Seville

The wide Guadalquivir

Broad gray hats
long slow capes

Ay—Guadalquivir—

They come from the distant
countries of sorrow

The wide Guadalquivir

They enter the maze
Love glass and stone

Ay—Guadalquivir—

Noche

Cirio, candil,
farol y luciérnaga.

La constelación
de la saeta.

Ventanitas de oro
tiemblan,
y en la aurora se mecen
cruces superpuestas.

Cirio, candil,
farol y luciérnaga.

Night

Candle lantern
streetlamp firefly

Constellation
of the saeta—

Little gold windows
flicker
and at dawn
the crosses
crisscross
swaying

Candle lantern
streetlamp firefly

Sevilla

Sevilla es una torre
llena de arqueros finos.

Sevilla para herir.
Córdoba para morir.

Una ciudad que acecha
largos ritmos,
y los enrosca
como laberintos.
Como tallos de parra
encendidos.

¡Sevilla para herir!

Bajo el arco del cielo,
sobre su llano limpio,
dispara la constante
saeta de su río.

¡Córdoba para morir!

Y loca de horizonte
mezcla en su vino,
lo amargo de Don Juan
y lo perfecto de Dionisio.

Sevilla para herir.
¡Siempre Sevilla para herir!

Seville

Seville is a tower
full of fine archers

Wounded in Seville
Dead in Cordoba

A city that waits
for long rhythms
and coils them
like labyrinths or
vinestalks
flaming

Wounded in Seville

Under the arched sky
on the bare plain
she shoots the steady
arrow of her river

Dead in Cordoba

Crazed by horizons
her wine is a mix
of bitter Don Juan
and perfect Dionysius

Wounded in Seville
Forever wounded in Seville

Procesión

Por la calleja vienen
extraños unicornios.
¿De qué campo,
de qué bosque mitológico?
Más cerca,
ya parecen astrónomos.
Fantásticos Merlines
y el Ecce Homo,
Durandarte encantado,
Orlando furioso.

Paso

Virgen con miriñaque,
Virgen de la Soledad,
abierta como un inmenso
tulipán.
En tu barco de luces
vas
por la alta marea
de la ciudad,
entre saetas turbias
y estrellas de cristal.
Virgen con miriñaque
tú vas
por el río de la calle,
¡hasta el mar!

Procession

Up the alley come
strange unicorns
From what field
—what mythical forest
At close range
they look like astronomers
fabulous Merlins
and the Ecce Homo
enchanted Durandal
and Orlando Furioso

Float

Virgin in a crinoline
virgin of Loneliness
as open as a vast
tulip
In your ship of lights
you float
on the city's
high tide
amid the swirl of saetas
and the glass stars
Virgin in a crinoline
you float
down the river of the street
to the sea

Saeta

Cristo moreno
pasa
de lirio de Judea
a clavel de España.

¡Miradlo por dónde viene!

De España.
Cielo limpio y oscuro,
tierra tostada,
y cauces donde corre
muy lenta el agua.
Cristo moreno,
con las guedejas quemadas,
los pómulos salientes
y las pupilas blancas.

¡Miradlo por dónde va!

Saeta

Gypsy Christ
changes
from Judea lily
into Spanish carnation

Look where he comes from—

Spain
Clear dark sky
scorched earth and
riverbeds where water
runs slowly
Gypsy Christ
with his burnt tresses
jutting cheekbones
white pupils

Look where he goes—

Balcón

La Lola
canta saetas.
Los toreritos
la rodean,
y el barberillo
desde su puerta,
sigue los ritmos
con la cabeza.
Entre la albahaca
y la hierbabuena,
la Lola canta
saetas.
La Lola aquella,
que se miraba
tanto en la alberca.

Balcony

Lola
sings saetas
the young toreros
all around her
and the barber
on his doorstep
nodding to her rhythms
Between the basil
and the mint
Lola
sings saetas
That same Lola
who stared at herself
so often
in the water trough

Madrugada

Pero como el amor
los saeteros
están ciegos.

Sobre la noche verde,
las saetas,
dejan rastros de lirio
caliente.

La quilla de la luna
rompe nubes moradas
y las aljabas
se llenan de rocío.

¡Ay, pero como el amor
los saeteros
están ciegos!

Before Dawn

But like love
the archers
are blind

The arrows
leave trails of hot
lily
in the green night

The moon-keel
shreds purple clouds
and the quivers
fill with dew

Ay—but the archers
are blind
like love

Gráfico de la Petenera

a Eugenio Montes

Campana
Bordón

En la torre
amarilla,
dobla una campana.

Sobre el viento
amarillo,
se abren las campanadas.

En la torre
amarilla,
cesa la campana.

El viento con el polvo,
hace proras de plata.

Chart of the Petenera

for Eugenio Montes

Bell
Refrain

In the yellow
tower
a bell rings

In the yellow
wind
the bell rings and rings

In the yellow
tower
the bell stops ringing

Wind shapes the dust
into silver prows

Camino

Cien jinetes enlutados,
¿dónde irán,
por el cielo yacente
del naranjal?
Ni a Córdoba ni a Sevilla
llegarán.
Ni a Granada la que suspira
por el mar.
Esos caballos soñolientos
los llevarán,
al laberinto de las cruces
donde tiembla el cantar.
Con siete ayes clavados,
¿dónde irán,
los cien jinetes andaluces
del naranjal?

Las seis cuerdas

La guitarra,
hace llorar a los sueños.
El sollozo de las almas
perdidas,
se escapa por su boca
redonda.
Y como la tarántula
teje una gran estrella
para cazar suspiros,
que flotan en su negro
aljibe de madera.

Road

One hundred horsemen in mourning
where will they go
in the hanging sky
over the orange grove
Not to Cordoba or Seville
will they go
Nor to Granada that sighs
for the sea
Those drowsy horses will carry them
to the labyrinth of crosses
quivering with song
With seven nailed cries—
where will they go
one hundred Andalusian horsemen
from the orange grove

Six Strings

The guitar
makes dreams cry
The sobbing of lost
souls
slips through its round
mouth
And like the tarantula
it weaves a great star
for catching the sighs
that float in its black
wooden cistern

Danza

En el huerto de la Petenera

En la noche del huerto,
seis gitanas,
vestidas de blanco
bailan.

En la noche del huerto,
coronadas,
con rosas de papel
y biznagas.

En la noche del huerto,
sus dientes de nácar,
escriben la sombra
quemada.

Y en la noche del huerto,
sus sombras se alargan,
y llegan hasta el cielo
moradas.

Dance
In the Petenera's Orchard

Night in the orchard
six gypsy women
all in white
dance

Night in the orchard
crowned
with paper
       roses
and jasmine
        biznagas

Night in the orchard
their pearl-white teeth
write
the burned shadows

Night in the orchard
their shadows grow long
turning purple
as they touch the sky

Muerte de la Petenera

En la casa blanca muere
la perdición de los hombres.

Cien jacas caracolean.
Sus jinetes están muertos.

Bajo las estremecidas
estrellas de los velones,
su falda de moaré tiembla
entre sus muslos de cobre.

Cien jacas caracolean.
Sus jinetes están muertos.

Largas sombras afiladas
vienen del turbio horizonte,
y el bordón de una guitarra
se rompe.

Cien jacas caracolean.
Sus jinetes están muertos.

Death of the Petenera

In the white villa
the passions of men die

One hundred horses frisk
Their riders are dead

Lit by the shaken
stars of the oil lamps
her moiré skirt moves
between her copper thighs

One hundred horses frisk
Their riders are dead

Long thin shadows
rise from the roiled horizon
A guitar's bass string
snaps

One hundred horses frisk
Their riders are dead

Falseta

¡Ay, Petenera gitana!
¡Yayay Petenera!
Tu entierro no tuvo niñas
buenas.
Niñas que le dan a Cristo muerto
sus guedejas,
y llevan blancas mantillas
en las ferias.
Tu entierro fue de gente
siniestra.
Gente con el corazón
en la cabeza,
que te siguió llorando
por las callejas.
¡Ay, Petenera gitana!
¡Yayay Petenera!

"De profundis"

Los cien enamorados
duermen para siempre
bajo la tierra seca.
Andalucía tiene
largos caminos rojos.
Córdoba, olivos verdes
donde poner cien cruces,
que los recuerden.
Los cien enamorados
duermen para siempre.

Falseta

Ay gypsy Petenera—
Ay yay Petenera
There were no nice girls
at your burial
Girls who give their tresses
to the dead Christ
and wear white mantillas
at the fair
There were mean folks
at your burial
Folks with their hearts
in their heads
who went on crying for you
in the alleys
Ay gypsy Petenera—
Ay yay Petenera

De Profundis

The one hundred lovers
sleep and sleep
under the dry dirt
Andalusia has
long red roads
Cordoba has green olive groves
for the one hundred crosses
planted in their memory
The one hundred lovers
sleep and sleep

Clamor

En las torres
amarillas,
doblan las campanas.

Sobre los vientos
amarillos,
se abren las campanadas.

Por un camino va
la Muerte, coronada,
de azahares marchitos.
Canta y canta
una canción
en su vihuela blanca,
y canta y canta y canta.

En las torres amarillas,
cesan las campanas.

El viento con el polvo,
hacen proras de plata.

Bells for the Dead

In the yellow
towers
bells ring

In the yellow
winds
bells ring and ring

Death goes by
on the road
crowned with withered
orange blossoms
She sings and sings
a song
with her white lute
and sings and sings and sings

In the yellow towers
the bells stop ringing

Wind shapes the dust
into silver prows

Dos muchachas

a Máximo Quijano

La Lola

Bajo el naranjo lava
pañales de algodón.
Tiene verdes los ojos
y violeta la voz.

¡Ay, amor,
bajo el naranjo en flor!

El agua de la acequia
iba llena de sol.
En el olivarito
cantaba un gorrión.

¡Ay, amor,
bajo el naranjo en flor!

Luego cuando la Lola
gaste todo el jabón,
vendrán los torerillos.

¡Ay, amor,
bajo el naranjo en flor!

Two Girls

for Máximo Quijano

Lola

Under the orange tree
she washes cotton cloths
Her eyes are green
and her voice is violet

Ay love
under the flowering orange tree

The water in the ditch
flowed by full of sun
In the olive grove
a sparrow sang

Ay love
under the flowering orange tree

And later when Lola
has used up the soap
the young toreros will come

Ay love
under the flowering orange tree!

Amparo

Amparo,
¡qué sola estás en tu casa
vestida de blanco!

(Ecuador entre el jazmín
y el nardo.)

Oyes los maravillosos
surtidores de tu patio,
y el débil trino amarillo
del canario.

Por la tarde ves temblar
los cipreses con los pájaros,
mientras bordas lentamente
letras sobre el cañamazo.

Amparo,
¡qué sola estás en tu casa
vestida de blanco!

Amparo,
¡y qué dificil decirte:
yo te amo!

Amparo

Amparo
alone in your house
wearing white

(Equator between jasmine
and nard)

You hear the courtyard's
wondrous fountains
and the canary's
weak yellow cheep

At dusk you watch the cypresses
quiver with birds
while slowly stitching
letters on burlap

Amparo
alone in your house
wearing white

Amparo
how hard it is to tell you
I love you

Viñetas flamencas

a Manuel Torres, "Niño de Jerez,"
que tiene tronco de Faraón

Retrato de Silverio Franconetti

Entre italiano
y flamenco,
¿cómo cantaría
aquel Silverio?
La densa miel de Italia
con el limón nuestro,
iba en el hondo llanto
del siguiriyero.
Su grito fue terrible.
Los viejos
dicen que se erizaban
los cabellos,
y se abría el azogue
de los espejos.
Pasaba por los tonos
sin romperlos.
Y fue un creador
y un jardinero.
Un creador de glorietas
para el silencio.
Ahora su melodía
duerme con los ecos.
Definitiva y pura.
¡Con los últimos ecos!

Flamenco Vignettes

for Manuel Torres ("The boy from Jerez")
descendant of the Pharaohs

Portrait of Silverio Franconetti

Part Italian
part flamenco
how did Silverio
sing?
Thick Italian honey
and our lemon
went
into the deep wail
of his siguiriya
His cry was formidable
The old folks say
that their hair stood on end
and that the mirrors
spilled mercury
He slid over the sounds
without breaking them
An artist
and a gardener
he built gazebos
to silence
Now his song
sleeps with the echoes
Final and pure—
with the last echoes

Juan Breva

Juan Breva tenía
cuerpo de gigante
y voz de niña.
Nada como su trino.
Era la misma
pena cantando
detrás de una sonrisa.
Evoca los limonares
de Málaga la dormida,
y hay en su llanto dejos
de sal marina.
Como Homero cantó
ciego. Su voz tenía,
algo de mar sin luz
y naranja exprimida.

Juan Breva

Juan Breva had
the body of a giant
and a little girl's voice
Nothing like his trill
which was sorrow
itself
singing
behind a smile
and conjuring
the lemon groves
of drowsy Málaga—
a dash of sea salt
in his lament
Like Homer
he sang blind
His voice carried
a lilt of the sea
without light
and a hint of squeezed orange

Café cantante

Lámparas de cristal
y espejos verdes.

Sobre el tablado oscuro,
la Parrala sostiene
una conversación
con la Muerte.
La llama,
no viene,
y la vuelve a llamar.
Las gentes
aspiran los sollozos.
Y en los espejos verdes,
largas colas de seda
se mueven.

Café Cantante

Glass lamps
and green mirrors

On the dark stage
La Parrala
sings a colloquy
with Death
She sings for it to come—
it doesn't come
so she sings again
The drinkers
swallow sobs
In the green mirrors
long silken tails
swish

Lamentación de la muerte

a Miguel Benítez

Sobre el cielo negro,
culebrinas amarillas.

Vine a este mundo con ojos
y me voy sin ellos.
¡Señor del mayor dolor!
Y luego,
un velón y una manta
en el suelo.

Quise llegar adonde
llegaron los buenos.
¡Y he llegado, Dios mío! . . .
Pero luego,
un velón y una manta
en el suelo.

Limoncito amarillo,
limonero.
Echad los limoncitos
al viento.
¡Ya lo sabéis! . . . Porque luego,
luego,
un velón y una manta
en el suelo.

Sobre el cielo negro,
culebrinas amarillas.

Death Lament

for Miguel Benítez

Yellow jags
in the black sky

I came into this world
with eyes
and I'm leaving without them
Lord of great sorrow—!
And now
a lamp and a blanket
on the ground

I wanted to reach the place
for those who are good
And I have reached it—oh Lord—
But now
a lamp and a blanket
on the ground

Little yellow lemon
lemon tree
Toss your little lemons
to the wind
Now you all know! Now—now—
a lamp and a blanket
on the ground

Yellow jags
in the black sky

Conjuro

La mano crispada
como una Medusa
ciega el ojo doliente
del candil.

As de bastos.
Tijeras en cruz.

Sobre el humo blanco
del incienso, tiene
algo de topo y
mariposa indecisa.

As de bastos.
Tijeras en cruz.

Aprieta un corazón
invisible, ¿la veis?
Un corazón
reflejado en el viento.

As de bastos.
Tijeras en cruz.

Conjury

The hand contorted
like a Medusa
blinds the suffering eye
of the lamp

Ace of wands
Scissors crossed

Above the smoking
white incense
it looks like a mole
and a nervous butterfly

Ace of wands
Scissors crossed

It squeezes
an unseen heart—do you see it—
A heart
that gleams in the wind

Ace of wands
Scissors crossed

Memento

Cuando yo me muera,
enterradme con mi guitarra
bajo la arena.

Cuando yo me muera,
entre los naranjos
y la hierbabuena.

Cuando yo me muera,
enterradme, si queréis,
en una veleta.

¡Cuando yo me muera!

Memento

When I die
bury me with my guitar
beneath the sand

When I die
among the orange trees
and the mint

When I die
bury me—if you care—
in a weathervane

When I die

Tres ciudades

a Pilar Zubiaurre

Malagueña

La muerte
entra y sale
de la taberna.

Pasan caballos negros
y gente siniestra
por los hondos caminos
de la guitarra.

Y hay un olor a sal
y a sangre de hembra,
en los nardos febriles
de la marina.

La muerte
entra y sale,
y sale y entra
la muerte
de la taberna.

Three Cities

for Pilar Zubiaurre

Malagueña

Death
comes in and out
of the tavern

Black horses
and rough folks
travel
on the deep paths
of the guitar

Feverish nard flowers
by the harbor
have the smell of salt
and female blood

Death
comes in and out
of the tavern
and out and in
comes death

Barrio de Córdoba

Tópico nocturno

En la casa se defienden
de las estrellas.
La noche se derrumba.
Dentro hay una niña muerta
con una rosa encarnada
oculta en la cabellera.
Seis ruiseñores la lloran
en la reja.

Las gentes van suspirando
con las guitarras abiertas.

Neighborhood in Cordoba
Night Theme

Inside the house they fend off
the stars
The night falls down
Inside there's a dead girl
with a deep-red rose
hidden in her hair
At the window grate
six nightingales
cry for her

Going by
the people sigh
carrying guitars

Baile

La Carmen está bailando
por las calles de Sevilla.
Tiene blancos los cabellos
y brillantes las pupilas.

¡Niñas,
corred las cortinas!

En su cabeza se enrosca
una serpiente amarilla,
y va soñando en el baile
con galanes de otros días.

¡Niñas,
corred las cortinas!

Las calles están desiertas
y en los fondos se adivinan,
corazones andaluces
buscando viejas espinas.

¡Niñas,
corred las cortinas!

Dance

Carmen is dancing
down the streets of Seville
Her hair is white
and her pupils glitter

Girls—
draw the curtains

A yellow snake
coils on her head
As she dances she dreams
of old sweethearts

Girls—
draw the curtains

The streets are lonely
and in the shadows
lurk Andalusian hearts
hunting for old thorns

Girls—
draw the curtains!

Gypsy Ballads

Romance de la luna, luna

a Conchita García Lorca

La luna vino a la fragua
con su polisón de nardos.
El niño la mira, mira.
El niño la está mirando.
En el aire conmovido
mueve la luna sus brazos
y enseña, lúbrica y pura,
sus senos de duro estaño.
Huye luna, luna, luna.
Si vinieran los gitanos,
harían con tu corazón
collares y anillos blancos.
Niño, déjame que baile.
Cuando vengan los gitanos,
te encontrarán sobre el yunque
con los ojillos cerrados.
Huye luna, luna, luna,
que ya siento sus caballos.
Niño, déjame, no pises
mi blancor almidonado.

El jinete se acercaba
tocando el tambor del llano.
Dentro de la fragua el niño,
tiene los ojos cerrados.
Por el olivar venían,
bronce y sueño, los gitanos.
Las cabezas levantadas
y los ojos entornados.

I

Ballad of the Moon Moon

for Conchita García Lorca

Moon came to the forge
in her petticoat of nard
The boy looks and looks
the boy looks at the Moon
In the turbulent air
Moon lifts up her arms
showing—pure and sexy—
her beaten-tin breasts
Run Moon run Moon Moon
If the gypsies came
white rings and white necklaces
they would beat from your heart
Boy will you let me dance
When the gypsies come
they'll find you on the anvil
with your little eyes shut
Run Moon run Moon Moon
I hear the horses' hoofs
Leave me boy! Don't walk
on my lane of white starch

The horseman came beating
the drum of the plains
The boy at the forge
has his little eyes shut
Through the olive groves
in bronze and in dreams
here the gypsies come
their heads riding high
their eyelids hanging low

Cómo canta la zumaya,
¡ay cómo canta en el árbol!
Por el cielo va la luna
con un niño de la mano.

Dentro de la fragua lloran,
dando gritos, los gitanos.
El aire la vela, vela.
El aire la está velando.

How the night heron sings
how it sings in the tree
Moon crosses the sky
with a boy by the hand

At the forge the gypsies
cry and then scream
The wind watches watches
the wind watches the Moon

2

Preciosa y el aire

a Dámaso Alonso

Su luna de pergamino
Preciosa tocando viene,
por un anfibio sendero
de cristales y laureles.
El silencio sin estrellas,
huyendo del sonsonete,
cae donde el mar bate y canta
su noche llena de peces.
En los picos de la sierra
los carabineros duermen
guardando las blancas torres
donde viven los ingleses.
Y los gitanos del agua
levantan por distraerse,
glorietas de caracolas
y ramas de pino verde.

*

Su luna de pergamino
Preciosa tocando viene.
Al verla se ha levantado
el viento, que nunca duerme.
San Cristobalón desnudo,
lleno de lenguas celestes,
mira a la niña tocando
una dulce gaita ausente.

Niña, deja que levante
tu vestido para verte.
Abre en mis dedos antiguos
la rosa azul de tu vientre.

2

Preciosa and the Wind

for Dámaso Alonso

Playing her parchment moon
Preciosa comes dancing
down a path by the sea
of crystal and laurel
Silence of no stars
flees from her singsong
and falls where the crashing sea
sings a night full of fish
On the peaks of the sierra
armed men are asleep
They guard the white towers
where the Englishmen live
Gypsies of the water
raise up for joy
arbors made of conch shells
and branches of green pine

*

Playing her parchment moon
Preciosa comes dancing
Seeing her the wind rises
the wind that never sleeps
Big San Cristóbal naked
covered in skyblue tongues
watches the girl playing
a sweet absent flute

Girl let me lift your skirt
so I can see you down there
Open in my ancient fingers
the blue rose of your womb

Preciosa tira el pandero
y corre sin detenerse.
El viento-hombrón la persigue
con una espada caliente.

Frunce su rumor el mar.
Los olivos palidecen.
Cantan las flautas de umbría
y el liso gong de la nieve.

¡Preciosa, corre, Preciosa,
que te coge el viento verde!
¡Preciosa, corre, Preciosa!
¡Míralo por dónde viene!
Sátiro de estrellas bajas
con sus lenguas relucientes.

*

Preciosa, llena de miedo,
entra en la casa que tiene
más arriba de los pinos,
el cónsul de los ingleses.

Asustado por los gritos
tres carabineros vienen,
sus negras capas ceñidas
y los gorros en las sienes.

El inglés da a la gitana
un vaso de tibia leche,
y una copa de ginebra
que Preciosa no se bebe.

Y mientras cuenta, llorando,
su aventura a aquella gente,
en las tejas de pizarra
el viento, furioso, muerde.

Flinging her tambourine
Preciosa runs and runs
The Big Windman follows
waving his hot sword

The sea crimps its murmur
the olive trees turn white
Flutes of shadow sing
and the smooth gong of snow

Run run Preciosa
from the hands of the wind!
Run run Preciosa
Look at the green wind come!
Low stars of a Satyr
with his shining tongues

*

Preciosa full of fear
runs into the house
of the English consul
high above the pines

Startled by the shouts
three armed men come
caps over their temples
black capes wrapped tight

The consul gives the gypsy
a glass of warm milk
and a cup of cold gin
that Preciosa won't drink

She sobs telling her tale
to the consul's house
while the raging wind bites
at the slates of the roof

3

Reyerta

a Rafael Méndez

En la mitad del barranco
las navajas de Albacete,
bellas de sangre contraria,
relucen como los peces.
Una dura luz de naipe
recorta en el agrio verde,
caballos enfurecidos
y perfiles de jinetes.
En la copa de un olivo
lloran dos viejas mujeres.
El toro de la reyerta
se sube por las paredes.
Ángeles negros traían
pañuelos y agua de nieve.
Ángeles con grandes alas
de navajas de Albacete.
Juan Antonio el de Montilla
rueda muerto la pendiente,
su cuerpo lleno de lirios
y una granada en las sienes.
Ahora monta cruz de fuego
carretera de la muerte.

*

El juez, con guardia civil,
por los olivares viene.
Sangre resbalada gime
muda canción de serpiente.

3

Brawl

for Rafael Méndez

Halfway down the gully
the blades from Albacete
glisten like fishes
flush with fighting blood
Hard light of the cards
in the bitter green
trims the rearing horses
and the riders' silhouettes
Up in an olive tree
two old women weep
The bull of the brawl
bucks against the walls
Black angels have brought
snow-water and hankies
Angels whose great wings
are blades from Albacete
Dead down the gully
Juan Antonio rolls
the one from Montilla
all of lilies his body
pomegranate his brow
He rides a burning cross
on the high road to death

*

Judge and civil guards
cross the olive groves
The shed blood moans
mute song of a snake

Señores guardias civiles:
aquí pasó lo de siempre.
Han muerto cuatro romanos
y cinco cartagineses.

*

La tarde loca de higueras
y de rumores calientes,
cae desmayada en los muslos
heridos de los jinetes.
Y ángeles negros volaban
por el aire del poniente.
Ángeles de largas trenzas
y corazones de aceite.

Civil guardsmen—sirs—
it has happened again
Four from Rome are dead
and five from Carthage

*

Dusk wild with fig trees
and sultry murmurs
falls faint on the wounds
in the riders' thighs
Black angels went flying
through the western sky
Angels with long braids
and oil in their hearts

4

Romance sonámbulo

a Gloria Giner y a Fernando de los Ríos

Verde que te quiero verde.
Verde viento. Verdes ramas.
El barco sobre la mar
y el caballo en la montaña.
Con la sombra en la cintura,
ella sueña en su baranda
verde carne, pelo verde,
con ojos de fría plata.
Verde que te quiero verde.
Bajo la luna gitana,
las cosas la están mirando
y ella no puede mirarlas.

*

Verde que te quiero verde.
Grandes estrellas de escarcha,
vienen con el pez de sombra
que abre el camino del alba.
La higuera frota su viento
con la lija de sus ramas,
y el monte, gato garduño,
eriza sus pitas agrias.
¿Pero quién vendrá? ¿Y por dónde?. . .
Ella sigue en su baranda
verde carne, pelo verde,
soñando en la mar amarga.

*

4

Dreamwalking Ballad

for Gloria Giner and Fernando de los Ríos

Green I want you green
green wind green branches
Boat on the sea and
horse on the mountain
Shadow on her waist
she dreams at her railing
green flesh green hair
eyes of cold silver
Green I want you green
Under the gypsy moon
things are seeing her
but she can't see them

*

Green I want you green
The great stars of frost
come with fish of shadow
paving the path to dawn
The fig tree rasps the wind
with its rough branches
and the wildcat mountain
bares its sour agaves
Who will come—from where—?
At her railing she gazes
green flesh green hair
dream of the bitter sea

*

Compadre, quiero cambiar,
mi caballo por su casa,
mi montura por su espejo,
mi cuchillo por su manta.
Compadre, vengo sangrando,
desde los puertos de Cabra.
Si yo pudiera, mocito,
este trato se cerraba.
Pero yo ya no soy yo,
ni mi casa es ya mi casa.
Compadre, quiero morir
decentemente en mi cama.
De acero, si puede ser,
con las sábanas de holanda.
¿No ves la herida que tengo
desde el pecho a la garganta?
Trescientas rosas morenas
lleva tu pechera blanca.
Tu sangre rezuma y huele
alrededor de tu faja.
Pero yo ya no soy yo.
Ni mi casa es ya mi casa.
Dejadme subir al menos
hasta las altas barandas,
¡dejadme subir!, dejadme
hasta las verdes barandas.
Barandales de la luna
por donde retumba el agua.

*

Ya suben los dos compadres
hacia las altas barandas.
Dejando un rastro de sangre.
Dejando un rastro de lágrimas.

Compadre can I swap
my horse for your house
saddle for your mirror
knife for your blanket
compadre I come bleeding
from the Cabra passes
If I could young friend
the deal would be done
But I'm no longer me
my house isn't mine
Compadre let me die
decent in my bed
A steel bed if you please
laid with dutch linen
Don't you see the slash
from my breast to my throat
Three hundred dark roses
on your white shirtfront
Blood oozes and stinks
in the sash at your waist
But I'm no longer me
my house isn't mine
Let me climb way up
to the high terrace
Let me climb let me
to the green terrace
Railing of moonlight
and the rushing water

                    *

Two compadres climb
to the high terrace
leaving a trail of blood
and a trail of tears

Temblaban en los tejados
farolillos de hojalata.
Mil panderos de cristal,
herían la madrugada.

*

Verde que te quiero verde,
verde viento, verdes ramas.
Los dos compadres subieron.
El largo viento, dejaba
en la boca un raro gusto
de hiel, de menta y de albahaca.
¡Compadre! ¿Dónde está, dime?
¿Dónde está tu niña amarga?
¡Cuántas veces te esperó!
¡Cuantas veces te esperara
cara fresca, negro pelo,
en esta verde baranda!

*

Sobre el rostro del aljibe,
se mecía la gitana.
Verde carne, pelo verde,
con ojos de fría plata.
Un carambano de luna,
la sostiene sobre el agua.
La noche se puso íntima
como una pequeña plaza.
Guardias civiles borrachos,
en la puerta golpeaban.
Verde que te quiero verde.
Verde viento. Verdes ramas.
El barco sobre la mar.
Y el caballo en la montaña.

Tin lanterns trembled
on the tops of roofs
A thousand glass tambourines
tore up the dawn

*

Green I want you green
green wind green branches
The two compadres climbed
The slow wind in their mouths
left a strange flavor
of bile basil and mint
Compadre where is she
Where's your bitter girl
How often has she waited
How often will she wait
fresh face and black hair
on the green terrace

*

Over the face of the cistern
the gypsy girl swayed
Green flesh green hair
eyes of cold silver
A moon icicle holds her
high over the water
The night was as cozy
as a small plaza
Drunken civil guards
pounded on the door
Green I want you green
Green wind green branches
Boat on the sea and
horse on the mountain

5

La monja gitana

a José Moreno Villa

Silencio de cal y mirto.
Malvas en las hierbas finas.
La monja borda alhelíes
sobre una tela pajiza.
Vuelan en la araña gris,
siete pájaros del prisma.
La iglesia gruñe a lo lejos
como un oso panza arriba.
¡Qué bien borda! ¡Con qué gracia!
Sobre la tela pajiza,
ella quisiera bordar
flores de su fantasía.
¡Qué girasol! ¡Qué magnolia
de lentejuelas y cintas!
¡Qué azafranes y qué lunas,
en el mantel de la misa!
Cinco toronjas se endulzan
en la cercana cocina.
Las cinco llagas de Cristo
cortadas en Almería.
Por los ojos de la monja
galopan dos caballistas.
Un rumor último y sordo
le despega la camisa,
y al mirar nubes y montes
en las yertas lejanías,
se quiebra su corazón
de azúcar y yerbaluisa.
¡Oh!, qué llanura empinada

5

The Gypsy Nun

for José Moreno Villa

Lull of whitewash and myrtle
mallow in the herbs
The nun stitches wallflowers
on straw-colored cloth
In the gray chandelier
seven prism-birds fly
The church grunts in the distance
like a bear belly up
What graceful stitching
on the straw-colored cloth
She longs to embroider
the flowers of her thoughts
Ah sunflower ah magnolia
of sequins and ribbons
Saffron-flowers and moons
on the altarcloth
Five grapefruits sweeten
in the kitchen nearby—
cut down in Almería
the five wounds of Christ
Through the eyes of the nun
two horsemen ride
A last muffled murmur
loosens her blouse
Watching hills and clouds
in the stark distance
her heart of sugar
and lemon tea breaks
Ah the steep fields

con veinte soles arriba.
¡Qué ríos puestos de pie
vislumbra su fantasía!
Pero sigue con sus flores,
mientras que de pie, en la brisa,
la luz juega el ajedrez
alto de la celosía.

with twenty suns above
Ah the standing rivers
that her fantasy sees
She goes on stitching flowers
while high in the wind
the light in the lattices
plays a game of chess

6

La casada infiel

a Lydia Cabrera y a su negrita

Y que yo me la llevé al río
creyendo que era mozuela,
pero tenía marido.

Fue la noche de Santiago
y casi por compromiso.
Se apagaron los faroles
y se encendieron los grillos.
En las últimas esquinas
toqué sus pechos dormidos,
y se me abrieron de pronto
como ramos de jacintos.
El almidón de su enagua
me sonaba en el oído,
como una pieza de seda
rasgada por diez cuchillos.
Sin luz de plata en sus copas
los árboles han crecido
y un horizonte de perros
ladra muy lejos del río.

*

Pasadas las zarzamoras,
los juncos y los espinos,
bajo su mata de pelo
hice un hoyo sobre el limo.
Yo me quité la corbata.
Ella se quitó el vestido.

6

The Cheating Wife

for Lydia Cabrera and her little black girl

And I took her to the river
although she had a husband
I thought she was a maid

It was the night of Santiago
and as though by plan
The streetlamps guttered out
and the crickets lit up
At the edge of town
I touched her sleeping breasts
They opened at once
like stalks of hyacinth
Starch of her petticoat
sounded in my ear
like a piece of silk
scraped by ten knives
The trees loom tall
no silver in their tips
and far from the river
barks a horizon of dogs

*

Beyond the blackberries
the hawthorns and reeds
under her bush of hair
I made a hole in the mud
I lifted off my tie
She stripped off her dress

Yo el cinturón con revólver.
Ella sus cuatro corpiños.
Ni nardos ni caracolas
tienen el cutis tan fino,
ni los cristales con luna
relumbran con ese brillo.
Sus muslos se me escapaban
como peces sorprendidos,
la mitad llenos de lumbre,
la mitad llenos de frío.
Aquella noche corrí
el mejor de los caminos,
montado en potra de nácar
sin bridas y sin estribos.
No quiero decir, por hombre,
las cosas que ella me dijo.
La luz del entendimiento
me hace ser muy comedido.
Sucia de besos y arena
yo me la llevé del río.
Con el aire se batían
las espadas de los lirios.

Me porté como quien soy.
Como un gitano legítimo.
Le regalé un costurero
grande, de raso pajizo,
y no quise enamorarme
porque teniendo marido
me dijo que era mozuela
cuando le llevaba al río.

I my belt with revolver
she her four underthings
Not nard or snails
have such tender skin
nor does glass in moonlight
shine with such a glow
Her thighs fled from me
like startled fishes
half streaming with fire
half streaming with cold
That night I went tearing
down the best of the roads
on a pearly young mare
no bridle or stirrups
I don't want—as a man—
to tell you what she said
The light of what I know
has sealed up my lips
I brought her from the river
dirty from kisses and sand
The swords of the lilies
made war on the wind

I did as the man I am
a legitimate gypsy
I gave her a sewing case
made of straw satin
And since she was a wife
I didn't fall in love
When I took her to the river
she said she was a maid

7

Romance de la pena negra

a José Navarro Pardo

Las piquetas de los gallos
cavan buscando la aurora,
cuando por el monte oscuro
baja Soledad Montoya.
Cobre amarillo, su carne,
huele a caballo y a sombra.
Yunques ahumados sus pechos,
gimen canciones redondas.
Soledad: ¿por quién preguntas
sin compaña y a estas horas?
Pregunte por quien pregunte,
dime: ¿a ti qué se te importa?
Vengo a buscar lo que busco,
mi alegría y mi persona.
Soledad de mis pesares,
caballo que se desboca,
al fin encuentra la mar
y se lo tragan las olas.
No me recuerdes el mar
que la pena negra, brota
en las tierras de aceituna
bajo el rumor de las hojas.
¡Soledad, qué pena tienes!
¡Qué pena tan lastimosa!
Lloras zumo de limón
agrio de espera y de boca.
¡Qué pena tan grande! Corro
mi casa como una loca,

7

Ballad of the Black Sorrow

for José Navarro Pardo

The roosters' pickaxes
scratch seeking the dawn
when down the dark mountain
Soledad Montoya comes
Her skin yellow copper
reeks of shadow and horse
Her breasts smoking anvils
moan their round songs
Who are you seeking
Soledad Soledad
all alone at this hour
Whomever I'm seeking
tell me why you care
Whatever I'm seeking
my bliss and my soul
Soledad of my sorrows
a runaway horse
comes at last to the sea
and drowns in the waves
Don't tell me of the sea
Black sorrow wells up
in the lands of the olive
under the rustling leaves
Soledad how you sorrow
Such terrible sorrow
You shed lemon-rind tears
sour waiting sour mouth
In sorrow I scurry
through my house like a fiend

mis dos trenzas por el suelo
de la cocina a la alcoba.
¡Qué pena! Me estoy poniendo
de azabache, carne y ropa.
¡Ay mis camisas de hilo!
¡Ay mis muslos de amapola!
Soledad: lava tu cuerpo
con agua de las alondras,
y deja tu corazón
en paz, Soledad Montoya.

*

Por abajo canta el río:
volante de cielo y hojas.
Con flores de calabaza,
la nueva luz se corona.
¡Oh pena de los gitanos!
Pena limpia y siempre sola.
¡Oh pena de cauce oculto
y madrugada remota!

from kitchen to bedroom
two braids on the floor
I'm blackened by sorrow
my skin and my clothes
Ay my linen blouses
Ay my poppy thighs
Wash your body Soledad
with the water of larks
Soledad Montoya
give your heart some peace

*

The river sings below
ruffle of sky and leaves
The new light is crowned
with pumpkin flowers
Sorrow of the gypsies
clean sorrow all alone—
of the secret riverbed
and the distant dawn

8

San Miguel
Granada

a Diego Buigas de Dalmau

SAN MIGUEL

Se ven desde las barandas,
por el monte, monte, monte,
mulos y sombras de mulos
cargados de girasoles.

Sus ojos en las umbrías
se empañan de inmensa noche.
En los recodos del aire,
cruje la aurora salobre.

Un cielo de mulos blancos
cierra sus ojos de azogue
dando a la quieta penumbra
un final de corazones.
Y el agua se pone fría
para que nadie la toque.
Agua loca y descubierta
por el monte, monte, monte.

*

San Miguel lleno de encajes
en la alcoba de su torre,
enseña su bellos muslos
ceñidos por los faroles.

Arcángel domesticado
en el gesto de las doce,

8

San Miguel
Granada

for Diego Buigas de Dalmau

SAN MIGUEL

Seen from the balcony
on the hill hill hill
mules and mule shadows
sunflowers on their backs

Their eyes in the shadows
well up with vast night
In the bends of the wind
the salty dawn creaks

A sky of white mules
closes its mercury eyes
giving the quiet dark
a finale of hearts
The water turns cold
so no one will touch it
Wild open water
on the hill hill hill

*

San Miguel dressed in lace
in his tower chamber
shows his pretty thighs
smoothed by the lamps

Archangel tamed
at the sweep of twelve

finge una cólera dulce
de plumas y ruiseñores.
San Miguel canta en los vidrios;
Efebo de tres mil noches,
fragante de agua colonia
y lejano de las flores.

*

El mar baila por la playa,
un poema de balcones.
Las orillas de la luna
pierden juncos, ganan voces.
Vienen manolas comiendo
semillas de girasoles,
los culos grandes y ocultos
como planetas de cobre.
Vienen altos caballeros
y damas de triste porte,
morenas por la nostalgia
de un ayer de ruiseñores.
Y el obispo de Manila
ciego de azafrán y pobre,
dice misa con dos filos
para mujeres y hombres.

*

San Miguel se estaba quieto
en la alcoba de su torre,
con las enaguas cuajadas
de espejitos y entredoses.

San Miguel, rey de los globos
y de los números nones,
en el primor berberisco
de gritos y miradores.

fakes a sweet tantrum
of nightingales and plumes
He sings in the windows
Ephebe of three thousand nights
reeking of cologne
and far from the flowers

*

On the beach the sea frolics—
a balcony poem
The edges of the moon
shed reeds and take voices
Flashy gals from Madrid
munch sunflower seeds
their big secret rumps
like coppery planets
Tall gentlemen come
and somber ladies
dark with nostalgia
for a nightingale past
The bishop of Manila
poor and saffron-blind
says a two-bladed mass
for women and for men

*

San Miguel sat still
in his chamber room
wearing petticoats clotted
with mirrors and entredós

O king of balloons
king of odd numbers
in the Berber elegance
of miradors and shouts

9

San Rafael
Córdoba

a Juan Izquierdo Croselles

SAN RAFAEL

Coches cerrados llegaban
a las orillas de juncos
donde las ondas alisan
romano torso desnudo.
Coches, que el Guadalquivir
tiende en su cristal maduro,
entre láminas de flores
y resonancias de nublos.
Los niños tejen y cantan
el desengaño del mundo
cerca de los viejos coches
perdidos en el nocturno.
Pero Córdoba no tiembla
bajo el misterio confuso,
pues si la sombra levanta
la arquitectura del humo,
un pie de mármol afirma
su casto fulgor enjuto.
Pétalos de lata débil
recaman los grises puros
de la brisa, desplegada
sobre los arcos de triunfo.
Y mientras el puente sopla
diez rumores de Neptuno,
vendedores de tabaco
huyen por el roto muro.

9

San Rafael
Cordoba

for Juan Izquierdo Croselles

SAN RAFAEL

Closed cars drove up
to the reedy riverbanks
where waves smooth out
a naked Roman bust
Cars the Guadalquivir
holds on its ripe glass
between patinas of flowers
and the rumbling clouds
Boys weave and sing
their world weariness
near the old cars
lost in the nocturne
Cordoba isn't fazed
by the hazy mystery
for if the shadows raise
an architecture of smoke
the marble foot confirms
its pure dry radiance
Petals of flimsy tin
emboss the pure grays
of the wind unfurling
over victory arches
When the bridge exhales
ten Neptunian roars
all the tobacco hawkers
flee through the broken wall

Un solo pez en el agua
que a las dos Córdobas junta.
Blanda Córdoba de juncos.
Córdoba de arquitectura.
Niños de cara impasible
en la orilla se desnudan,
aprendices de Tobías
y Merlines de cintura,
para fastidiar al pez
en irónica pregunta
si quiere flores de vino
o saltos de media luna.
Pero el pez que dora el agua
y los mármoles enluta,
les da lección y equilibrio
de solitaria columna.
El Arcángel aljamiado
de lentejuelas oscuras,
en el mitin de las ondas
buscaba rumor y cuna.

*

Un solo pez en el agua.
Dos Córdobas de hermosura.
Córdoba quebrada en chorros.
Celeste Córdoba enjuta.

One fish in the water
joins two Cordobas
Gentle city of reeds
city of architecture
Inscrutable boys
undress by the river
students of Tobias
and Merlins of the waist
They bother the fish
with ironic questions—
do you want wine-flowers
or half-moon leaps?
But the fish gilds the water
and darkens the marble
teaching them the poise
of a single column
Archangel dark-sequinned
with Arabic script
seeks a murmur and a cradle
in the meeting of the waves

*

One fish in the water
two Cordobas of beauty
Cordoba cracked and gushing
Blue dry Cordoba

10

San Gabriel
Sevilla

a D. Agustín Viñuales

SAN GABRIEL

Un bello niño de junco,
anchos hombros, fino talle,
piel de nocturna manzana,
boca triste y ojos grandes,
nervio de plata caliente,
ronda la desierta calle.
Sus zapatos de charol
rompen las dalias del aire,
con los dos ritmos que cantan
breves lutos celestiales.
En la ribera del mar
no hay palma que se le iguale,
ni emperador coronado
ni lucero caminante.
Cuando la cabeza inclina
sobre su pecho de jaspe,
la noche busca llanuras
porque quiere arrodillarse.
Las guitarras suenan solas
para San Gabriel Arcángel,
domador de palomillas
y enemigo de los sauces.
San Gabriel: El niño llora
en el vientre de su madre.
No olvides que los gitanos
te regalaron el traje.

10

San Gabriel
Seville

for D. Agustín Viñuales

SAN GABRIEL

A beautiful reedy boy
wide shoulders slim hips
skin of a night apple
sad mouth and big eyes
nerve of hot silver
prowls the empty street
His patent-leather shoes
break the dahlias of the wind
with two rhythms playing
short celestial laments
No palm tree rivals him
on the shore of the sea
no emperor with a crown
or bright star on foot
When his head bends
over his jasper chest
night searches for a field
to kneel down in
Guitars play all alone
for Archangel Gabriel
tamer of little doves
and enemy of willows
San Gabriel: the boy
weeps in his mother's womb
Don't forget that gypsies
gave you your clothes

Anunciación de los Reyes
bien lunada y mal vestida,
abre la puerta al lucero
que por la calle venía.
El Arcángel San Gabriel
entre azucena y sonrisa,
biznieto de la Giralda,
se acercaba de visita.
En su chaleco bordado
grillos ocultos palpitan.
Las estrellas de la noche,
se volvieron campanillas.
San Gabriel: Aquí me tienes
con tres clavos de alegría.
Tu fulgor abre jazmines
sobre mi cara encendida.
Dios te salve, Anunciación.
Morena de maravilla.
Tendrás un niño más bello
que los tallos de la brisa.
¡Ay San Gabriel de mis ojos!
¡Gabrielillo de mi vida!
para sentarte yo sueño
un sillón de clavellinas.
Dios te salve, Anunciación,
bien lunada y mal vestida.
Tu niño tendrá en el pecho
un lunar y tres heridas.
¡Ay San Gabriel que reluces!
¡Gabrielillo de mi vida!
En el fondo de mis pechos
ya nace la leche tibia.
Dios te salve, Anunciación.

Annunciation of the Kings
halfmoon and ragged
opens her door for the star
coming down the street
The Archangel Gabriel
between a lily and a smile
grandson of the Giralda
coming for a visit
In his embroidered vest
hidden crickets pulse
The stars of the night
turned into tiny bells
San Gabriel: here I am
with three nails of joy
Your fire opens jasmines
in my gleaming face
God save you Annunciation
Dark eyes and dark hair
Your boy will be more handsome
than the stalks of wind
Ay Gabriel of my eyes
Darling Gabriel my life!
I dream of seating you
on a throne of maiden pinks
God save you Annunciation
halfmoon and ragged
On the chest of your child
a mole and three wounds
Ay Gabriel how you shine
Darling Gabriel my life
Warm milk is welling
deep inside my breasts
God save you Annunciation—

Madre de cien dinastías.
Áridos lucen tus ojos,
paisajes de caballista.

*

El niño canta en el seno
de Anunciación sorprendida.
Tres balas de almendra verde
tiemblan en su vocecita.
Ya San Gabriel en el aire
por una escala subía.
Las estrellas de la noche
se volvieron siemprevivas.

mother of dynasties
Landscapes of horsemen
gleam in your arid eyes

*

To Annunciation's surprise
a child sings at her breast
Three green-almond bullets
quaver in his voice
On a ladder Gabriel
climbed into the wind
Into everlastings turned
the stars of the night

Prendimiento de Antoñito el Camborio en el camino de Sevilla

a Margarita Xirgu

Antonio Torres Heredia,
hijo y nieto de Camborios,
con una vara de mimbre
va a Sevilla a ver los toros.
Moreno de verde luna
anda despacio y garboso.
Sus empavonados bucles
le brillan entre los ojos.
A la mitad del camino
cortó limones redondos,
y los fue tirando al agua
hasta que la puso de oro.
Y a la mitad del camino,
bajo las ramas de un olmo,
Guardia Civil caminera
lo llevó codo con codo.

*

El día se va despacio
la tarde colgada a un hombro,
dando una larga torera
sobre el mar y los arroyos.
Las aceitunas aguardan
la noche de Capricornio,
y una corta brisa, ecuestre,
salta los montes de plomo.
Antonio Torres Heredia,
hijo y nieto de Camborios,

11

Capture of Antoñito el Camborio
on the Road to Seville

for Margarita Xirgu

Antonio Torres Heredia
son and grand' of Camborios
goes to Seville for the bulls
with a wicker switch
Dark as the green moon
he walks slow and elegant
His slick blue ringlets
shine between his eyes
Halfway to Seville
he cut some round lemons
and tossed them in the water
until it turned to gold
Halfway to Seville
under the boughs of an elm
they hooked him by the elbows
a patrol of civil guards

*

Afternoon goes by slowly
hanging from a shoulder
long sweep of a cape
over the sea and creeks
The olives are waiting
for the Capricorn night
and a short horsy breeze
leaps up the hills of lead
Antonio Torres Heredia
son and grand' of Camborios

viene sin vara de mimbre
entre los cinco tricornios.

Antonio, ¿quién eres tú?
Si te llamaras Camborio,
hubieras hecho una fuente
de sangre, con cinco chorros.
Ni tú eres hijo de nadie,
ni legítimo Camborio.
¡Se acabaron los gitanos
que iban por el monte solos!
Están los viejos cuchillos,
tiritando bajo el polvo.

*

A las nueve de la noche
lo llevan al calabozo,
mientras los guardias civiles
beben limonada todos.
Y a las nueve de la noche
le cierran al calabozo,
mientras el cielo reluce
como la grupa de un potro.

walks without his switch
between five tricorne hats

Antonio—who are you?
Were you a Camborio
you'd have made a fountain
of blood with five jets
You're the son of no one—
you're no Camborio
Gone are the gypsies
who walked the hills alone
The old knives shudder
lying beneath the dust

*

At nine o'clock that evening
they walk him to the jail
All the civil guardsmen
drink their lemonade
At nine o'clock that evening
they lock him in the jail
The sky above gleams
like the rump of a colt

Muerte de Antoñito el Camborio

a José Antonio Rubio Sacristán

Voces de muerte sonaron
cerca del Guadalquivir.
Voces antiguas que cercan
voz de clavel varonil.
Les clavó sobre las botas
mordiscos de jabalí.
En la lucha daba saltos
jabonados de delfín.
Bañó con sangre enemiga
su corbata carmesí,
pero eran cuatro puñales
y tuvo que sucumbir.
Cuando las estrellas clavan
rejones al agua gris,
cuando los erales sueñan
verónicas de alhelí,
voces de muerte sonaron
cerca del Guadalquivir.

*

Antonio Torres Heredia,
Camborio de dura crin,
moreno de verde luna,
voz de clavel varonil:
¿Quién te ha quitado la vida
cerca del Guadalquivir?
Mis cuatro primos Heredias,
hijos de Benamejí.
Lo que en otros no envidiaban,

12

Death of Antoñito el Camborio

for José Antonio Rubio Sacristán

Blood cries rang out
near the Guadalquivir
Ancient cries corralling
the cry of a carnation
He gnashed at their boots
like a wild boar
He leapt in the brawl
sleek as a dolphin
He drenched his tie red
in the enemy's blood
but there were four blades
and he had to give it up
When stars thrust their spurs
into the gray water
when young bulls dream
of the sweep of a flower
blood cries rang out
near the Guadalquivir

*

Antonio Torres Heredia
a horsehaired Camborio
dark as a green moon
cry of a carnation
Who took away your life
near the Guadalquivir
My cousins the Heredias
four sons of Benamejí
They didn't covet in others

ya lo envidiaban en mí.
Zapatos color corinto,
medallones de marfil,
y este cutis amasado
con aceituna y jazmín.
¡Ay Antoñito el Camborio
digno de una Emperatriz!
Acuérdate de la Virgen
porque te vas a morir.
¡Ay Federico García!
llama a la Guardia Civil.
Ya mi talle se ha quebrado
como caña de maíz.
Tres golpes de sangre tuvo,
y se murió de perfil.
Viva moneda que nunca
se volverá a repetir.
Un ángel marchoso pone
su cabeza en un cojín.
Otros de rubor cansado,
encendieron un candil.
Y cuando los cuatro primos
llegan a Benamejí,
voces de muerte cesaron
cerca del Guadalquivir.

what they coveted in me
Shoes red as currants
cut-ivory cameos
and skin rubbed down
with jasmine and olives
Ay Antonio el Camborio
worthy of a Queen
Remember the Virgin
for you're going to die
Ay Federico García
call out the Civil Guard
Now my waist is broken
like a stalk of corn
He took three blood blows
died head to the side
His profile on a coin
never to be again
One busy angel places
his head on a pillow
Others flushed and tired
light the wick of a lamp
When the four cousins
get home to Benamejí
the death cries ceased
near the Guadalquivir

13

Muerto de amor

a Margarita Manso

¿Qué es aquello que reluce
por los altos corredores?
Cierra la puerta, hijo mío,
acaban de dar las once.
En mis ojos, sin querer,
relumbran cuatro faroles.
Será la gente aquella,
estará fregando el cobre.

*

Ajo de agónica plata
la luna menguante, pone
cabelleras amarillas
a las amarillas torres.
La noche llama temblando
al cristal de los balcones
perseguida por los mil
perros que no la conocen,
y un olor de vino y ámbar
viene de los corredores.

*

Brisas de caña mojada
y rumor de viejas voces,
resonaban por el arco
roto de la media noche.
Bueyes y rosas dormían.

13

Dying for Love

for Margarita Manso

What is that shining
in the balconies above?
Shut the door my son
it just struck eleven
Four lamps are gleaming
unwanted in my eyes
Maybe it's those people
scrubbing copper pots

*

Garlic of dying silver
the waning moon hangs
manes of yellow hair
on the yellow towers
Night calls out shaking
the balcony glass
chased by the thousand dogs
that don't know who she is
Scent of wine and amber
comes down from above

*

Breeze of wet reeds
and babble of old voices
hummed through the broken
arc of midnight
The oxen and roses
slept and slept

Sólo por los corredores
las cuatro luces clamaban
con el furor de San Jorge.
Tristes mujeres del valle
bajaban su sangre de hombre,
tranquila de flor cortada
y amarga de muslo joven.
Viejas mujeres del río
lloraban al pie del monte,
un minuto intransitable
de cabelleras y nombres.
Fachadas de cal, ponían
cuadrada y blanca la noche.
Serafines y gitanos
tocaban acordeones.
Madre, cuando yo me muera
que se enteren los señores.
Pon telegramas azules
que vayan del sur al norte.

Siete gritos, siete sangres,
siete adormideras dobles,
quebraron opacas lunas
en los oscuros salones.
Lleno de manos cortadas
y coronitas de flores,
el mar de los juramentos
resonaba, no sé dónde.
Y el cielo daba portazos
al brusco rumor del bosque,
mientras clamaban las luces
en los altos corredores.

Up in the balconies
lusty as San Jorge
four lights cried out
Sad women of the valley
sloughed their mannish blood
as calm as cut flowers
and bitter in young thighs
Old women of the river
wept near the hills
one insurmountable minute
of names and long hair
Whitewashed housefronts
made night square and white
On their accordions
seraphs and gypsies played
Mother when I die
let the gentlemen know
Send out blue telegrams
down south and up north

Seven cries seven of blood
seven double poppies
cracked the dull moons
in the darkened parlors
Full of cut-off hands
and coronets of flowers
the sea of curses sang
—where I don't know—
The sky slammed doors
on the drone of the woods
while up in the balconies
the lights cried out

14

El emplazado

para Emilio Aladrén

ROMANCE DEL EMPLAZADO

¡Mi soledad sin descanso!
Ojos chicos de mi cuerpo
y grandes de mi caballo,
no se cierran por la noche
ni miran al otro lado
donde se aleja tranquilo
un sueño de trece barcos.
Sino que limpios y duros
escuderos desvelados,
mis ojos miran un norte
de metales y peñascos
donde mi cuerpo sin venas
consulta naipes helados.

*

Los densos bueyes del agua
embisten a los muchachos
que se bañan en las lunas
de sus cuernos ondulados.
Y los martillos cantaban
sobre los yunques sonámbulos,
el insomnio del jinete
y el insomnio del caballo.

*

El veinticinco de junio
le dijeron a el Amargo:
Ya puedes cortar, si gustas,

14

The Marked Man

for Emilio Aladrén

BALLAD OF THE MARKED MAN

Loneliness without rest!
Small eyes of my body
big eyes of my horse
They never shut at night
or gaze across the way
where a thirteen-boat dream
floats serenely by—
My eyes are clean hard
servants without sleep
staring toward the north
of metals and crags
where my veinless body
consults the frozen cards

*

The heavy water oxen
charge after the boys
who swim in the moons
of their rippling horns
And the hammers sang
on sleepwalking anvils
sleepless night of the rider
sleepless night of the horse

*

On June twenty-fifth
they said to Amargo
if you like you can cut

las adelfas de tu patio.
Pinta una cruz en la puerta
y pon tu nombre debajo,
porque cicutas y ortigas
nacerán en tu costado,
y agujas de cal mojada
te morderán los zapatos.
Será de noche, en lo oscuro,
por los montes imantados
donde los bueyes del agua
beben los juncos soñando.
Pide luces y campanas.
Aprende a cruzar las manos,
y gusta los aires fríos
de metales y peñascos.
Porque dentro de dos meses
yacerás amortajado.

*

Espadón de nebulosa
mueve en el aire Santiago.
Grave silencio, de espalda,
manaba el cielo combado.

*

El veinticinco de junio
abrió sus ojos Amargo,
y el veinticinco de agosto
se tendió para cerrarlos.
Hombres bajaban la calle
para ver al emplazado,
que fijaba sobre el muro
su soledad con descanso.
Y la sábana impecable,
de duro acento romano,
daba equilibrio a la muerte
con las rectas de sus paños.

the oleanders in your yard
Paint a cross on the door
with your name beneath
For hemlock and nettle
will grow from your side
and needles of wet lime
will bite at your shoes
Night and dark will come
in the magnetic hills
where dreamy water oxen
drink up the reeds
Ask for lights and bells
learn to clasp your hands
and to love the cool wind
of metals and crags
Two months from now
you'll lie in a shroud

*

Great sword of the nebula
swings in the Santiago wind
Grave silence with its back turned
flowed from the curving sky

*

On June twenty-fifth
Amargo opened his eyes
On August twenty-fifth
he lay down and shut them
Men came down the street
to see the marked man
who saw on the wall
his loneliness at rest
And the perfect sheet
with a hard Roman design
squared up his death
with the line of the seams

15

Romance de la Guardia Civil española

a Juan Guerrero, Consul general de la poesía

Los caballos negros son.
Las herraduras son negras.
Sobre las capas relucen
manchas de tinta y de cera.
Tienen, por eso no lloran,
de plomo las calaveras.
Con el alma de charol
vienen por la carretera.
Jorobados y nocturnos,
por donde animan ordenan
silencios de goma oscura
y miedos de fina arena.
Pasan, si quieren pasar,
y ocultan en la cabeza
una vaga astronomía
de pistolas inconcretas.

*

¡Oh ciudad de los gitanos!
En las esquinas banderas.
La luna y la calabaza
con las guindas en conserva.
¡Oh ciudad de los gitanos!
¿Quién te vió y no te recuerda?
Ciudad de dolor y almizcle
con las torres de canela.

*

15

Ballad of the Spanish Civil Guard

for Juan Guerrero, Consul General of Poetry

Black are the horses
black are the horseshoes
On their capes shine
splotches of ink and wax
They do not cry—
they have skulls of lead
and souls of patent-leather
riding down the road
Hunched in the night
where they go they command
silence of dark rubber
and fear of fine sand
They go where they will
hiding in their heads
a blurred astronomy
of abstract guns

*

O city of gypsies!
Flags on the corners
The moon and the pumpkin
and sour cherry jam
O city of gypsies!
Who that has seen you
will ever forget?
City of pain and musk
with cinnamon towers

*

Cuando llegaba la noche
noche que noche nochera,
los gitanos en sus fraguas
forjaban soles y flechas.
Un caballo malherido,
llamaba a todas las puertas.
Gallos de vidrio cantaban
por Jerez de la Frontera.
El viento, vuelve desnudo
la esquina de la sorpresa,
en la noche platinoche
noche, que noche nochera.

*

La Virgen y San José
perdieron sus castañuelas,
y buscan a los gitanos
para ver si las encuentran.
La Virgen viene vestida
con un traje de alcaldesa
de papel de chocolate
con los collares de almendras.
San José mueve los brazos
bajo una capa de seda.
Detrás va Pedro Domecq
con tres sultanes de Persia.
La media luna, soñaba
un éxtasis de cigüeña.
Estandartes y faroles
invaden las azoteas.
Por los espejos sollozan
bailarinas sin caderas.
Agua y sombra, sombra y agua
por Jerez de la Frontera.

*

When the night came
night as nightnight
the gypsies at their forges
forged arrows and suns
A wounded horse
called at all the doors
Glass roosters sang
at Jerez de la Frontera
The naked wind turns
the corner of surprise
in the night silvernight
night as nightnight

*

The Virgin and San José
lost their castanets
Now they hunt gypsies
to get them back
The Virgin comes wearing
the suit of a mayoress
made of chocolate paper
with almond necklaces
San José moves his arms
under his silken cape
Next comes Pedro Domecq
with three Persian sultans
A half moon was dreaming
the bliss of a stork
Flags and lanterns
invade the roofs
In the mirrors sob
dancers without hips
Water shadow water
at Jerez de la Frontera

*

¡Oh ciudad de los gitanos!
En las esquinas banderas.
Apaga tus verdes luces
que viene la benemérita.
¡Oh ciudad de los gitanos!
¿Quién te vió y no te recuerda?
Dejadla lejos del mar
sin peines para sus crenchas.

*

Avanzan de dos en fondo
a la ciudad de la fiesta.
Un rumor de siemprevivas,
invade las cartucheras.
Avanzan de dos en fondo.
Doble nocturno de tela.
El cielo, se les antoja,
una vitrina de espuelas.

*

La ciudad libre de miedo,
multiplicaba sus puertas.
Cuarenta guardias civiles
entran a saco por ellas.
Los relojes se pararon,
y el coñac de las botellas
se disfrazó de noviembre
para no infundir sospechas.
Un vuelo de gritos largos
se levantó en las veletas.
Los sables cortan las brisas
que los cascos atropellan.
Por las calles de penumbra,

O city of gypsies
flags on the corners
Turn off your green lights—
here comes the Civil Guard
O city of gypsies!
Who that has seen you
can ever forget?
Leave her far from the sea
no combs to part her hair

*

They walk two by two
to the festival city
The rustle of everlastings
invades their cartridge belts
They walk two by two
double cloth nocturne
They like to think the sky
is a showcase of spurs

*

The city with no fear
had more and more doors
Forty civil guardsmen
stalked right through
Clocks came to a stop
and bottles of cognac
posed as November
not to raise an eye
In the weathervanes rose
a flight of long cries
Sabers cut the breeze
trampled by hoofs
Down shadowy streets

huyen las gitanas viejas
con los caballos dormidos
y las orzas de monedas.
Por las calles empinadas
suben las capas siniestras,
dejando detrás fugaces
remolinos de tijeras.

En el Portal de Belén,
los gitanos se congregan.
San José, lleno de heridas,
amortaja a una doncella.
Tercos fusiles agudos
por toda la noche suenan.
La Virgen cura a los niños
con salivilla de estrella.
Pero la Guardia Civil
avanza sembrando hogueras,
donde joven y desnuda
la imaginación se quema.
Rosa la de los Camborios,
gime sentada en su puerta
con sus dos pechos cortados
puestos en una bandeja.
Y otras muchachas corrían
perseguidas por sus trenzas,
en un aire donde estallan
rosas de pólvora negra.
Cuando todos los tejados
eran surcos en la tierra,
el alba meció sus hombros
en largo perfil de piedra.

*

flee the gypsy crones
with their sleeping horses
and pots full of coins
Up the steep streets
climb the evil capes
with scissors twirling
behind them as they come

At the Christmas manger
gypsies gather round
San José with many wounds
lays a shroud on a girl
Rifles stiff and pointed
ring out all night
The Virgin cures children
with drool from the stars
But the civil guardsmen
walk on lighting fires
where young and naked
imagination burns
Rosa de Camborio
moans seated at her door
her two lopped breasts
lying on a tray
Some girls were running
chased by their braids
through blackpowder roses
bursting in the wind
When all the roofs
were furrows in the dirt
dawn swayed its shoulders
in a long stone silhouette

*

¡Oh ciudad de los gitanos!
La Guardia Civil se aleja
por un túnel de silencio
mientras las llamas te cercan.

¡Oh ciudad de los gitanos!
¿Quién te vió y no te recuerda?
Que te busquen en mi frente.
Juego de luna y arena.

O city of gypsies!
The civil guardsmen walk on
through a tunnel of silence
while the flames encroach

O city of gypsies!
Who that has seen you
can ever forget?
May they find you on my brow
Game of moon and sand

Tres romances históricos

16

Martirio de Santa Olalla

a Rafael Martínez Nadal

I

PANORAMA DE MÉRIDA

Por la calle brinca y corre
caballo de larga cola,
mientras juegan o dormitan
viejos soldados de Roma.
Medio monte de Minervas
abre sus brazos sin hojas.
Agua en vilo redoraba
las aristas de las rocas.
Noche de torsos yacentes
y estrellas de nariz rota,
aguarda grietas del alba
para derrumbarse toda.
De cuando en cuando sonaban
blasfemias de cresta roja.
Al gemir la santa niña,
quiebra el cristal de las copas.
La rueda afila cuchillos
y garfios de aguda comba:
brama el toro de los yunques,
y Mérida se corona
de nardos casi despiertos
y tallos de zarzamora.

Three Historical Ballads

16

Martyrdom of Santa Olalla

for Rafael Martínez Nadal

I

PANORAMA OF MÉRIDA

A long-tailed horse
capers through the street
while old Roman soldiers
play cards or sleep
Half hill of Minervas
spreads its leafless arms
Flying water gilded
the rims of the rocks
Night of fallen torsos
and brokennosed stars
waits for dawn to crack
and all crumble down
Redcrested curses
rang out here and there
The saint girl moaned
and goblets shattered
A wheel hones knives
and the curves of hooks
The bull-in-the-anvil roars—
Mérida wears a crown
of white nard awaking
and blackberry stalks

II

EL MARTIRIO

Flora desnuda se sube
por escalerillas de agua.
El Cónsul pide bandeja
para los senos de Olalla.
Un chorro de venas verdes
le brota de la garganta.
Su sexo tiembla enredado
como un pájaro en las zarzas.
Por el suelo, ya sin norma,
brincan sus manos cortadas
que aún pueden cruzarse en tenue
oración decapitada.
Por los rojos agujeros
donde sus pechos estaban
se ven cielos diminutos
y arroyos de leche blanca.
Mil arbolillos de sangre
le cubren toda la espalda
y oponen húmedos troncos
al bisturí de las llamas.
Centuriones amarillos
de carne gris, desvelada,
llegan al cielo sonando
sus armaduras de plata.
Y mientras vibra confusa
pasión de crines y espadas,
el Cónsul porta en bandeja
senos ahumados de Olalla.

II

THE MARTYRDOM

Flora climbs naked
up the water stairs
The consul commands a tray
for Olalla's breasts
A tangle of green veins
spurts from her throat
Her sex quivers like a bird
caught in the brambles
Lawless on the ground
her lopped hands leap
and yet they join together
in frail beheaded prayer
Through the red holes
where her breasts were
you can see tiny skies
and creeks of white milk
A thousand blood trees
cover her back
pitting damp trunks
against the scalpel of flames
Yellow centurions
with weary gray skin
reach the sky clanging
coats of silver mail
Passion of manes and swords
blurs trembling—
on a tray the consul bears
Olalla's steaming breasts

III

INFIERNO Y GLORIA

Nieve ondulada reposa.
Olalla pende del árbol.
Su desnudo de carbón
tizna los aires helados.
Noche tirante reluce.
Olalla muerta en el árbol.
Tinteros de las ciudades
vuelcan la tinta despacio.
Negros maniquís de sastre
cubren la nieve del campo
en largas filas que gimen
su silencio mutilado.
Nieve partida comienza.
Olalla blanca en el árbol.
Escuadras de níquel juntan
los picos en su costado.

*

Una Custodia reluce
sobre los cielos quemados,
entre gargantas de arroyo
y ruiseñores en ramos.
¡Saltan vidrios de colores!
Olalla blanca en lo blanco.
Ángeles y serafines
dicen: Santo, Santo, Santo.

III

HELL AND GLORY

Snow lies undulant
Olalla hangs from a tree
Her bare burned body
chars the icy wind
The tense night gleams
Olalla dead in the tree
Inkpots in the cities
slowly spill their ink
Tailors' black mannequins
dot the snowy fields
in long lines moaning
her mutilated hush
Snow is falling again
Olalla white in the tree
Chrome brackets link
the spikes in her side

*

A Monstrance gleams
over the burned skies
on the narrowing creeks
and nightingales in trees
The stained glass leaps
Olalla white on white
Holy   Holy   Holy
angels and seraphs chant

17

Burla de Don Pedro a caballo
Romance con lagunas

a Jean Cassou

Por una vereda
venía Don Pedro.
¡Ay cómo lloraba
el caballero!
Montado en un ágil
caballo sin freno,
venía en la busca
del pan y del beso.
Todas las ventanas
preguntan al viento,
por el llanto oscuro
del caballero.

PRIMERA LAGUNA

Bajo el agua
siguen las palabras.
Sobre el agua
una luna redonda
se baña,
dando envidia a la otra
¡tan alta!
En la orilla,
un niño,
ve las lunas y dice:
¡Noche; toca los platillos!

17

Burla of Don Pedro on Horseback
Ballad with Lagoons

for Jean Cassou

Don Pedro
came down a path
Ay how the gentleman
wept and wept
Riding a nimble
horse with no bridle
he comes along looking
for bread and a kiss
All the windows
ask the wind
about his dark weeping
why the gentleman weeps

FIRST LAGOON

Under the water
the words carry on
On top of the water
a round moon
swims
rousing the envy
of the other
high-up moon!
A boy on the shore
looks at the moons
Play the cymbals!
he says to the night

SIGUE

A una ciudad lejana
ha llegado Don Pedro.
Una ciudad lejana
entre un bosque de cedros.
¿Es Belén? Por el aire
yerbaluisa y romero.
Brillan las azoteas
y las nubes. Don Pedro
pasa por arcos rotos.
Dos mujeres y un viejo
con velones de plata
le salen al encuentro.
Los chopos dicen: No.
Y el ruiseñor: Veremos.

SEGUNDA LAGUNA

Bajo el agua
siguen las palabras.
Sobre el peinado del agua
un círculo de pájaros y llamas.
Y por los cañaverales,
testigos que conocen lo que falta.
Sueño concreto y sin norte
de madera de guitarra.

SEGUE

Don Pedro has come
to a far city
Far city in a cedar grove—
is it Bethlehem?
Clouds and roofs gleam
Rosemary and lemon grass
scent the wind
Under broken arches
Don Pedro rides in
Out to greet him come
two women one old man
bearing silver lamps
The poplars say: no
And the nightingale: maybe

SECOND LAGOON

Under the water
the words carry on
Over combed water
a ring of birds and flames
Out in the canefields
the witnesses
know what is missing
Vivid wandering dream
of the wood
of a guitar

SIGUE

Por el camino llano
dos mujeres y un viejo
con velones de plata
van al cementerio.
Entre los azafranes
han encontrado muerto
el sombrío caballo
de Don Pedro.
Voz secreta de tarde
balaba por el cielo.
Unicornio de ausencia
rompe en cristal su cuerno.
La gran ciudad lejana
está ardiendo
y un hombre va llorando
tierras adentro.
Al Norte hay una estrella.
Al Sur un marinero.

ÚLTIMA LAGUNA

Bajo el agua
están las palabras.
Limo de voces perdidas.
Sobre la flor enfriada,
está Don Pedro olvidado
¡ay! jugando con las ranas.

SEGUE

On the wide road
two women one old man
go to the graveyard
with silver lamps
Deep in the saffron
they found Don Pedro's
somber horse dead
Secret voice of dusk
bleated through the sky
Unicorn of non-being
breaks its glass horn
The great far city
is burning
and a man is crying
on the inland roads
In the south a sailor
in the north a star

LAST LAGOON

Words lie
under the water
Silt of lost voices
On the cold flower
Don Pedro forgotten
Ay! playing with frogs

18

Thamar y Amnón

para Alfonso García Valdecasas

La luna gira en el cielo
sobre las tierras sin agua
mientras el verano siembra
rumores de tigre y llama.
Por encima de los techos
nervios de metal sonaban.
Aire rizado venía
con los balidos de lana.
La tierra se ofrece llena
de heridas cicatrizadas,
o estremecida de agudos
cauterios de luces blancas.

*

Thamar estaba soñando
pájaros en su garganta,
al son de panderos fríos
y cítaras enlunadas.
Su desnudo en el alero,
agudo norte de palma,
pide copos a su vientre
y granizo a sus espaldas.
Thamar estaba cantando
desnuda por la terraza.
Alrededor de sus pies,
cinco palomas heladas.
Amnón, delgado y concreto,
en la torre la miraba,

18

Tamar and Amnon

for Alfonso García Valdecasas

The moon rolls in the sky
over lands without water
while the summer scatters
purr of tiger and flame
Over the rooftops
nerves of metal sang
Curly wind blew in
with the bleating wool
The land stretches out
under scars of old wounds
or trembles in the sharp
white cauteries of light

*

Tamar was dreaming
birds in her throat
to the thrum of cold timbrels
and moonstruck zithers
Naked under the eaves
sharp north of the palm
she wants snow for her belly
and hail for her back
Tamar was singing
naked on the terrace
and all around her feet
lay five frozen doves
Amnon lean and solid
watched from the tower

llenas las ingles de espuma
y oscilaciones la barba.
Su desnudo iluminado
se tendía en la terraza,
con un rumor entre dientes
de flecha recién clavada.
Amnón estaba mirando
la luna redonda y baja,
y vio en la luna los pechos
durísimos de su hermana.

*

Amnón a las tres y media
se tendió sobre la cama.
Toda la alcoba sufría
con sus ojos llenos de alas.
La luz maciza, sepulta
pueblos en la arena parda,
o descubre transitorio
coral de rosas y dalias.
Linfa de pozo oprimida,
brota silencio en las jarras.
En el musgo de los troncos
la cobra tendida canta.
Amnón gime por la tela
fresquísima de la cama.
Yedra del escalofrío
cubre su carne quemada.
Thamar entró silenciosa
en la alcoba silenciada,
color de vena y Danubio,
turbia de huellas lejanas.
Thamar, bórrame los ojos
con tu fija madrugada.

his groin full of foam
his beard full of ripples
Naked and gleaming
he lay on the terrace
in his teeth the shudder
of an arrow just struck
Amnon was watching
the moon round and low
he glimpsed in the moon
his sister's taut breasts

*

At half past three Amnon
lay down on his bed
All the chamber suffered
with eyes full of wings
The thick light buries
villages in gray sand
or finds the fleeting
rose-and-dahlia coral
Hidden juice of the well
gushes silence in the jugs
In the moss of tree trunks
the long cobra sings
Amnon moans in his bed
on the fresh linens
Ivy of a shiver
sheathes his burning skin
Tamar came hushed
into the hushed chamber
color of veins and Danube
and thrum of ancient feet
Tamar rub out my eyes
with your infinite dawn

Mis hilos de sangre tejen
volantes sobre tu falda.
Déjame tranquila, hermano.
Son tus besos en mi espalda,
avispas y vientecillos
en doble enjambre de flautas.
Thamar, en tus pechos altos
hay dos peces que me llaman
y en las yemas de tus dedos
rumor de rosa encerrada.

*

Los cien caballos del rey
en el patio relinchaban.
Sol en cubos resistía
la delgadez de la parra.
Ya la coge del cabello,
ya la camisa le rasga.
Corales tibios dibujan
arroyos en rubio mapa.

*

¡Oh qué gritos se sentían
por encima de las casas!
Qué espesura de puñales
y túnicas desgarradas.
Por las escaleras tristes
esclavos suben y bajan.
Émbolos y muslos juegan
bajo las nubes paradas.
Alrededor de Thamar
gritan vírgenes gitanas
y otras recogen las gotas
de su flor martirizada.

My threads of blood weave
flounces for your skirt
Let me alone brother
your kisses on my back
are wasps and light winds
in two swarms of flutes
On your high breasts Tamar
two fishes are calling me
the tips of your fingers
croon like a secret rose

*

The king's hundred horses
whinnied in the yard
Squares of sun struggled
with the slender vine
He grabs her by the hair
he tears off her shirt
Warm corals draw creeks
in her blond map

*

Ay what cries were heard
out over the houses
A thicket of daggers
and tattered tunics
On the sad stairways
slaves run up and down
Thighs and pistons play
beneath the halted clouds
All around Tamar
gypsy maidens scream
Some gather the drops
of her martyred flower

Paños blancos, enrojecen
en las alcobas cerradas.
Rumores de tibia aurora
pámpanos y peces cambian.

*

Violador enfurecido,
Amnón huye con su jaca.
Negros le dirigen flechas
en los muros y atalayas.
Y cuando los cuatro cascos
eran cuatro resonancias,
David con sus tijeras
cortó las cuerdas del arpa.

The white cloths turn red
in the shut chambers
Fish and vineshoots swap
the sounds of sultry dawn

*

Mad rapist Amnon
tears away on his horse
Black archers shoot arrows
from the towers and walls
When the four hoofbeats
were four reverberations
David with his scissors
cut the strings of the harp

The Tamarit Diwan

Gacelas

I. Del amor imprevisto

Nadie comprendía el perfume
de la oscura magnolia de tu vientre.
Nadie sabía que martirizabas
un colibrí de amor entre los dientes.

Mil caballitos persas se dormían
en la plaza con luna de tu frente,
mientras que yo enlazaba cuatro noches
tu cintura, enemiga de la nieve.

Entre yeso y jazmines, tu mirada
era un pálido ramo de simientes.
Yo busqué, para darte, por mi pecho
las letras de marfil que dicen *siempre*.

Siempre siempre: jardin de mi agonía,
tu cuerpo fugitivo para siempre,
la sangre de tus venas en mi boca,
tu boca ya sin luz para mi muerte.

Gacelas

I.   Of Sudden Love

No one understood the fragrance
dark magnolia of your groin
No one knew you martyred
love's hummingbird in your teeth

A thousand Persian ponies slept
in the moonlit plaza of your brow
For four nights I lassoed
your waist—enemy of snow—

Amid the plaster and jasmine
your gaze was a pale bouquet of seeds
I searched my heart to give you
the ivory letters that say forever

ever ever garden of my dying
your body shunning me forever
in my mouth the blood of your veins
your mouth with no light for my death

II.   De la terrible presencia

Yo quiero que el agua se quede sin cauce.
Yo quiero que el viento se quede sin valles.

Quiero que la noche se quede sin ojos
y mi corazón sin la flor del oro;

que los bueyes hablen con las grandes hojas
y que la lombriz se muera de sombra;

que brillen los dientes de la calavera
y los amarillos inunden la seda.

Puedo ver el duelo de la noche herida
luchando enroscada con el mediodía.

Resisto un ocaso de verde veneno
y los arcos rotos donde sufre el tiempo.

Pero no ilumines tu limpio desnudo
como un negro cactus abierto en los juncos.

Déjame en un ansia de oscuros planetas,
pero no me enseñes tu cintura fresca.

II.   Of the Powerful Presence

I want the water without a riverbed
I want the wind without valleys

I want the night without eyes
and my heart without the golden flower

the oxen to talk to the giant leaves
and the worm to die of shadow

the teeth in the skull to gleam
and yellows to flood the silk

I can see the grief of the wounded night
coiled and grappling with noon

I can bear a poison-green sunset
and the cracked arches of suffering time

But do not shine in your stark body
like a black cactus splayed among the reeds

Leave me with this desire for dark planets
but do not show me your fresh waist

III. Del amor desesperado

La noche no quiere venir
para que tú no vengas,
ni yo pueda ir.

Pero yo iré,
aunque un sol de alacranes me coma la sien.

Pero tú vendrás
con la lengua quemada por la lluvia de sal.

El día no quiere venir
para que tú no vengas,
ni yo pueda ir.

Pero yo iré
entregando a los sapos mi mordido clavel.

Pero tú vendrás
por las turbias cloacas de la oscuridad.

Ni la noche ni el día quieren venir
para que por ti muera
y tú mueras por mí.

III.   Of Tormented Love

Night does not want to come
so that you will not come
and I can't go

But I will go
though a scorpion sun eat my temple

But you will come
with your tongue burned by the salt rain

Day does not want to come
so that you will not come
and I can't go

But I will go
and give my nibbled carnation to the toads

But you will come
through the tunnels of murky darkness

Neither night nor day wants to come
so that I will die for you
and you for me

IV.   Del amor que no se deja ver

Solamente por oír
la campana de la Vela
te puse una corona de verbena.

Granada era una luna
ahogada entre las yedras.

Solamente por oír
la campana de la Vela
desgarré mi jardín de Cartagena.

Granada era una corza
rosa por las veletas.

Solamente por oír
la campana de la Vela
me abrasaba en tu cuerpo
sin saber de quién era.

IV. Of Love That Won't Be Seen

Only to hear
the bell of the Vela
I gave you a crown of verbena

Granada was a moon
drowning in ivy

Only to hear
the bell of the Vela
I tore up my Cartagena garden

Granada was a pink doe
among the weathervanes

Only to hear
the bell of the Vela
I burned in your body
not knowing whose it was

V.   Del niño muerto

Todas las tardes in Granada,
todas las tardes se muere un niño.
Todas las tardes el agua se sienta
a conversar con sus amigos.

Los muertos llevan alas de musgo
El viento nublado y el viento limpio
son dos faisanes que vuelan por las torres
y el día es un muchacho herido.

No quedaba en el aire ni una brizna de alondra
cuando yo te encontré por las grutas del vino.
No quedaba en la tierra ni una miga de nube
cuando te ahogabas por el río.

Un gigante de agua cayó sobre los montes
y el valle fue rodando con perros y con lirios.
Tu cuerpo, con la sombra violeta de mis manos,
era, muerto en la orilla, un arcángel de frío.

V.   Of the Dead Boy

Every evening in Granada
every evening a little boy dies
Every evening the water sits down
to talk with its friends

The dead have wings of moss
The cloudy wind and the clean wind
are two pheasants flying among the towers
and the day is a wounded boy

Not a wisp of a lark left in the air
when I found you in the wine grottoes
Not a scrap of cloud left in the world
when you drowned in the river

A colossus of water fell on the hills
and the valley rolled with lilies and dogs
Your body in the violet shadow of my hands
was a cold archangel on the riverbank

VI.   De la raíz amarga

Hay una raíz amarga
y un mundo de mil terrazas.

Ni la mano más pequeña
quiebra la puerta del agua.

¿Dónde vas, adónde, dónde?
Hay un cielo de mil ventanas
—batalla de abejas lívidas—
y hay una raíz amarga.

Amarga.

Duele en la planta del pie
el interior de la cara,
y duele en el tronco fresco
de noche recién cortada.

¡Amor, enemigo mío,
muerde tu raíz amarga!

VI.   Of the Bitter Root

There is a bitter root
and a thousand terraces in the world

Not the smallest hand
breaks the door of water

Where are you going where where
A thousand windows in the sky
—a battle of angry bees—
and a bitter root

Bitter

It hurts in the sole of my foot
and inside my face
and it hurts in the freshcut
trunk of the night

Love my enemy
bite your bitter root

VII.   Del recuerdo de amor

No te lleves tu recuerdo.
Déjalo solo en mi pecho,

temblor de blanco cerezo
en el martirio de enero.

Me separa de los muertos
un muro de malos sueños.

Doy pena de lirio fresco
para un corazón de yeso.

Toda la noche, en el huerto
mis ojos, como dos perros.

Toda la noche, comiendo
los membrillos de veneno.

Algunas veces el viento
es un tulipán de miedo,

es un tulipán enfermo,
la madrugada de invierno.

Un muro de malos sueños
me separa de los muertos.

La hierba cubre en silencio
el valle gris de tu cuerpo.

Por el arco del encuentro
la cicuta está creciendo.

Pero deja tu recuerdo,
déjalo solo en mi pecho.

VII.   Of the Memory of Love

Don't take my memory of you
leave it in my heart

trembling white cherry tree
January's martyr

A wall of bad dreams
divides me from the dead

I'm as pained as a fresh lily
before a plaster heart

All night in the orchard
my eyes are like two dogs

All night eating
the poison quinces

Sometimes the wind
is a tulip of fear

a sick tulip
in the winter dawn

A wall of bad dreams
divides me from the dead

Silent grass covers
your body's gray valley

Near the arch where we meet
hemlock is growing

Leave me my memory of you
leave it in my heart

VIII.   De la muerte oscura

Quiero dormir el sueño de las manzanas,
alejarme del tumulto de los cementerios.
Quiero dormir el sueño de aquel niño
que quería cortarse el corazón en alta mar.

No quiero que me repitan que los muertos no pierden la sangre;
que la boca podrida sigue pidiendo agua.
No quiero enterarme de los martirios que da la hierba,
ni de la luna con boca de serpiente
que trabaja antes del amanecer.

Quiero dormir un rato,
un rato, un minuto, un siglo;
pero que todos sepan que no he muerto;
que hay un establo de oro en mis labios;
que soy el pequeño amigo del viento oeste;
que soy la sombra inmensa de mis lágrimas.

Cúbreme por la aurora con un velo,
porque me arrojará puñados de hormigas,
y moja con agua dura mis zapatos
para que resbale la pinza de su alacrán.

Porque quiero dormir el sueño de las manzanas
para aprender un llanto que me limpie de tierra;
porque quiero vivir con aquel niño oscuro
que quería cortarse el corazón en alta mar.

VIII.   Of the Dark Death

Let me sleep the sleep of apples
far from the tumult of cemeteries
Let me sleep the sleep of the boy
who longed to cut out his heart at sea

Let them not say the dead lose no blood
or that rotten mouths beg for water
Let me never know the torments of the grass
or the moon with the mouth of a snake
that starts its day before dawn

Let me sleep for a moment
a moment a minute a century
but let them all know I have not died
that there's a stable of gold on my lips
that I'm the great shadow of my tears
and the west wind's little friend

Wrap me in a veil when the sunrise
pelts me with fistfuls of ants
and soak my shoes in hard water
so that its scorpion claw will slip

Let me sleep the sleep of apples
and learn a lament that will clean off the dirt
let me live with that dark boy
who longed to cut out his heart at sea

IX.   Del amor maravilloso

Con todo el yeso
de los malos campos,
eras junco de amor, jazmín mojado.

Con sur y llama
de los malos cielos,
eras rumor de nieve por mi pecho.

Cielos y campos
anudaban cadenas en mis manos

Campos y cielos
azotaban las llagas de mi cuerpo.

IX.   Of Wonderful Love

You had all the chalk
of the bad fields—
and even so
you were a love reed a wet jasmine

You had south and flame
from the bad skies—
and even so
you were the sound of snow in my heart

Skies and fields
knotted chains around my hands

Fields and skies
whipped the wounds on my body

X.   De la huida

Me he perdido muchas veces por el mar
con el oído lleno de flores recién cortadas,
con la lengua llena de amor y de agonía.
Muchas veces me he perdido por el mar,
como me pierdo en el corazón de algunos niños.

No hay nadie que, al dar un beso,
no sienta la sonrisa de la gente sin rostro,
ni hay nadie que, al tocar un recién nacido,
olvide las inmóviles calaveras del caballo.

Porque las rosas buscan en la frente
un duro paisaje de hueso
y las manos del hombre no tienen más sentido
que imitar a las raíces bajo tierra.

Como me pierdo en el corazón de algunos niños,
me he perdido muchas veces por el mar.
Ignorante del agua, voy buscando
una muerte de luz que me consuma.

X.   Of Wandering

I have often wandered by the sea
my ears full of freshcut flowers
my tongue full of love and dying
I have often wandered by the sea
as I wander in the hearts of some children

Anyone who offers a kiss
feels the smile of those without faces
Anyone who touches a newborn
knows the stiff skulls of horses

Roses are searching foreheads
for a hard landscape of bone
and the only purpose of human hands
is as roots beneath the earth

As I wander in the hearts of some children
I have often wandered by the sea
Knowing nothing about water
I long to die consumed by light

XI.   Del amor con cien años

Suben por la calle
los cuatro galanes.

Ay, ay, ay, ay.

Por la calle abajo
van los tres galanes.

Ay, ay, ay.

Se ciñen el talle
esos dos galanes.

Ay, ay.

¡Cómo vuelve el rostro
un galán y el aire!

Ay.

Por los arrayanes
se pasea nadie.

XI.   Of Love with One Hundred Years

Four loverboys
walk up the street

ay ay ay ay

Three loverboys
walk down the street

ay ay ay

Two loverboys
walk arm in arm

ay ay

One loverboy and the wind
turn and look back

ay

No one walks
among the myrtle trees

Casidas

I.   Del herido por el agua

Quiero bajar al pozo,
quiero subir los muros de Granada,
para mirar el corazón pasado
por el punzón oscuro de las aguas.

El niño herido gemía
con una corona de escarcha.
Estanques, aljibes y fuentes
levantaban al aire sus espadas.
¡Ay qué furia de amor, qué hiriente filo,
qué nocturno rumor, qué muerte blanca!
¡Qué desiertos de luz iban hundiendo
los arenales de la madrugada!
El niño estaba solo
con la ciudad dormida en la garganta.
Un surtidor que viene de los sueños
lo defiende del hambre de las algas.
El niño y su agonía, frente a frente,
eran dos verdes lluvias enlazadas.
El niño se tendía por la tierra
y su agonía se curvaba.

Quiero bajar al pozo,
quiero morir mi muerte a bocanadas,
quiero llenar mi corazón de musgo,
para ver al herido por el agua.

Casidas

I. Of the Boy Wounded by Water

I want to go down to the well
I want to climb the walls of Granada
I want to see the heart struck
by the water's dark dagger

The wounded boy moaned
in a crown of frost
Pools tanks and fountains
lifted their swords to the wind
What a love fury—what a wounding blade—
what a night murmur and a white death
What deserts of light drowning
the dunes of the dawn
The boy was alone
while the city slept in his throat
Water spurting from dreams
fought off the seaweed's hunger
The boy and his dying—face to face—
were two green rains twined together
The boy lay down on the dirt
and his dying arced—

I want to climb down the well
die my death in great gulps
fill up my heart with moss
and see the boy wounded by water

II.   Del llanto

He cerrado mi balcón
porque no quiero oír el llanto,
pero por detrás de los grises muros
no se oye otra cosa que el llanto.

Hay muy pocos ángeles que canten,
hay muy pocos perros que ladren,
mil violines caben en la palma de mi mano.

Pero el llanto es un perro inmenso,
el llanto es un ángel inmenso,
el llanto es un violín inmenso,
las lágrimas amordazan al viento,
y no se oye otra cosa que el llanto.

II. Of Crying

I've shut my balcony
because I don't want to hear the crying
but behind the gray walls
all you hear is crying

There are so few angels that sing
there are so few dogs that bark
a thousand violins fit in the palm of my hand

but the crying is a huge dog
the crying is a giant angel
the crying is a vast violin
the tears muzzle the wind
and all you hear is crying

III. De los ramos

Por las arboledas del Tamarit
han venido los perros de plomo
a esperar que se caigan los ramos,
a esperar que se quiebren ellos solos.

El Tamarit tiene un manzano
con una manzana de sollozos.
Un ruiseñor agrupa los suspiros
y un faisán los ahuyenta por el polvo.

Pero los ramos son alegres,
los ramos son como nosotros.
No piensan en la lluvia y se han dormido,
como si fueran árboles, de pronto.

Sentados con el agua en las rodillas
dos valles aguardaban al otoño.
La penumbra con paso de elefante
empujaba las ramas y los troncos.

Por las arboledas del Tamarit
hay muchos niños de velado rostro
a esperar que se caigan mis ramos,
a esperar que se quiebren ellos solos.

III.   Of the Branches

Through the groves of Tamarit
came the leaden dogs
waiting for branches to fall
waiting for them to break

In the Tamarit an apple tree
has an apple of sobs
A nightingale scoops up sighs
a pheasant strews them in the dust

But the branches are joyous
the branches are like us
They do not think of rain
they doze off—fast—like trees

With water to their knees
two valleys wait for autumn
Dusk walks like an elephant
pushing branches and trees

In the groves of Tamarit
many children wear veils
waiting for my branches to fall
waiting for them to break

IV.   De la mujer tendida

Verte desnuda es recordar la Tierra,
la Tierra lisa, limpia de caballos.
La Tierra sin un junco, forma pura
cerrada al porvenir: confín de plata.

Verte desnuda es comprender el ansia
de la lluvia que busca débil talle,
o la fiebre del mar de inmenso rostro
sin encontrar la luz de su mejilla.

La sangre sonará por las alcobas
y vendrá con espadas fulgurantes,
pero tú no sabrás dónde se ocultan
el corazón de sapo o la violeta.

Tu vientre es una lucha de raíces,
tus labios son un alba sin contorno.
Bajo las rosas tibias de la cama
los muertos gimen esperando turno.

IV.   Of the Woman Lying Down

Seeing you naked I think of Land
smooth land with no horses
pure shape of land with no reeds
silver horizon with no future

Seeing you naked I feel the longing
of rain that seeks a tender waist
or the feverish sea with the vast face
that finds no light on its cheek

Blood will ring in the bedrooms
it will rise with blazing swords
but the toad's heart and the violet—
you won't know where they hide

Your belly is a tussle of roots
your lips a nebulous dawn
Under the bed's warm roses
the dead moan and wait their turn

V.   Del sueño al aire libre

Flor de jazmín y toro degollado.
Pavimento infinito. Mapa. Sala. Arpa. Alba.
La niña sueña un toro de jazmines
y el toro es un sangriento crepúsculo que brama.

Si el cielo fuera un niño pequeñito,
los jazmines tendrían mitad de noche oscura,
y el toro circo azul sin lidiadores,
y un corazón al pie de una columna.

Pero el cielo es un elefante,
el jazmín es un agua sin sangre
y la niña es un ramo nocturno
por el inmenso pavimento oscuro.

Entre el jazmín y el toro
o garfios de marfil o gente dormida.
En el jazmín un elefante y nubes
y en el toro el esqueleto de la niña.

V.   Of Dreaming in the Night Air

Jasmine flower and beheaded bull
Vast ring Map Hall Harp Dawn
The girl dreams of a jasmine bull
the bull is a bloody dawn braying

If the sky were a tiny boy
the jasmine would own half the night
the bull a blue ring with no bullfighters
at the foot of the column a heart

But the sky is an elephant
jasmine is water without blood
and the girl is a dark bouquet
on the great ring of the night

Between the jasmine and the bull
are ivory hooks or people asleep
Elephant and clouds in the jasmine
the girl's skeleton in the bull

VI.   De la mano imposible

Yo no quiero más que una mano,
una mano herida, si es posible.
Yo no quiero más que una mano,
aunque pase mil noches sin lecho.

Sería un pálido lirio de cal,
sería una paloma amarrada a mi corazón,
sería el guardián que en la noche de mi tránsito
prohibiera en absoluto la entrada a la luna.

Yo no quiero más que esa mano
para los diarios aceites y la sábana blanca de mi agonía.
Yo no quiero más que esa mano
para tener un ala de mi muerte.

Lo demás todo pasa.
Rubor sin nombre ya. Astro perpetuo.
Lo demás es lo otro; viento triste,
mientras las hojas huyen en bandadas.

VI.   Of the Hand That Can Never Be

All I want is a hand
a wounded hand if that can be
All I want is a hand
though I may live a thousand nights without a bed

Whether a pale lily of whitewash
or a dove lashed to my heart
or the watchman who on the night of my passing
forbids all entry to the moon

All I want is this hand
for the daily unctions and the white sheet of my dying
All I want is this hand
to hold the wing of my death

All else passes
Suffering has no more name Star everlasting
All else is other Sad wind
while the flocks of leaves scatter

VII.   De la rosa

La rosa,
no buscaba la aurora:
casi eterna en su ramo,
buscaba otra cosa.

La rosa,
no buscaba ni ciencia ni sombra:
confín de carne y sueño,
buscaba otra cosa.

La rosa,
no buscaba la rosa:
inmóvil por el cielo
buscaba otra cosa.

VII.   Of the Rose

The rose
wasn't looking for dawn
almost eternal on its stem
it was looking for something else

The rose
wasn't looking for science or shadow
frontier of flesh and dream
it was looking for something else

The rose
wasn't looking for the rose
poised there in the sky
it was looking for something else

VIII.   De la muchacha dorada

La muchacha dorada
se bañaba en el agua
y el agua se doraba.

Las algas y las ramas
en sombra la asombraban,
y el ruiseñor cantaba
por la muchacha blanca.

Vino la noche clara,
turbia de plata mala,
con peladas montañas
bajo la brisa parda.

La muchacha mojada
era blanca en el agua
y el agua, llamarada.

Vino el alba sin mancha
con cien caras de vaca,
yerta y amortajada
con heladas guirnaldas.

La muchacha de lágrimas
se bañaba entre llamas,
y el ruiseñor lloraba
con las alas quemadas.

La muchacha dorada
era una blanca garza
y el agua la doraba.

VIII.   Of the Gold Girl

The gold girl
was swimming in the water
and the water turned gold

Waterweeds and branches
in shadow shadowed her
and the nightingale sang
for the white girl

The clear night came
dark with bad silver
and the bare hills
under the dusky wind

The wet girl
was white in the water
and the water blazed

The dawn came spotless
with a hundred cow heads
stiff and shrouded
in frozen garlands

The girl of tears
swam in the flames
and the nightingale wept
in its burned wings

The gold girl
was a white heron
the water turned gold

IX.　De las palomas oscuras

a Claudio Guillén

Por las ramas del laurel
vi dos palomas oscuras.
La una era el sol,
la otra la luna.
"Vecinitas," les dije,
" ¿dónde está mi sepultura?"
"En mi cola," dijo el sol.
"En mi garganta," dijo la luna.
Y yo que estaba caminando
con la tierra por la cintura
vi dos águilas de nieve
y una muchacha desnuda.
La una era la otra
y la muchacha era ninguna.
"Aguilitas," les dije,
" ¿dónde está mi sepultura?"
"En mi cola," dijo el sol.
"En mi garganta," dijo la luna.
Por las ramas del laurel
vi dos palomas desnudas.
La una era la otra
y las dos eran ninguna.

IX.   Of the Dark Doves

for Claudio Guillén

In the branches of the laurel tree
I saw two dark doves
One was the sun
and one the moon
Little neighbors I said
where is my grave—
In my tail said the sun
On my throat said the moon
And I who was walking
with the land around my waist
saw two snow eagles
and a naked girl
One was the other
and the girl was none
Little eagles I said
where is my grave—
In my tail said the sun
On my throat said the moon
In the branches of the laurel tree
I saw two naked doves
One was the other
and both were none

Lament for Ignacio Sánchez Mejías

for my dear friend Encarnación Lápez Júlvez

La cogida y la muerte

A las cinco de la tarde.
Eran las cinco en punto de la tarde.
Un niño trajo la blanca sábana
a las cinco de la tarde.
Una espuerta de cal ya prevenida
a las cinco de la tarde.
Lo demás era muerte y sólo muerte
a las cinco de la tarde.

El viento se llevó los algodones
a las cinco de la tarde.
Y el óxido sembró cristal y níquel
a las cinco de la tarde.
Ya luchan la paloma y el leopardo
a las cinco de la tarde.
Y un muslo con un asta desolada
a las cinco de la tarde.
Comenzaron los sones de bordón
a las cinco de la tarde.
Las campanas de arsénico y el humo
a las cinco de la tarde.

En las esquinas grupos de silencio
a las cinco de la tarde.
¡Y el toro solo corazón arriba!
a las cinco de la tarde.
Cuando el sudor de nieve fue llegando
a las cinco de la tarde,
cuando la plaza se cubrió de yodo
a las cinco de la tarde,
la muerte puso huevos en la herida

I

The Goring and the Death

At five in the afternoon
At the stroke of five
The boy brought the white sheet
at five o'clock
A basket of lime all ready
at five o'clock
The rest was death and only death
at five o'clock

Wind carried off the cotton balls
at five o'clock
Rust scattered chrome and glass
at five o'clock
The dove and the leopard fought
at five o'clock
And a thigh with a desolate horn in it
at five o'clock
The bass strings began to thrum
at five o'clock
The bells of arsenic and smoke
at five o'clock

On the corners crowds of silence
at five o'clock
The bull alone with lifted heart
at five o'clock
When the icy sweat began to flow
at five o'clock
when iodine filled the bullring
at five o'clock
and death laid eggs in the wound

a las cinco de la tarde.
A las cinco de la tarde.
A las cinco en punto de la tarde.

Un ataúd con ruedas es la cama
a las cinco de la tarde.
Huesos y flautas suenan en su oído
a las cinco de la tarde.
El toro ya mugía por su frente
a las cinco de la tarde.
El cuarto se irisaba de agonía
a las cinco de la tarde.
A lo lejos ya viene la gangrena
a las cinco de la tarde.
Trompa de lirio por las verdes ingles
a las cinco de la tarde.
Las heridas quemaban como soles
a las cinco de la tarde,
y el gentío rompía las ventanas
a las cinco de la tarde.
A las cinco de la tarde.
¡Ay qué terribles cinco de la tarde!
¡Eran las cinco en todos los relojes!
¡Eran las cinco en sombra de la tarde!

at five o'clock
At five o'clock
At the stroke of five

The bed is a coffin on wheels
at five o'clock
Bones and flutes sing in his ear
at five o'clock
The bull roared from his brow
at five o'clock
The room was a death rainbow
at five o'clock
The gangrene began from afar
at five o'clock
Trumpet of a lily in his green groin
at five o'clock
The wounds burned like suns
at five o'clock
and the mob broke the windows
at five o'clock
At five o'clock
Ay what terrible fives
It was five on all the clocks
In the afternoon shadows

2

La sangre derramada

¡Que no quiero verla!

Dile a la luna que venga,
que no quiero ver la sangre
de Ignacio sobre la arena.

¡Que no quiero verla!

La luna de par en par,
caballo de nubes quietas,
y la plaza gris del sueño
con sauces en las barreras.

¡Que no quiero verla!
Que mi recuerdo se quema.
¡Avisad a los jazmines
con su blancura pequeña!

¡Que no quiero verla!

La vaca del viejo mundo
pasaba su triste lengua
sobre un hocico de sangres
derramadas en la arena,
y los toros de Guisando,
casi muerte y casi piedra,
mugieron como dos siglos,
hartos de pisar la tierra.

2

The Spilled Blood

I don't want to look

Tell the moon to come
I don't want to behold
Ignacio's blood in the ring

I don't want to look

The moon shines clear
horse of quiet clouds
the gray bullring of dreams
with willows by the gates

I don't want to look
My memory is burning
Tell the jasmine flowers
so small and so white

I don't want to look

Cow of the old world
licked its sad tongue
over a snoutful of blood
spilled in the ring
and the bulls of Guisando
half dead and half stone
roared like two centuries
tired of treading the dirt

No.
¡Que no quiero verla!

Por las gradas sube Ignacio
con toda su muerte a cuestas.
Buscaba el amanecer,
y el amanecer no era.
Busca su perfil seguro,
y el sueño lo desorienta.
Buscaba su hermoso cuerpo
y encontró su sangre abierta.
¡No me digáis que la vea!
No quiero sentir el chorro
cada vez con menos fuerza;
ese chorro que ilumina
los tendidos y se vuelca
sobre la pana y el cuero
de muchedumbre sedienta.
¿Quién me grita que me asome?
¡No me digáis que la vea!

No se cerraron los ojos
cuando vio los cuernos cerca,
pero las madres terribles
levantaron la cabeza.
Y a través de las ganaderías
hubo un aire de voces secretas,
que gritaban a toros celestes,
mayorales de pálida niebla.

No hubo príncipe en Sevilla
que comparársele pueda,
ni espada como su espada

No
I don't want to look

Ignacio mounts the steps
with his death on his back
He was searching for dawn
but day wasn't dawning
He searches for his strong face
and gets lost in a dream
He searched for his fine body
and found his spilled blood
Don't tell me to look
I won't watch the blood
run slower and slower
the blood that glistens
on the rows and spills
on the leather and corduroy
of the thirsting crowd—
Who shouts at me to look
Don't tell me to look

His eyes didn't close
as the horns came near
but the terrible mothers
raised up their heads
And over the herds
the secret voices flew
shouting to the bulls in heaven
herders of pale fog

No prince in Seville
could rival him—
no sword like his sword

ni corazón tan de veras.
Como un río de leones
su maravillosa fuerza,
y como un torso de mármol
su dibujada prudencia.
Aire de Roma andaluza
le doraba la cabeza
donde su risa era un nardo
de sal y de inteligencia.
¡Qué gran torero en la plaza!
¡Qué buen serrano en la sierra!
¡Qué blando con las espigas!
¡Qué duro con las espuelas!
¡Qué tierno con el rocío!
¡Qué deslumbrante en la feria!
¡Qué tremendo con las últimas
banderillas de tiniebla!

Pero ya duerme sin fin.
Ya los musgos y la hierba
abren con dedos seguros
la flor de su calavera.
Y su sangre ya viene cantando:
cantando por marismas y praderas,
resbalando por cuernos ateridos,
vacilando sin alma por la niebla,
tropezando con miles de pezuñas
como una larga, oscura, triste lengua,
para formar un charco de agonía
junto al Guadalquivir de las estrellas.

¡Oh blanco muro de España!
¡Oh negro toro de pena!
!Oh sangre dura de Ignacio!
¡Oh ruiseñor de sus venas!

no heart so true
Like a river of lions
his prodigious strength
Like a marble torso
his etched poise
A hint of Andalusian Rome
gilded his head
and his laughter was a white nard
of salt and wit
How grand the bullfighter
as he moved in the ring
Such a man of the sierra
How sweet with the wheat
How hard with the spurs
How tender with the dew
How splendid at the fair
How fierce with the last
banderillas of the dusk

But now he sleeps
Now the moss and grass
open the flower of his skull
with their steady fingers
His blood comes singing
over marshlands and fields
slipping on the frozen horns
wavering soulless in the fog
stumbling on a thousand hoofs
like a long dark sad tongue
and pooling and dying
beside the Guadalquivir
river of the stars

O white wall of Spain
O black bull of sorrow
O Ignacio's hard blood
O nightingale of his veins

No.
¡Que no quiero verla!
Que no hay cáliz que la contenga,
que no hay golondrinas que se la beban,
no hay escarcha de luz que la enfríe,
no hay canto ni diluvio de azucenas,
no hay cristal que la cubra de plata.
No.
¡¡Yo no quiero verla!!

No
I don't want to look
For no cup will hold it
no swallows will sip it
nor can it be cooled
by a shimmering frost
Nor can flood of lilies
or crystal or song
coat it in silver
No
I don't want to look

3

Cuerpo presente

La piedra es una frente donde los sueños gimen
sin tener agua curva ni cipreses helados.
La piedra es una espalda para llevar al tiempo
con árboles de lágrimas y cintas y planetas.

Yo he visto lluvias grises correr hacia las olas
levantando sus tiernos brazos acribillados,
para no ser cazadas por la piedra tendida
que desata sus miembros sin empapar la sangre.

Porque la piedra coge simientes y nublados,
esqueletos de alondras y lobos de penumbra;
pero no da sonidos, ni cristales, ni fuego,
sino plazas y plazas y otras plazas sin muros.

Ya está sobre la piedra Ignacio el bien nacido.
Ya se acabó; ¿qué pasa? Contemplad su figura:
la muerte lo ha cubierto de pálidos azufres
y le ha puesto cabeza de oscuro minotauro.

Ya se acabó. La lluvia penetra por su boca.
El aire como loco deja su pecho hundido,
y el Amor, empapado con lágrimas de nieve,
se calienta en la cumbre de las ganaderías.

¿Qué dicen? Un silencio con hedores reposa.
Estamos con un cuerpo presente que se esfuma,
con una forma clara que tuvo ruiseñores
y la vemos llenarse de agujeros sin fondo.

3

The Body Lies Here

The stone is a forehead of grieving dreams
with no curling water or icy cypresses
The stone is a shoulder for carrying time
and trees of tears and ribbons and planets

I have seen the gray rain chase the waves
that lift their gentle and riddled arms
so as not to be hunted by the heavy stone
that wastes the body and soaks up no blood

For the stone takes the seeds and the clouds
and the lark-skeletons and shadow-wolves
but it gives no sound no glass and no fire
only the bullrings and some have no walls

Here on the stone lies noble Ignacio
It's over And what now Look at his body
Death has painted him with pale sulfurs
and cast him the head of a dark minotaur

It's over Rain leaks in through his mouth
Air in a frenzy flees his sagging chest
and Love—soaked in tears of snow—
warms up with the best of the herds

What did they say Silence and a stench
rest Here is a body that lifts away
in the bright shape once a nightingale
and we watch it fill with infinite holes

¿Quién arruga el sudario? ¡No es verdad lo que dice!
Aquí no canta nadie, ni llora en el rincón,
ni pica las espuelas, ni espanta la serpiente:
aquí no quiero más que los ojos redondos
para ver ese cuerpo sin posible descanso.

Yo quiero ver aquí los hombres de voz dura.
Los que doman caballos y dominan los ríos:
los hombres que les suena el esqueleto y cantan
con una boca llena de sol y pedernales.

Aquí quiero yo verlos. Delante de la piedra.
Delante de este cuerpo con las riendas quebradas.
Yo quiero que me enseñen dónde está la salida
para este capitán atado por la muerte.

Yo quiero que me enseñen un llanto como un río
que tenga dulces nieblas y profundas orillas,
para llevar el cuerpo de Ignacio y que se pierda
sin escuchar el doble resuello de los toros.

Que se pierda en la plaza redonda de la luna
que finge cuando niña doliente res inmóvil;
que se pierda en la noche sin canto de los peces
y en la maleza blanca del humo congelado.

No quiero que le tapen la cara con pañuelos
para que se acostumbre con la muerte que lleva.
Vete, Ignacio: No sientas el caliente bramido.
Duerme, vuela, reposa: ¡También se muere el mar!

Who rumples the shroud He does not speak truth
Here no one sings or cries in a corner
or digs in his spurs or scares the snake
Here all I want is a pair of round eyes
for watching this body that will not rest

Here I want to see the men with hard voices
the men who tame horses and master rivers
the men who rattle their skeletons and sing
with their mouths full of sunshine and flint

Here I want to see them looking at the stone
Looking at this body with its broken reins
I want them to show me the door that leads out
for this captain who is lashed to his death

I want them to teach me to cry like a river
with sweet mist and deep riverbanks
for bearing away his body Let it be lost
and never hear the deep bray of the bulls

Let it be lost on the round bullring of the moon
that poses as a girl and a suffering bull
Let it be lost in the songless night of the fish
and in the white thicket of frozen smoke

Let them not hide his face under handkerchiefs
that teach him to bear the death he holds
Go Ignacio Do not hear the hot roar
Sleep Fly Rest Even the sea dies

4

Alma ausente

No te conoce el toro ni la higuera,
ni caballos ni hormigas de tu casa.
No te conoce el niño ni la tarde
porque te has muerto para siempre.

No te conoce el lomo de la piedra,
ni el raso negro donde te destrozas.
No te conoce tu recuerdo mudo
porque te has muerto para siempre.

El otoño vendrá con caracolas,
uva de niebla y montes agrupados,
pero nadie querrá mirar tus ojos
porque te has muerto para siempre.

Porque te has muerto para siempre,
como todos los muertos de la Tierra,
como todos los muertos que se olvidan
en un montón de perros apagados.

No te conoce nadie. No. Pero yo te canto.
Yo canto para luego tu perfil y tu gracia.
La madurez insigne de tu conocimiento.
Tu apetencia de muerte y el gusto de su boca.
La tristeza que tuvo tu valiente alegría.

Tardará mucho tiempo en nacer, si es que nace,
un andaluz tan claro, tan rico de aventura.
Yo canto su elegancia con palabras que gimen
y recuerdo una brisa triste por los olivos.

4

The Soul Is Gone

The bull doesn't know you or the fig tree
or the horses or the ants in your house
nor does the little boy or the afternoon
because you have died now forever

The spine of the stone doesn't know you
nor the black satin in which you lie wasted
Your untold memories don't know you
because you have died now forever

And the autumn will come with seashells
and misty grapes and gathering hills
but no one will want to look in your eyes
because you have died now forever

Because you have died now forever
like all other dead men on this earth
like all the dead men who lie forgotten
in a heap of annihilated dogs

No one knows you But I sing for you
I sing for your chiseled face and your grace
and the great seasoned age of your knowledge
your craving for death the savor of its mouth
and the sadness in your valiant joy

A long time will pass before another
Andalusian is born—if ever he is born—
so lucid and so rich in daring
I sing of his elegance with weeping words
and I remember a sad wind among the olives

Dark Love Sonnets

Soneto de la guirnalda de rosas

¡Esa guirnalda! ¡pronto! ¡que me muero!
¡Teje deprisa! ¡canta! ¡gime! ¡canta!
Que la sombra me enturbia la garganta
y otra vez viene y mil la luz de enero.

Entre lo que me quieres y te quiero,
aire de estrellas y temblor de planta,
espesura de anémonas levanta
con oscuro gemir un año entero.

Goza el fresco paisaje de mi herida,
quiebra juncos y arroyos delicados,
bebe en muslo de miel sangre vertida.

Pero ¡pronto! Que unidos, enlazados,
boca rota de amor y alma mordida,
el tiempo nos encuentre destrozados.

Sonnet of the Garland of Roses

Quick—I'm dying—the garland—
Weave fast—Sing—Moan—Sing—
The shadow darkens my throat—
January's light is thousandfold again

From you-love-me to I-love-you
a wind of stars a trembling plant
and a forest of anemones
with a dark moan lifts the year

Love the fresh land of my wound
break the delicate reeds and creeks
drink on honeythigh the streaming blood

But quick—May time (as we lie together
with lovetorn mouths and bitten souls)
find us here—destroyed—

Soneto de la dulce queja

Tengo miedo a perder la maravilla
de tus ojos de estatua y el acento
que me pone de noche en la mejilla
la solitaria rosa de tu aliento.

Tengo pena de ser en esta orilla
tronco sin ramas, y lo que más siento
es no tener la flor, pulpa o arcilla,
para el gusano de mi sufrimiento.

Si tú eres el tesoro oculto mío,
si eres mi cruz y mi dolor mojado,
si soy el perro de tu señorío,

no me dejes perder lo que he ganado
y decora las aguas de tu río
con hojas de mi Otoño enajenado.

Sonnet of the Sweet Lament

I'm afraid of losing the wonder
of your stony eyes and the spice
that the lonely rose of your breath
lays on my cheek at night

I'm sorry to be here on this shore
a tree with no branches and sorrier
to have no clay or pulp or flower
for the worm of my suffering

If you are my secret treasure
if you are my cross and my wet pain
if I am the dog of your realm

do not let me lose what I have won
and drape the waters of your river
with the leaves of my departing autumn

Llagas de amor

Esta luz, este fuego que devora,
este paisaje gris que me rodea,
este dolor por una sola idea,
esta angustia de cielo, mundo y hora,

este llanto de sangre que decora
lira sin pulso ya, lúbrica tea,
este peso del mar que me golpea,
este alacrán que por mi pecho mora,

son guirnalda de amor, cama de herido,
donde sin sueño, sueño tu presencia
entre las ruinas de mi pecho hundido.

Y aunque busco la cumbre de prudencia
me da tu corazón valle tendido
con cicuta y pasión de amarga ciencia.

Wounds of Love

This light this devastating fire
this gray land all around me
this ache of one idea
this torment of sky and world and hour

this sob of blood that decorates
my silent lyre O lusty torch
this heavy sea that pounds in me
this scorpion that lives in my chest

garland of love bed of my wound
where without a dream I dream of you
in the ruins of my sinking heart

And though I reach for the peak of reason
your heart gives me a long valley
and the hemlock and passion of bitter science

El poeta pide a su amor que le escriba

Amor de mis entrañas, viva muerte,
en vano espero tu palabra escrita
y pienso, con la flor que se marchita,
que si vivo sin mí quiero perderte.

El aire es inmortal. La piedra inerte
ni conoce la sombra ni la evita.
Corazón interior no necesita
la miel helada que la luna vierte.

Pero yo te sufrí. Rasgué mis venas,
tigre y paloma, sobre tu cintura
en duelo de mordiscos y azucenas.

Llena, pues, de palabras mi locura
o déjame vivir en mi serena
noche del alma para siempre oscura.

The Poet Asks His Love to Write to Him

Love of my soul oh living death
I'm waiting for your written word
and believe like the withering flower
that I want to lose you if I have no life

The air is immortal The inert stone
does not know the shadow or shun it
An inner heart does not need
the icy honey spilled by the moon

But for you I suffered I scraped my veins
on your waist tiger and dove
in a duel of lovebites and lilies

So fill up my madness with words
or let me live in my serene night
of the soul which will always be dark

El poeta dice la verdad

Quiero llorar mi pena y te lo digo
para que tú me quieras y me llores
en un anochecer de ruiseñores,
con un puñal, con besos y contigo.

Quiero matar al único testigo
para el asesinato de mis flores
y convertir mi llanto y mis sudores
en eterno montón de duro trigo.

Que no se acabe nunca la madeja
del te quiero me quieres, siempre ardida
con decrépito sol y luna vieja.

Que lo que no me des y no te pida
será para la muerte, que no deja
ni sombra por la carne estremecida.

The Poet Speaks the Truth

I want to cry out my sorrow I tell you
so that you will love me and cry for me
in an evening all of nightingales
and a dagger and kisses and you

I want to kill the only witness
to the assassination of my flowers
and turn my tears and my sweat
into an eternal stack of hard wheat

May it never end this tangled skein
of I-love-you and you-love-me that burns
under a withered sun and old moon

May what you don't give and I don't ask
be all for death which leaves not even
a shadow for the shaken flesh

El poeta habla por teléfono con el amor

Tu voz regó la duna de mi pecho
en la dulce cabina de madera.
Por el sur de mis pies fue primavera
y al norte de mi frente flor de helecho.

Pino de luz por el espacio estrecho
cantó sin alborada y sementera
y mi llanto prendió por vez primera
coronas de esperanza por el techo.

Dulce y lejana voz por mí vertida.
Dulce y lejana voz por mí gustada.
Lejana y dulce voz amortecida.

Lejana como oscura corza herida.
Dulce como un sollozo en la nevada.
¡Lejana y dulce en tuétano metida!

The Poet Speaks with Love on the Telephone

Your voice watered the dune of my heart
in a telephone booth of sweet wood
South of my feet it was springtime
a fern flower grew north of my brow

Pinetree of light in the narrow booth
sang with no seedtime and no dawn
and my crying took crowns of hope
from the ceiling as never before

Sweet and distant voice I uttered
sweet and distant voice I savored
distant sweet and muffled voice

Distant as the dark wounded doe
sweet like a sob in a snowfall
distant and sweet and in the marrow

El poeta pregunta a su amor por la "Ciudad Encantada" de Cuenca

¿Te gustó la ciudad que gota a gota
labró el agua en el centro de los pinos?
¿Viste sueños y rostros y caminos
y muros de dolor que el aire azota?

¿Viste la grieta azul de luna rota
que el Júcar moja de cristal y trinos?
¿Han besado tus dedos los espinos
que coronan de amor piedra remota?

¿Te acordaste de mí cuando subías
al silencio que sufre la serpiente
prisionera de grillos y de umbrías?

¿No viste por el aire transparente
una dalia de penas y alegrías
que te mandó mi corazón caliente?

The Poet Asks His Love About the "Enchanted City" of Cuenca

Did you like the city that drop by drop
worked water through the hearts of the pines
Did you see dreams and faces and paths
and walls of pain that the wind whips

Did you see the blue crack of the broken moon
that the Júcar soaks in crystal and birdsong
Have they kissed your fingers the whitethorns
that crown the distant stones with love

Did you think of me when you climbed
to the silence of the suffering serpent
prisoner of crickets and shadows

Did you see in the limpid air
the dahlia of bliss and sorrows
that my burning heart sent to you

Soneto gongorino en que el poeta manda a su amor una paloma

Este pichón del Turia que te mando,
de dulces ojos y de blanca pluma,
sobre laurel de Grecia vierte y suma
llama lenta de amor do estoy parando.

Su cándida virtud, su cuello blando,
en lirio doble de caliente espuma,
con un temblor de escarcha, perla y bruma
la ausencia de tu boca está marcando.

Pasa la mano sobre su blancura
y verás qué nevada melodía
esparce en copos sobre tu hermosura.

Así mi corazón de noche y día,
preso en la cárcel del amor oscura,
llora sin verte su melancolía.

Gongoresque Sonnet in Which the Poet Sends His Love a Dove

This dove I send you from the Turia
with sweet eyes and white feathers
(on Greek laurel leaves) translates
my love's slow flame in this hotel

Its spotless virtue and soft throat
—a double lily of hot foam—
trembling with frost and mist and pearl
denotes the absence of your mouth

Pass your hand over its white body
and you will see its snowy song
fall like snowflakes on your beauty

And so my heart of night and day
held in the dark prison of our love
without you weeps disconsolate

[¡Ay voz secreta del amor oscuro!]

¡Ay voz secreta del amor oscuro!
¡ay balido sin lanas! ¡ay herida!
¡ay aguja de hiel, camelia hundida!
¡ay corriente sin mar, ciudad sin muro!

¡Ay noche inmensa de perfil seguro,
montaña celestial de angustia erguida!
¡ay perro en corazón, voz perseguida!
¡silencio sin confín, lirio maduro!

Huye de mi, caliente voz de hielo,
no me quieras perder en la maleza
donde sin fruto gimen carne y cielo.

Deja el duro marfil de mi cabeza,
apiádate de mí, ¡rompe mi duelo!
¡que soy amor, que soy naturaleza!

[Ay secret cry of dark love—]

Ay secret cry of dark love—
Ay wound—Ay bleating with no wool—
Ay gall-needle—drowned camellia—
Ay surge with no sea—city with no wall—

Ay vast night of the safe alibi—
celestial mountain of stiff anguish
Ay dog at heart—hunted cry—
Ay endless silence—ripe lily—

Flee from me—hot icy cry—
don't lose me in the wilderness
where my body and the sky moan with no purpose

Leave the hard ivory of my head
Take pity on me—break my grief—
For I am love—I am nature—

El amor duerme en el pecho del poeta

Tú nunca entenderás lo que te quiero
porque duermes en mí y estás dormido.
Yo te oculto llorando, perseguido
por una voz de penetrante acero.

Norma que agita igual carne y lucero
traspasa ya mi pecho dolorido
y las turbias palabras han mordido
las alas de tu espíritu severo.

Grupo de gente salta en los jardines
esperando tu cuerpo y mi agonía
en caballos de luz y verdes crines.

Pero sigue durmiendo, vida mía.
¡Oye mi sangre rota en los violines!
¡Mira que nos acechan todavía!

Love Sleeps in the Poet's Chest

You'll never know how I love you
because you sleep in me and are asleep
Weeping I hide you—haunted
by a voice of penetrating steel

Law that shakes the flesh and a star
by now has entered my aching heart
and disturbing words have bitten
the wings of your stern self

People leap in the gardens
looking for your body and my death
on horses of light with green manes

But stay asleep—O my life—
Hear the violins sing my shattered blood
Do you see them watching us?

Noche del amor insomne

Noche arriba los dos con luna llena,
yo me puse a llorar y tú reías.
Tu desdén era un dios, las quejas mías
momentos y palomas en cadena.

Noche abajo los dos. Cristal de pena,
llorabas tú por hondas lejanías.
Mi dolor era un grupo de agonías
sobre tu débil corazón de arena.

La aurora nos unió sobre la cama,
las bocas puestas sobre el chorro helado
de una sangre sin fin que se derrama.

Y el sol entró por el balcón cerrado
y el coral de la vida abrió su rama
sobre mi corazón amortajado.

Night of Sleepless Love

High night for us both and full moon
I began to cry and you were laughing
Your scorn was a god and my laments
were moments and doves in chains

Low night for us both sorrow crystal
you cried for the deep distances
and my pain was a heap of dying
on your weak heart of sand

Dawn entangled us in bed
mouths pressing on the icy flow
of endlessly spilling blood

Sun streaked through the shuttered balcony
and the coral of life unfurled its branch
above my shrouded heart

Fragment of a dark love sonnet

[¡Oh cama del hotel! ¡oh dulce cama!]

¡Oh cama del hotel! ¡oh dulce cama!
Sábana de blancuras y rocío.
¡Oh rumor de tu cuerpo con el mío!
¡Oh gruta de algodón, penumbra y llama!

¡Oh lira doble que el amor enrama
con tus muslos de lumbre y nardo frío!
¡Oh barca vacilante, claro río,
a veces ruiseñor y a veces rama!

[Oh hotel bed oh this sweet bed]

Oh hotel bed oh this sweet bed
Oh sheet of whitenesses and dew
Hum of your body with my body
Cave of cotton flame and shadow

Oh double lyre that my love branches
around your thighs of fire and cold white nard
Oh tipping raft—oh bright river—
now a branch and now a nightingale

Love poem to a young man

[Aquel rubio de Albacete]

Aquel rubio de Albacete
vino, madre, y me miró.
¡No lo puedo mirar yo!
Aquel rubio de los trigos
hijo de la verde aurora,
alto, solo y sin amigos
pisó mi calle a deshora.
La noche se tiñe y dora
de un delicado fulgor
¡No lo puedo mirar yo!
Aquel lindo de cintura
sentí galán sin amigo;
sembró por mi noche oscura
su amarillo jazminero
tanto me quiere y le quiero
que mis ojos se llevó.
¡No lo puedo mirar yo!
Aquel joven de la Mancha
vino, madre, y me miró.
¡No lo puedo mirar yo!

[That blond from Albacete]

That blond from Albacete
came Mama & looked at me
I can't look at him—no—
That wheaten blond
son of the green sunrise
tall lonesome soul
walked down my street
at the wrong hour
Night turns dark & gold
with a delicate glow
I can't look at him—no—
His waist so handsome
I knew he was a lover
sowing in the dark night
his yellow jasmine
He loves me so & I him
that he took away my eyes
I can't look at him—no—
That lad from La Mancha
came Mama & looked at me
I can't look at him—no—

Blood Wedding

Tragedy in Three Acts and Seven Scenes

CAST OF CHARACTERS · PERSONAJES

Mother	La madre
Bride	La novia
Mother-in-law	La suegra
Leonardo's wife	La mujer de Leonardo
Maid	La criada
Neighbor	La vecina
Girls	Muchachas
Leonardo	Leonardo
Groom	El novio
Father of the bride	El padre de la novia
Moon	La luna
Death (as a beggar)	La muerte (como mendiga)
Woodcutters	Leñadores
Boys	Mozos

Acto primero

CUADRO PRIMERO

Habitación pintada de amarillo.

Novio: (*Entrando.*) Madre.

Madre: ¿Qué?

Novio: Me voy.

Madre: ¿Adónde?

Novio: A la viña. (*Va a salir.*)

Madre: Espera.

Novio: ¿Quiere algo?

Madre: Hijo, el almuerzo.

Novio: Déjelo. Comeré uvas. Déme la navaja.

Madre: ¿Para qué?

Novio: (*Riendo.*) Para cortarlas.

Madre: (*Entre dientes y buscándola.*) La navaja, la navaja . . . Malditas sean todas y el bribón que las inventó.

Novio: Vamos a otro asunto.

Madre: Y las escopetas y las pistolas y el cuchillo más pequeño, y hasta las azadas y los bieldos de la era.

Novio: Bueno.

Madre: Todo lo que puede cortar el cuerpo de un hombre. Un hombre hermoso, con su flor en la boca, que sale a las viñas o va a sus olivos propios, porque son de él, heredados . . .

Novio: (*Bajando la cabeza.*) Calle usted.

Madre: . . . y ese hombre no vuelve. O si vuelve es para ponerle una palma encima o un plato de sal gorda para que no se hinche. No sé cómo te atreves a llevar una navaja en tu cuerpo, ni cómo yo dejo a la serpiente dentro del arcón.

Novio: ¿Está bueno ya?

Madre: Cien años que yo viviera, no hablaría de otra cosa. Primero tu padre; que me olía a clavel y lo disfruté tres años escasos. Luego tu

Act One

Room painted yellow.

Groom: (*Entering.*) Mother.

Mother: Yes?

Groom: I'm going now.

Mother: Where?

Groom: To the vineyards. (*He turns to leave.*)

Mother: But wait.

Groom: What is it?

Mother: Your lunch, son.

Groom: No need. I'll eat grapes. Give me the knife.

Mother: For what?

Groom: (*Laughing.*) For cutting the grapes off the vine.

Mother: (*Between her teeth, while searching for it.*) The knife, the knife . . . Damn all the knives and the scoundrel who invented them.

Groom: Let's talk about something else.

Mother: And the shotguns, the pistols, the littlest knife—even the hoes and pitchforks.

Groom: All right.

Mother: Anything that cuts a man's body. A beautiful man in the flower of his life, going out to the vineyards or to his own olive grove, because they are his—his inheritance.

Groom: (*Lowering his head.*) Hush.

Mother: And the man never comes home. Or he comes home for a palm branch to lay on his dead body, or a plate of coarse salt to stop the swelling. I don't know how you can carry a knife against your body, or how I can live with a snake in the cupboard.

Groom: That's enough now.

Mother: If I live a hundred years I'll talk about nothing else. First your father, who smelled like a carnation—I had him barely three

hermano. ¿Y es justo y puede ser que una cosa pequeña como una pistola o una navaja pueda acabar con un hombre, que es un toro? No callaría nunca. Pasan los meses y la desesperación me pica en los ojos y hasta en las puntas del pelo.

Novio: (*Fuerte.*) ¿Vamos a acabar?

Madre: No. No vamos a acabar. ¿Me puede alguien traer a tu padre? ¿Y a tu hermano? Y luego el presidio. ¿Qué es el presidio? ¡Allí comen, allí fuman, allí tocan los instrumentos! Mis muertos están llenos de hierba, sin hablar, hechos polvo; dos hombres que eran dos geranios . . . Los matadores, en presidio, frescos, viendo los montes . . .

Novio: ¿Es que quiere usted que los mate?

Madre: No . . . Si hablo es porque . . . ¿Cómo no voy a hablar viéndote salir por esa puerta? Es que no me gusta que lleves navaja. Es que . . . que no quisiera que salieras al campo.

Novio: (*Riendo.*) ¡Vamos!

Madre: Que me gustaría que fueras una mujer. No te irías al arroyo ahora y bordaríamos las dos cenefas y perritos de lana.

Novio: (*Coge de un brazo a la madre y ríe.*) Madre, ¿y si yo la llevara conmigo a las viñas?

Madre: ¿Qué hace en las viñas una vieja? ¿Me ibas a meter debajo de los pámpanos?

Novio: (*Levantándola en sus brazos.*) Vieja, revieja, requetevieja.

Madre: Tu padre sí que me llevaba. Eso es buena casta. Sangre. Tu abuelo dejó un hijo en cada esquina. Eso me gusta. Los hombres, hombres; el trigo, trigo.

Novio: ¿Y yo, madre?

Madre: ¿Tú, qué?

Novio: ¿Necesito decírselo otra vez?

Madre: (*Seria.*) ¡Ah!

Novio: ¿Es que le parece mal?

Madre: No.

Novio: ¿Entonces?

Madre: No lo sé yo misma. Así, de pronto, siempre me sorprende. Yo sé que la muchacha es buena. ¿Verdad que sí? Modosa. Trabajadora. Amasa su pan y cose sus faldas, y siento sin embargo cuando la nombro, como si me dieran una pedrada en la frente.

years. Then your brother. Is it right and possible that a little thing like a pistol or a knife can destroy a man who is a bull? I will never hush. The months go by and the despair stings my eyes and the ends of my hair.

Groom: (*Forceful.*) Isn't that enough?

Mother: No, that is not enough. Can anyone bring me back your father and your brother? So they go to jail. What is jail? They eat, they smoke, they play the guitar! My dead men are covered with grass, silent, turning to dust—two men who were two geraniums. And the killers in jail, healthy and happy, gazing at the hills . . .

Groom: Do you want me to kill them?

Mother: No. If I talk, it's because . . . How can I not talk when I see you walking out that door? I don't want you to carry a knife . . . I don't want you to go into the fields.

Groom: (*Laughing.*) Come on now.

Mother: I wish you had been a girl. You wouldn't be going to the creek, and the two of us would stay home sewing ruffles and stuffed puppies.

Groom: (*Taking his mother's arm and laughing.*) Mama, should I take you with me to the vineyards?

Mother: What does an old woman do in the vineyards? Rest beneath the grapevines?

Groom: (*Lifting her up in his arms.*) Old old woman, little old woman.

Mother: Your father—he could lift me too. He was good stock, good blood. Your granddad left a kid on every corner. That's what I like. Men to be men, wheat to be wheat.

Groom: And me, mother?

Mother: What about you?

Groom: Do I have to say it again?

Mother: (*Serious.*) Ah.

Groom: Do you think it's a bad idea?

Mother: No.

Groom: And so?

Mother: I don't really know. I feel confused. I know she's a nice girl. Isn't she? Modest and hardworking. She kneads her bread and sews her skirts. But when I say her name, it's as though I'd been struck in the forehead by a stone.

Novio: Tonterías.

Madre: Más que tonterías. Es que me quedo sola. Ya no me quedas más que tú y siento que te vayas.

Novio: Pero usted vendrá con nosotros.

Madre: No. Yo no puedo dejar aquí solos a tu padre y a tu hermano. Tengo que ir todas las mañanas, y si me voy es fácil que muera uno de los Félix, uno de la familia de los matadores, y lo entierren al lado. ¡Y eso sí que no! ¡Ca! ¡Eso sí que no! Porque con las uñas los desentierro y yo sola los machaco contra la tapia.

Novio: (*Fuerte.*) Vuelta otra vez.

Madre: Perdóname. (*Pausa.*) ¿Cuánto tiempo llevas en relaciones?

Novio: Tres años. Ya pude comprar la viña.

Madre. Tres años. ¿Ella tuvo un novio, no?

Novio: No sé. Creo que no. Las muchachas tienen que mirar con quién se casan.

Madre: Sí. Yo no miré a nadie. Miré a tu padre, y cuando lo mataron miré a la pared de enfrente. Una mujer con un hombre, y ya está.

Novio: Usted sabe que mi novia es buena.

Madre: No lo dudo. De todos modos siento no saber cómo fue su madre.

Novio: ¿Qué más da?

Madre: (*Mirándolo.*) Hijo.

Novio: ¿Qué quiere usted?

Madre: ¡Que es verdad! ¡Que tienes razón! ¿Cuándo quieres que la pida?

Novio: (*Alegre.*) ¿Le parece bien el domingo?

Madre: (*Seria.*) Le llevaré los pendientes de azófar, que son antiguos, y tú le compras . . .

Novio: Usted entiende más . . .

Madre: Le compras unas medias caladas, y para ti dos trajes . . . ¡Tres! ¡No te tengo más que a ti!

Novio: Me voy. Mañana iré a verla.

Madre: Sí, sí, y a ver si me alegras con seis nietos, o los que te dé la gana, ya que tu padre no tuvo lugar de hacérmelos a mí.

Novio: El primero para usted.

Groom: Nonsense.

Mother: A lot more than nonsense. I'll be alone here. You're all I've got left, and I'm sorry to see you go.

Groom: But you'll come with us.

Mother: No. I can't leave your father and brother alone here. I have to visit them every morning! If I leave here, what if one of the Félixes dies—one of those killers—and they bury him beside them. I can't let that happen! Cha! No! I'll dig him up with my fingernails and I'll pound him against the wall.

Groom: (*Forceful.*) Back to that again.

Mother: I'm sorry. (*Pause.*) How long have you known her?

Groom: Three years. And I bought the vineyard.

Mother: Three years. She had another boyfriend, didn't she?

Groom: I don't know—don't think so. A girl needs to have a look at the man she's going to marry.

Mother: Yes. I looked at your father, no one else, and when they killed him I looked at the wall in front of me. One woman and one man, that's all.

Groom: You know my girl is nice.

Mother: I don't doubt it. But I wish I knew what her mother was like.

Groom: How will that help?

Mother: (*Looking at him.*) Son.

Groom: Why does it matter?

Mother: That's true! You're right! When do you want me to speak to her father?

Groom: (*Happily.*) How does Sunday sound?

Mother: (*Solemn.*) I will take her the antique brass earrings, and you will buy her . . .

Groom: You'll know best . . .

Mother: For her, you can buy lace stockings—and for you, two suits . . . or three! I have only you.

Groom: I'm off now. I'll go see her tomorrow.

Mother: Yes, yes, and make me happy with six grandchildren, or as many as you like—since your father never had the chance to give them to me.

Groom: The first boy will be for you.

Madre: Sí, pero que haya niñas. Que yo quiero bordar y hacer encaje y estar tranquila.

Novio: Estoy seguro que usted querrá a mi novia.

Madre: La querré. (*Se dirige a besarlo y reacciona.*) Anda, ya estás muy grande para besos. Se los das a tu mujer. (*Pausa. Aparte.*) Cuando lo sea.

Novio: Me voy.

Madre: Que caves bien la parte del molinillo, que la tienes descuidada.

Novio: ¡Lo dicho!

Madre: Anda con Dios. (*Vase el novio. La madre queda sentada de espaldas a la puerta. Aparece en la puerta una vecina vestida de color oscuro, con pañuelo en la cabeza.*) Pasa.

Vecina: ¿Cómo estás?

Madre: Ya ves.

Vecina: Yo bajé a la tienda y vine a verte. ¡Vivimos tan lejos!

Madre: Hace veinte años que no he subido a lo alto de la calle.

Vecina: Tú estás bien.

Madre: ¿Lo crees?

Vecina: Las cosas pasan. Hace dos días trajeron al hijo de mi vecina con los dos brazos cortados por la máquina. (*Se sienta.*)

Madre: ¿A Rafael?

Vecina: Si. Y allí lo tienes. Muchas veces pienso que tu hijo y el mío están mejor donde están, dormidos, descansando, que no expuestos a quedarse inútiles.

Madre: Calla. Todo eso son invenciones, pero no consuelos.

Vecina: ¡Ay!

Madre: ¡Ay!

Madre: ¡Ay! (*Pausa.*)

Vecina: (*Triste.*) ¿Y tu hijo?

Madre: Salió.

Vecina: ¡Al fin compró la viña!

Madre: Tuvo suerte.

Vecina: Ahora se casará.

Madre. (*Como despertando y acercando su silla a la silla de la vecina.*) Oye.

Vecina: (*En plan confidencial.*) Dime.

Madre: ¿Tú conoces a la novia de mi hijo?

Mother: Yes, but give me girls too. I want to sit in peace, making embroidery and lace.

Groom: I'm sure you will love my bride.

Mother: I will love her. (*She goes to kiss him and stops.*) Go on, you're too old for kisses—give them to your wife. (*Pauses. Aside.*) When she is your wife.

Groom: I'm going now.

Mother: Do some hoeing near the little mill—you've neglected it.

Groom: Yes, mother.

Mother: God bless you. (*The groom goes out. The mother remains seated with her back to the door. A neighbor appears in the doorway dressed in a dark color, with a kerchief on her head.*) Come in.

Neighbor: How are you?

Mother: Still here.

Neighbor: I was coming down to the shop so I stopped to see you. We live so far apart!

Mother: Twenty years since I climbed to the top of the street.

Neighbor: You look well.

Mother: Do you think?

Neighbor: Things happen. Two days ago they brought back my neighbor's son—the machine maimed his arms. (*She sits down.*)

Mother: Was it Rafael?

Neighbor: Yes. And there he is. I often think your son and mine are better off as they are, sleeping, resting—out of danger. They will never be useless.

Mother: Don't say that. It's nonsense—not a consolation.

Neighbor: Ay.

Mother: Ay. (*She pauses.*)

Neighbor: (*Sad.*) And your son?

Mother: He went out.

Neighbor: At last he bought the vineyard!

Mother: He was lucky.

Neighbor: Now he will marry.

Mother: (*Perking up and moving her chair closer to her neighbor's.*) Tell me.

Neighbor: (*Confidingly.*) What?

Mother: Do you know my son's girlfriend?

Vecina: ¡Buena muchacha!

Madre: Sí, pero . . .

Vecina: Pero quien la conozca a fondo no hay nadie. Vive sola con su padre allí, tan lejos, a diez leguas de la casa más cerca. Pero es buena. Acostumbrada a la soledad.

Madre: ¿Y su madre?

Vecina: A su madre la conocí. Hermosa. Le relucía la cara como a un santo; pero a mí no me gustó nunca. No quería a su marido.

Madre: (*Fuerte.*) Pero ¡cuántas cosas sabéis las gentes!

Vecina: Perdona. No quise ofender; pero es verdad. Ahora; si fue decente o no, nadie lo dijo. De esto no se ha hablado. Ella era orgullosa.

Madre: ¡Siempre igual!

Vecina: Tú me preguntaste.

Madre: Es que quisiera que ni a la viva ni a la muerta las conociera nadie. Que fueran como dos cardos, que ninguna persona les nombra y pinchan si llega el momento.

Vecina: Tienes razón. Tu hijo vale mucho.

Madre: Vale. Por eso lo cuido. A mí me habían dicho que la muchacha tuvo novio hace tiempo.

Vecina: Tendría ella quince años. Él se casó ya hace dos años con una prima de ella, por cierto. Nadie se acuerda del noviazgo.

Madre: ¿Cómo te acuerdas tú?

Vecina: ¡Me haces unas preguntas!

Madre: A cada uno le gusta enterarse de lo que le duele. ¿Quién fue el novio?

Vecina: Leonardo.

Madre: ¿Qué Leonardo?

Vecina: Leonardo el de los Félix.

Madre: (*Levantándose.*) ¡De los Félix!

Vecina: Mujer, ¿qué culpa tiene Leonardo de nada? Él tenía ocho años cuando las cuestiones.

Madre: Es verdad . . . Pero oigo eso de Félix y es lo mismo (*Entre dientes.*) Félix que llenárseme de cieno la boca (*Escupe.*) y tengo que escupir, tengo que escupir por no matar.

Vecina: Repórtate; ¿qué sacas con eso?

Madre: Nada. Pero tú lo comprendes.

Neighbor: A nice girl.

Mother: Yes, but . . .

Neighbor: But no one knows her well. She lives alone with her father out there, thirty miles from the nearest house. But she's a nice girl—used to being alone.

Mother: And her mother?

Neighbor: I met her mother once. Beautiful. Her face shone like a saint's—but I never liked her. She didn't love her husband.

Mother: (*Forceful.*) How do you know so much!

Neighbor: I'm sorry, I didn't mean to upset you, but it's true. Whether she was proper or not, no one said. There was no talk. She was proud.

Mother: You never change.

Neighbor: You asked me.

Mother: I don't want anyone to know them—the one that's alive or the one that's dead. They should be two thistles, and prick anyone who speaks their names.

Neighbor: You're right. Your son means so much.

Mother: Yes, that's why I watch over him. I hear this girl had another admirer.

Neighbor: She was fifteen or so. He married one of her cousins two years ago. No one remembers she once had someone else.

Mother: How do you happen to remember?

Neighbor: The questions you ask!

Mother: Everyone wants to know what will hurt. Who was the boy?

Neighbor: Leonardo.

Mother: Which Leonardo?

Neighbor: Leonardo Félix.

Mother: (*Standing up.*) Félix!

Neighbor: Is Leonardo to blame? He was eight years old when those things happened.

Mother: That's true. But I hear the name Félix and it's always the same. (*Muttering.*) Félix—and my mouth tastes like mud. (*She spits.*) And I have to spit. If I don't spit I'll kill.

Neighbor: Calm down. What will that get you?

Mother: Nothing. But you can understand.

Vecina: No te opongas a la felicidad de tu hijo. No le digas nada. Tú estás vieja. Yo también. A ti y a mí nos toca callar.

Madre: No le diré nada.

Vecina: (*Besándola.*) Nada.

Madre: (*Serena.*) ¡Las cosas! . . .

Vecina: Me voy, que pronto llegará mi gente del campo.

Madre: ¿Has visto qué día de calor?

Vecina: Iban negros los chiquillos que llevan el agua a los segadores. Adiós, mujer.

Madre: Adiós.

(*La madre se dirige a la puerta de la izquierda. En medio del camino se detiene y lentamente se santigua.*)

TELÓN

Neighbor: Don't get in the way of your son's happiness. Say nothing to
    him. You are old, so am I. We must say nothing.

Mother: I'll say nothing.

Neighbor: (*Kissing her.*) Nothing.

Mother: (*Calm.*) These things happen . . .

Neighbor: I'm going now, my men will be coming in from the fields.

Mother: Such a hot day.

Neighbor: The boys carrying water to the harvesters—their skin was
    black from the sun. Goodbye.

Mother: Goodbye.

(*She walks toward the door on the left. Partway there she
stops and crosses herself slowly.*)

CURTAIN

Acto primero

CUADRO II

Habitación pintada de rosa con cobres y ramos de flores populares. En el centro, una mesa con mantel. Es la mañana.

(Suegra de Leonardo con un niño en brazos. Lo mece. La mujer, en la otra esquina, hace punto de media.)

Suegra:

> Nana, niño, nana
> del caballo grande
> que no quiso el agua.
> El agua era negra
> dentro de las ramas.
> Cuando llega al puente
> se detiene y canta.
> ¿Quién dirá, mi niño,
> lo que tiene el agua,
> con su larga cola
> por su verde sala?

Mujer: (*Bajo.*)

> Duérmete, clavel,
> que el caballo no quiere beber.

Suegra:

> Duérmete, rosal,
> que el caballo se pone a llorar.
> Las patas heridas,
> las crines heladas,
> dentro de los ojos
> un puñal de plata.

Act One

Room painted pink, with copper pots and bunches of common flowers. In the center of the room, a table with a tablecloth. Morning.

> *Leonardo's mother-in-law cradles a baby in her arms. In the opposite corner, his wife is knitting.*

Mother-in-law:

> Lullaby—little boy—
> of the great horse
> that didn't want water.
> The water was black
> inside the branches.
> Reaching the bridge
> it stops and sings.
> Who will say—little boy—
> what spoiled the water
> with its long tail
> in the green parlor.

Wife: (*Softly.*)

> Sleep, carnation,
> the horse won't drink.

Mother-in-law:

> Sleep, rosebush,
> the horse will weep.
> Wounded hooves,
> frozen mane,
> and in his eyes
> a silver dagger.

Bajaban al río.
¡Ay, cómo bajaban!
La sangre corría
más fuerte que el agua.

Mujer:

Duérmete, clavel,
que el caballo no quiere beber.

Suegra:

Duérmete, rosal,
que el caballo se pone a llorar.

Mujer:

No quiso tocar
la orilla mojada,
su belfo caliente
con moscas de plata.
A los montes duros
solo relinchaba
con el río muerto
sobre la garganta.
¡Ay, caballo grande
que no quiso el agua!
¡Ay dolor de nieve,
caballo del alba!

Suegra:

¡No vengas! Deténte,
cierra la ventana
con ramas de sueños
y sueño de ramas.

Mujer:

Mi niño se duerme.

Down to the river they went,
ay, how they went down.
The blood ran
stronger than water.

Wife:

Sleep, carnation,
the horse won't drink.

Mother-in-law:

Sleep, rosebush,
the horse will weep.

Wife:

He would not touch
the wet riverbank
with his hot muzzle
and silver whiskers.
All alone he neighed
at the hard hills
as the dead river
flowed over his throat.
Ay great horse
that didn't want water.
Ay ache of snow,
horse of the dawn.

Mother-in-law:

Don't come! Stop!
Close the window
with branches of dreams
and a dream of branches.

Wife:

My little boy sleeps.

Suegra:

Mi niño se calla.

Mujer:

Caballo, mi niño
tiene una almohada.

Suegra:

Su cuna de acero.

Mujer:

Su colcha de holanda.

Suegra:

Nana, niño, nana.

Mujer:

¡Ay caballo grande
que no quiso el agua!

Suegra:

¡No vengas, no entres!
Vete a la montaña.
Por los valles grises
donde está la jaca.

Mujer: (*Mirando.*)

Mi niño se duerme.

Suegra:

Mi niño descansa.

Mujer: (*Bajito.*)

Duérmete, clavel,
que el caballo no quiere beber.

Mother-in-law:

> My little boy hushes.

Wife:

> Horse, my little boy
> has a pillow.

Mother-in-law:

> His iron cradle.

Wife:

> His quilt of Dutch linen.

Mother-in-law:

> Lullaby—little boy—

Wife:

> Ay great horse
> that didn't want water!

Mother-in-law:

> Don't come, don't come in!
> Go to the hills!
> Through the gray valleys
> where the mare waits.

Wife: (*Looking at him.*)

> My little boy sleeps.

Mother-in-law:

> My little boy rests.

Wife: (*Softly.*)

> Sleep, carnation,
> the horse won't drink.

Suegra: (*Levantándose y muy bajito.*)

> Duérmete, rosal,
>
> que el caballo se pone a llorar.

(*Entran al niño. Entra Leonardo.*)

Leonardo: ¿Y el niño?

Mujer: Se durmió.

Leonardo: Ayer no estuvo bien. Lloró por la noche.

Mujer: (*Alegre.*) Hoy está como una dalia. ¿Y tú? ¿Fuiste a casa del herrador?

Leonardo: De allí vengo. ¿Querrás creer? Llevo más de dos meses poniendo herraduras nuevas al caballo y siempre se le caen. Por lo visto se las arranca con las piedras.

Mujer: ¿Y no será que lo usas mucho?

Leonardo: No. Casi no lo utilizo.

Mujer: Ayer me dijeron las vecinas que te habían visto al límite de los llanos.

Leonardo: ¿Quién lo dijo?

Mujer: Las mujeres que cogen las alcaparras. Por cierto que me sorprendió. ¿Eras tú?

Leonardo: No. ¿Qué iba a hacer yo allí, en aquel secano?

Mujer: Eso dije. Pero el caballo estaba reventando de sudar.

Leonardo: ¿Lo viste tú?

Mujer: No. Mi madre.

Leonardo: ¿Está con el niño?

Mujer: Sí. ¿Quieres un refresco de limón?

Leonardo: Con el agua bien fría.

Mujer: ¡Cómo no viniste a comer! . . .

Leonardo: Estuve con los medidores del trigo. Siempre entretienen.

Mujer: (*Haciendo el refresco y muy tierna.*) ¿Y lo pagan a buen precio?

Leonardo: El justo.

Mujer: Me hace falta un vestido y al niño una gorra con lazos.

Leonardo: (*Levantándose.*) Voy a verlo.

Mujer: Ten cuidado, que está dormido.

Mother-in-law: (*Standing up, and in a soft whisper.*)
> Sleep, rosebush.
> The horse weeps.

(*They take the baby out. Leonardo enters.*)

Leonardo: And the baby?

Wife: Asleep.

Leonardo: He wasn't well yesterday. He cried in the night.

Wife: (*Gaily.*) Today he's like a dahlia. And you? Did you see the blacksmith?

Leonardo: I've just come from there. Do you know what? For more than two months I've shoed that horse again and again—the stones must be nicking off the shoes.

Wife: Are you riding him too hard?

Leonardo: No, I hardly ride him.

Wife: Yesterday the neighbors said they saw you at the far edge of the plains.

Leonardo: Who said so?

Wife: The women who pick capers. I was surprised, of course. Was that you?

Leonardo: No. What would I do out on those parched plains?

Wife: That's what I said. But the horse was in a lather.

Leonardo: Did you see him?

Wife: No, my mother did.

Leonardo: Is she with the baby?

Wife: Yes. Would you like some lemonade?

Leonardo: With very cold water.

Wife: You didn't come to lunch!

Leonardo: I was getting the wheat weighed. They always keep me talking.

Wife: (*Making the lemonade, and speaking gently.*) And do they pay a good price?

Leonardo: A fair price.

Wife: I need a dress and the baby needs a cap with ties.

Leonardo: (*Rising.*) I'll go and take a look at him.

Wife: Go quietly, he's sleeping.

Suegra: (*Saliendo.*) Pero ¿quién da esas carreras al caballo? Está abajo tendido, con los ojos desorbitados como si llegara del fin del mundo.

Leonardo: (*Agrio.*) Yo.

Suegra: Perdona; tuyo es.

Mujer: (*Tímida.*) Estuvo con los medidores del trigo.

Suegra: Por mí, que reviente. (*Se sienta. Pausa.*)

Mujer: El refresco. ¿Está frío?

Leonardo: Sí.

Mujer: ¿Sabes que piden a mi prima?

Leonardo: ¿Cuándo?

Mujer: Mañana. La boda será dentro de un mes. Espero que vendrán a invitarnos.

Leonardo: (*Serio.*) No sé.

Suegra: La madre de él creo que no estaba muy satisfecha con el casamiento.

Leonardo: Y quizá tenga razón. Ella es de cuidado.

Mujer: No me gusta que penséis mal de una buena muchacha.

Suegra: Pero cuando dice eso es porque la conoce. ¿No ves que fue tres años novia suya? (*Con intención.*)

Leonardo: Pero la dejé. (*A su mujer.*) ¿Vas a llorar ahora? ¡Quita! (*Le aparta bruscamente las manos de la cara.*) Vamos a ver al niño.

(*Entran abrazados. Aparece la muchacha, alegre. Entra corriendo.*)

Muchacha: Señora.

Suegra: ¿Qué pasa?

Muchacha: Llegó el novio a la tienda y ha comprado todo lo mejor que había.

Suegra: ¿Vino solo?

Muchacha: No, con su madre. Seria, alta. (*La imita.*) Pero ¡qué lujo!

Suegra: Ellos tienen dinero.

Muchacha: ¡Y compraron unas medias caladas! ¡Ay, qué medias! ¡El sueño de las mujeres en medias! Mire usted: una golondrina aquí (*Señala al tobillo.*), un barco aquí (*Señala la pantorrilla.*), y aquí una rosa. (*Señala al muslo.*)

Mother-in-law: (*Entering.*) But who could be running the horse like that? He's sprawled out down there with his eyes bulging, as though he just came back from the ends of the earth.

Leonardo: (*Bitter.*) Me.

Mother-in-law: Pardon, he *is* yours.

Wife: (*Shy.*) He was getting the wheat weighed.

Mother-in-law: Run him into the ground, for all I care. (*She sits down. Pause.*)

Wife: Your lemonade. Is it cold enough?

Leonardo: Yes.

Wife: Did you know they're asking for my cousin's hand?

Leonardo: When?

Wife: Tomorrow. The wedding is within the month. I hope they'll come by and invite us.

Leonardo: (*Solemn.*) I'm not so sure.

Mother-in-law: I heard his mother wasn't happy about the marriage.

Leonardo: She could be right. That girl is special.

Wife: I don't like you thinking bad thoughts about a nice girl.

Mother-in-law: He says it because he knows her. She was his girl for three years, did you know? (*Meaningfully.*)

Leonardo: But I left her. (*Turning to his wife.*) Are you going to cry? Stop . . . (*He pulls her hands from her face brusquely.*) Let's go look at the baby.

> (*They go out holding each other. A girl enters, gaily. She's running.*)

Girl: Señora.

Mother-in-law: Yes?

Girl: The groom came to the shop and bought all the best they had.

Mother-in-law: Did he come alone?

Girl: No, he came with his mother. Tall and solemn. (*Imitating her.*) But what luxury!

Mother-in-law: They have money.

Girl: They bought lace stockings. Those stockings! The dream of all women who wear stockings! A swallow here (*pointing to her ankle*), a boat here (*pointing to her calf*), and a rose here (*pointing to her thigh*).

Suegra: ¡Niña!

Muchacha: ¡Una rosa con las semillas y el tallo! ¡Ay! ¡Todo en seda!

Suegra: Se van a juntar dos buenos capitales.

(*Aparecen Leonardo y su mujer.*)

Muchacha: Vengo a deciros lo que están comprando.

Leonardo: (*Fuerte.*) No nos importa.

Mujer: Déjala.

Suegra: Leonardo, no es para tanto.

Muchacha: Usted dispense. (*Se va llorando.*)

Suegra: ¿Qué necesidad tienes de ponerte a mal con las gentes?

Leonardo: No le he preguntado su opinión. (*Se sienta.*)

Suegra: Está bien. (*Pausa.*)

Mujer: (*A Leonardo.*) ¿Qué te pasa? ¿Qué idea te bulle por dentro de la cabeza? No me dejes así, sin saber nada . . .

Leonardo: Quita.

Mujer: No. Quiero que me mires y me lo digas.

Leonardo: Déjame. (*Se levanta.*)

Mujer: ¿Adónde vas, hijo?

Leonardo: (*Agrio.*) ¿Te puedes callar?

Suegra: (*Enérgica a su hija.*) ¡Cállate! (*Sale Leonardo.*) ¡El niño!

(*Entra y vuelve a salir con él en brazos. La mujer ha permanecido de pie, inmóvil.*)

> Las patas heridas,
> las crines heladas,
> dentro de los ojos
> un puñal de plata.
> Bajaban al río.
> ¡Ay, cómo bajaban!
> La sangre corría
> más fuerte que el agua.

Mother-in-law: Young lady!

Girl: A rose with seeds and stem! All silk!

Mother-in-law: Two fine fortunes are going to marry.

(*Leonardo and his wife come back in.*)

Girl: I came to tell you what they're buying.

Leonardo: (*Forceful.*) That's not our affair.

Wife: Let her.

Mother-in-law: Leonardo, don't make so much of it.

Girl: Sorry! (*She goes out, crying.*)

Mother-in-law: Why do you need to upset people?

Leonardo: I didn't ask for your view. (*He sits down.*)

Mother-in-law: Fine. (*Pause.*)

Wife: (*To Leonardo.*) What is it? What are you brooding about? Don't leave me like this, knowing nothing . . .

Leonardo: Let me alone.

Wife: No—I want you to look at me and tell me.

Leonardo: Let me be. (*He rises.*)

Wife: Where are you going?

Leonardo: (*Bitter.*) Can you hush.

Mother-in-law: (*Sharply, to her daughter.*) Hush! (*Leonardo goes out.*) The baby!

(*She goes out and comes back in again with the child in her arms. The wife stands still, without moving.*)

> Wounded hooves,
> frozen mane,
> and in his eyes
> a silver knife.
> Down to the river they went,
> ay, how they went down.
> The blood ran
> stronger than water.

Mujer: (*Volviéndose lentamente y como soñando.*)
>> Duérmete, clavel,
>> que el caballo se pone a beber.

Suegra:
>> Duérmete, rosal,
>> que el caballo se pone a llorar.

Mujer:
>> Nana, niño, nana.

Suegra:
>> ¡Ay, caballo grande,
>> que no quiso el agua!

Mujer: (*Dramática.*)
>> ¡No vengas, no entres!
>> ¡Vete a la montaña!
>> ¡Ay dolor de nieve,
>> caballo del alba!

Suegra: (*Llorando.*)
>> Mi niño se duerme . . .

Mujer: (*Llorando y acercándose lentamente.*)
>> Mi niño descansa . . .

Suegra:
>> Duérmete, clavel,
>> que el caballo no quiere beber.

Mujer: (*Llorando y apoyándose sobre la mesa.*)
>> Duérmete, rosal,
>> que el caballo se pone a llorar.

TELÓN

Wife: (*Turning slowly as though in a dream.*)
>Sleep, carnation,
>the horse will drink.

Mother-in-law:
>Sleep, rosebush,
>the horse will weep.

Wife:
>Lullaby, little boy.

Mother-in-law:
>Ay great horse
>that didn't want water!

Wife: (*Dramatic.*)
>Don't come, don't come in!
>Go to the hills!
>Ay ache of snow,
>horse of the dawn!

Mother-in-law: (*Weeping.*)
>My little boy sleeps.

Wife: (*Weeping and drawing slowly closer.*)
>My little boy rests.

Mother-in-law:
>Sleep, carnation,
>the horse won't drink.

Wife: (*Weeping as she leans on the table.*)
>Sleep, rosebush,
>the horse will weep.

CURTAIN

Acto primero

CUADRO III

Interior de la cueva donde vive la novia. Al fondo, una cruz de grandes flores rosa. Las puertas redondas con cortinas de encaje y lazos rosa. Por las paredes de material blanco y duro, abanicos redondos, jarros azules y pequeños espejos.

Criada: Pasen . . . (*Muy afable, llena de hipocresía humilde. Entran el novio y su madre. La madre viste de raso negro y lleva mantilla de encaje. El novio, de pana negra con gran cadena de oro.*) ¿Se quieren sentar? Ahora vienen. (*Sale.*)

       (*Quedan madre e hijo sentados inmóviles como estatuas. Pausa larga.*)

Madre: ¿Traes el reloj?

Novio: Sí. (*Lo saca y lo mira.*)

Madre: Tenemos que volver a tiempo. ¡Qué lejos vive esta gente!

Novio: Pero estas tierras son buenas.

Madre: Buenas; pero demasiado solas. Cuatro horas de camino y ni una casa ni un árbol.

Novio: Éstos son los secanos.

Madre: Tu padre los hubiera cubierto de árboles.

Novio: ¿Sin agua?

Madre: Ya la hubiera buscado. Los tres años que estuvo casado conmigo, plantó diez cerezos. (*Haciendo memoria.*) Los tres nogales del molino, toda una viña y una planta que se llama Júpiter, que da flores encarnadas, y se secó. (*Pausa.*)

Novio: (*Por la novia.*) Debe estar vistiéndose.

Act One

SCENE THREE

Inside the cave room where the bride lives. At the back, big pink flowers in the form of a cross. Arched doorways, hung with lace curtains tied with pink ribbons. On the hard white walls hang round fans, blue pitchers and small mirrors.

Maid: Come in . . . (*Friendly, full of false humility. The groom and his mother enter. The mother in black satin with a lace mantilla. The groom in black corduroy with a big gold chain.*) Would you like to sit down? They'll be here in a moment. (*She goes out.*)

>(*Mother and son stay seated, as still as statues. Long pause.*)

Mother: Did you bring the watch?
Groom: Yes. (*He takes it out and looks at it.*)
Mother: We have to get back on time. They live so far away!
Groom: But this is fine land.
Mother: Fine, but lonesome. Four hours traveling, and not a house or a tree.
Groom: This land has no water.
Mother: Your father would have covered it with trees.
Groom: Without water?
Mother: He would have found water. In his three years married to me, he planted ten cherry trees. (*Remembering.*) The three walnut trees near the mill, a vineyard, and a Jupiter plant—with red flowers— but it dried up. (*Pause.*)
Groom: (*Referring to the bride.*) She must be dressing.

(Entra el padre de la novia. Es anciano, con el cabello blanco reluciente. Lleva la cabeza inclinada. La madre y el novio se levantan y se dan las manos en silencio.)

Padre: ¿Mucho tiempo de viaje?

Madre: Cuatro horas. *(Se sientan.)*

Padre: Habéis venido por el camino más largo.

Madre: Yo estoy ya vieja para andar por las terreras del río.

Novio: Se marea. *(Pausa.)*

Padre: Buena cosecha de esparto.

Novio: Buena de verdad.

Padre: En mi tiempo, ni esparto daba esta tierra. Ha sido necesario castigarla y hasta llorarla, para que nos dé algo provechoso.

Madre: Pero ahora da. No te quejes. Yo no vengo a pedirte nada.

Padre: *(Sonriendo.)* Tú eres más rica que yo. Las viñas valen un capital. Cada pámpano una moneda de plata. Lo que siento es que las tierras . . . ¿entiendes? estén separadas. A mí me gusta todo junto. Una espina tengo en el corazón, y es la huertecilla esa metida entre mis tierras, que no me quieren vender por todo el oro del mundo.

Novio: Eso pasa siempre.

Padre: Si pudiéramos con veinte pares de bueyes traer tus viñas aquí y ponerlas en la ladera. ¡Qué alegría! . . .

Madre: ¿Para qué?

Padre: Lo mío es de ella y lo tuyo de él. Por eso. Para verlo todo junto, ¡que junto es una hermosura!

Novio: Y sería menos trabajo.

Madre: Cuando yo me muera, vendéis aquello y compráis aquí al lado.

Padre: Vender, ¡vender! ¡Bah!; comprar, hija, comprarlo todo. Si yo hubiera tenido hijos hubiera comprado todo este monte hasta la parte del arroyo. Porque no es buena tierra; pero con brazos se la hace buena, y como no pasa gente no te roban los frutos y puedes dormir tranquilo. *(Pausa.)*

Madre: Tú sabes a lo que vengo.

Padre: Sí.

Madre: ¿Y qué?

Padre: Me parece bien. Ellos lo han hablado.

(*The bride's father comes in. He is old, with shining white hair. His head is bowed. The mother and the groom rise and shake his hand in silence.*)

Father: Long journey?

Mother: Four hours. (*They sit down.*)

Father: You must have come the long way.

Mother: I'm too old for the banks of the creek.

Groom: They make her dizzy. (*Pause.*)

Father: Good harvest of esparto.

Groom: Very good.

Father: In my day, this land didn't give even esparto. We had to punish it, cry over it, so it would give us something we could use.

Mother: Now it gives. But don't worry, I'm not here to ask you for anything.

Father: (*Smiling.*) You're richer than I am. The vineyards are worth good money. Each vine a silver coin. Though I worry that our lands are so far apart, you understand? I like to have them all in one place. I've got a thorn in my heart—the little orchard in the middle of my land, which they won't sell me for all the gold in the world.

Groom: It's always that way.

Father: With twenty pairs of oxen, we could bring your vines here and plant them along the creek. What happiness!

Mother: But why?

Father: What is mine is hers and what is yours is his. That would be why. To see it all together. A glory!

Groom: And much less work.

Mother: When I die, you can sell mine and buy some out here.

Father: Sell, sell! Bah! Buy, my dear, buy it all. If I had sons I'd have bought this land as far as the creek. It's not good land, but with strong arms it gets better, and since no one comes out this way, no one steals your fruit, and you can get some quiet sleep. (*Pause.*)

Mother: You know why I've come.

Father: Yes.

Mother: And so?

Father: It sounds good to me. They have spoken about it.

Madre: Mi hijo tiene y puede.

Padre: Mi hija también.

Madre: Mi hijo es hermoso. No ha conocido mujer. La honra más limpia que una sábana puesta al sol.

Padre: Qué te digo de la mía. Hace las migas a las tres, cuando el lucero. No habla nunca; suave como la lana, borda toda clase de bordados y puede cortar una maroma con los dientes.

Madre: Dios bendiga su casa.

Padre: Que Dios la bendiga.

(*Aparece la criada con dos bandejas. Una con copas y la otra con dulces.*)

Madre: (*Al hijo.*) ¿Cuándo queréis la boda?

Novio: El jueves próximo.

Padre: Día en que cumple veintidós años justos.

Madre: ¡Veintidós años! Esa edad tendría mi hijo mayor si viviera. Que viviría caliente y macho como era, si los hombres no hubieran inventado las navajas.

Padre: En eso no hay que pensar.

Madre: Cada minuto. Métete la mano en el pecho.

Padre: Entonces el jueves. ¿No es así?

Novio: Así es.

Padre: Los novios y nosotros iremos en coche hasta la iglesia, que está muy lejos, y el acompañamiento en los carros y en las caballerías que traigan.

Madre: Conformes.

(*Pasa la criada.*)

Padre: Dile que ya puede entrar. (*A la madre.*) Celebraré mucho que te guste.

(*Aparece la novia. Trae las manos caídas en actitud modesta y la cabeza baja.*)

Mother: My son is rich and strong.

Father: My daughter too.

Mother: My son is handsome. He has never known a woman. His honor is cleaner than a sheet hung out to dry in the sun.

Father: What can I say about my daughter. She bakes bread at three, when the morning star rises. She never speaks. As soft as wool, she embroiders all sorts of embroidery and can cut a rope with her teeth.

Mother: May God bless her house.

Father: May God bless it.

(*The maid arrives with two trays. One with goblets, and the other with sweets.*)

Mother: (*To her son.*) When do you want to marry?

Groom: Next Thursday.

Father: The day of her twenty-second birthday.

Mother: Twenty-two! That would be the age of my oldest son had he lived. He would still be with us, alive and feisty, had men not invented knives.

Father: It's better not to think about that.

Mother: At every moment. Put your hand over your heart.

Father: Thursday then. No?

Groom: Yes.

Father: The church is far from here. We'll go in the carriage with the bride and groom, and the wedding party will follow with their horses and carts.

Mother: Agreed.

(*The maid passes by.*)

Father: Tell her she can come in. (*To the mother.*) I'll be so glad if she pleases you.

(*The bride comes in. She holds her hands modestly at her sides, and her head is lowered.*)

Madre: Acércate. ¿Estás contenta?

Novia: Sí, señora.

Padre: No debes estar seria. Al fin y al cabo ella va a ser tu madre.

Novia: Estoy contenta. Cuando he dado el sí es porque quiero darlo.

Madre: Naturalmente. (*Le coge la barbilla.*) Mírame.

Padre: Se parece en todo a mi mujer.

Madre: ¿Sí? ¡Qué hermoso mirar! ¿Tú sabes lo que es casarse, criatura?

Novia: (*Seria.*) Lo sé.

Madre: Un hombre, unos hijos y una pared de dos varas de ancha para todo lo demás.

Novio: ¿Es que hace falta otra cosa?

Madre: No. Que vivan todos, ¡eso! ¡Que vivan!

Novia: Yo sabré cumplir.

Madre: Aquí tienes unos regalos.

Novia: Gracias.

Padre: ¿No tomamos algo?

Madre: Yo no quiero. (*Al novio.*) ¿Y tú?

Novio: Tomaré. (*Toma un dulce. La novia toma otro.*)

Padre: (*Al novio.*) ¿Vino?

Madre: No lo prueba.

Padre: ¡Mejor!

(*Pausa. Todos están en pie.*)

Novio: (*A la novia.*) Mañana vendré.

Novia: ¿A qué hora?

Novio: A las cinco.

Novia: Yo te espero.

Novio: Cuando me voy de tu lado siento un despego grande y así como un nudo en la garganta.

Novia: Cuando seas mi marido ya no lo tendrás.

Novio: Eso digo yo.

Madre: Vamos. El sol no espera. (*Al padre.*) ¿Conformes en todo?

Padre: Conformes.

Madre: (*A la criada.*) Adiós, mujer.

Mother: Come near. Are you happy?

Bride: Yes, señora.

Father: No need to be so formal. After all, she will be your mother.

Bride: I'm happy. I said yes because I wanted to say yes.

Mother: Of course. (*She takes the bride's chin in her hand.*) Look at me.

Father: She looks like my wife in every way.

Mother: She does? What a beautiful gaze. Do you know what it means to marry, my dear?

Bride: (*Solemn.*) Yes, I do.

Mother: A man, children, and a wall two yards thick for all else.

Groom: What else would we need?

Mother: Nothing. And let them all live and thrive!

Bride: I'll do all I can.

Mother: Take these gifts.

Bride: Thank you.

Father: Something to eat or drink?

Mother: Not for me. (*To the groom.*) And you?

Groom: Thank you. (*He takes a sweet, the bride takes another.*)

Father: (*To the groom.*) Wine?

Mother: He doesn't touch it.

Father: So much the better!

(*Pause. All are standing.*)

Groom: (*To the bride.*) I'll come by tomorrow.

Bride: At what time?

Groom: Five.

Bride: I'll be waiting for you.

Groom: When I leave your side I feel a great emptiness and a knot in my throat.

Bride: Once you're my husband you won't feel that anymore.

Groom: That's what I tell myself.

Mother: Let's go. The sun doesn't wait. (*To the father.*) Do we agree in all ways?

Father: We agree.

Mother: (*To the maid.*) Goodbye.

Criada: Vayan ustedes con Dios.

(*La madre besa a la novia y van saliendo en silencio.*)

Madre: (*En la puerta.*) Adiós, hija. (*La novia contesta con la mano.*)
Padre: Yo salgo con vosotros. (*Salen.*)
Criada: Que reviento por ver los regalos.
Novia: (*Agria.*) Quita.
Criada: Ay, niña, enséñamelos.
Novia: No quiero.
Criada: Siquiera las medias. Dicen que son todas caladas. ¡Mujer!
Novia: ¡Ea, que no!
Criada: Por Dios. Está bien. Parece como si no tuvieras ganas de casarte.
Novia: (*Mordiéndose la mano con rabia.*) ¡Ay!
Criada: Niña, hija, ¿qué te pasa? ¿Sientes dejar tu vida de reina? No pienses en cosas agrias. ¿Tienes motivo? Ninguno. Vamos a ver los regalos. (*Coge la caja.*)
Novia: (*Cogiéndola de las muñecas.*) Suelta.
Criada: ¡Ay, mujer!
Novia: Suelta he dicho.
Criada: Tienes más fuerza que un hombre.
Novia: ¿No he hecho yo trabajos de hombre? ¡Ojalá fuera!
Criada: ¡No hables así!
Novio: Calla he dicho. Hablemos de otro asunto.

(*La luz va desapareciendo de la escena. Pausa larga.*)

Criada: ¿Sentiste anoche un caballo?
Novia: ¿A qué hora?
Criada: A las tres.
Novia: Sería un caballo suelto de la manada.
Criada: No. Llevaba jinete.
Novia: ¿Por qué lo sabes?
Criada: Porque lo vi. Estuvo parado en tu ventana. Me chocó mucho.
Novia: ¿No sería mi novio? Algunas veces ha pasado a esas horas.
Criada: No.

Maid: Go with God.

(*The mother kisses the bride and they go out in silence.*)

Mother: (*In the doorway.*) Goodbye, daughter. (*The bride lifts her hand in reply.*)

Father: I'll see you out. (*They go out.*)

Maid: I'm dying to see the gifts.

Bride: (*Bitter.*) Go away.

Maid: Ay, show me them!

Bride: I don't want to.

Maid. Not even the stockings? I hear they're all lace.

Bride: What! I said no.

Maid: Good God. Fine then. It seems as if you don't want to marry.

Bride: (*Biting her own hand angrily.*) Ay!

Maid: What is it, darling? Are you sorry to leave your life of a queen? Don't think bitter thoughts. Do you have a reason? None. Come and see the gifts. (*She takes the box.*)

Bride: (*Seizing her wrists.*) Let it go.

Maid: Ay.

Bride: I said let it go.

Maid: You're stronger than a man.

Bride: Haven't I done the work of a man? I wish I were one!

Maid: Don't talk like that!

Bride: Hush, I said. Let's talk about something else.

(*The stage is growing darker. Long pause.*)

Maid: Did you hear a horse last night?

Bride: At what time?

Maid: At three.

Bride: It must have been a horse that broke away from the herd.

Maid: No, it had a rider.

Bride: How do you know?

Maid: I saw him. He stopped at your window. I was startled.

Bride: Wasn't it my fiancé? He sometimes comes by at that hour.

Maid: No.

Novia: ¿Tú lo viste?
Criada: Sí.
Novia: ¿Quién era?
Criada: Era Leonardo.
Novia: (*Fuerte.*) ¡Mentira! ¡Mentira! ¿A qué viene aquí?
Criada: Vino.
Novia: ¡Cállate! ¡Maldita sea tu lengua!

(*Se siente el ruido de un caballo.*)

Criada: (*En la ventana.*) Mira, asómate. ¿Era?
Novia: ¡Era!

TELÓN RÁPIDO

Bride: Did you see him?
Maid: Yes.
Bride: Who was it?
Maid: Leonardo.
Bride: (*Forcefully.*) Lie! Lie! Why would he come here?
Maid: He came.
Bride: Hush! Damn your tongue.

(*Hoofbeats are heard.*)

Maid: (*At the window.*) Come here, look out. Was that him?
Bride: Yes it was!

CURTAIN FALLS FAST

Acto segundo

Zaguán de casa de la novia. Portón al fondo. Es de noche. La novia sale con enaguas blancas encañonadas, llenas de encajes y puntas bordadas y un corpiño blanco, con los brazos al aire. La criada, lo mismo.

Criada: Aquí te acabaré de peinar.

Novia: No se puede estar ahí dentro del calor.

Criada: En estas tierras no refresca ni al amanecer.

> (*Se sienta la novia en una silla baja y se mira en su espejito de mano. La criada la peina.*)

Novia: Mi madre era de un sitio donde había muchos árboles. De tierra rica.

Criada: ¡Así era ella de alegre!

Novia: Pero se consumió aquí.

Criada: El sino.

Novia: Como nos consumimos todas. Echan fuego las paredes. ¡Ay!, no tires demasiado.

Criada: Es para arreglarte mejor esta onda. Quiero que te caiga sobre la frente. (*La novia se mira en el espejo.*) Qué hermosa estás. ¡Ay! (*La besa apasionadamente.*)

Novia: (*Seria.*) Sigue peinándome.

Criada: (*Peinándola.*) ¡Dichosa tú que vas a abrazar a un hombre, que lo vas a besar, que vas a sentir su peso!

Novia: Calla.

Criada: Y lo mejor es, cuando te despiertes y lo sientas al lado y que él te roza los hombros con su aliento, como con una plumilla de ruiseñor.

Novia: (*Fuerte.*) ¿Te quieres callar?

Act Two

Entrance of the bride's house. Big doorway at the back of the stage. Night. The bride enters in white pleated petticoats covered with lace and embroidered ruffles, and a white bodice; her arms are bare. The maid is dressed the same.

Maid: I'll finish combing your hair out here.
Bride: Can't stay indoors in all this heat.
Maid: There's no cool air, even at dawn.

> (*The bride sits in a low chair and gazes into a hand mirror. The maid combs her hair.*)

Bride: My mother came from a place with many trees. And rich soil.
Maid: She was like that too: happy.
Bride: She withered here.
Maid: That was her fate.
Bride: We all wither. The walls are burning. Ay, don't pull so hard.
Maid: Just fixing a curl. I want it to fall over your forehead. (*The bride looks in the mirror.*) How beautiful you are. Ay! (*She kisses her feelingly.*)
Bride: (*Solemn.*) Go on combing me.
Maid: (*Combing.*) Happy you! You'll have a man in your arms, you'll kiss him, you'll feel his weight on your body!
Bride: Hush.
Maid: The best is waking and feeling him at your side and his breath brushes your shoulders like the feather of a nightingale.
Bride: (*Forceful.*) Will you hush!

Criada: ¡Pero, niña! ¿Una boda, qué es? Un boda es esto y nada más. ¿Son los dulces? ¿Son los ramos de flores? No. Es una cama relumbrante y un hombre y una mujer.

Novia: No se debe decir.

Criada: Eso es otra cosa. ¡Pero es bien alegre!

Novia: O bien amargo.

Criada: El azahar te lo voy a poner desde aquí, hasta aquí, de modo que la corona luzca sobre el peinado. (*Le prueba el ramo de azahar.*)

Novia: (*Se mira en el espejo.*) Trae. (*Coge el azahar y lo mira y deja caer la cabeza abatida.*)

Criada: ¿Qué es esto?

Novia: Déjame.

Criada: No son horas de ponerte triste. (*Animosa.*) Trae el azahar. (*Novia tira el azahar.*) ¡Niña! Qué castigo pides tirando al suelo la corona? ¡Levanta esa frente! ¿Es que no te quieres casar? Dilo. Todavía te puedes arrepentir. (*Se levanta.*)

Novia: Son nublos. Un mal aire en el centro. ¿Quién no lo tiene?

Criada: Tú quieres a tu novio.

Novio: Lo quiero.

Criada: Sí, sí estoy segura.

Novia: Pero éste es un paso muy grande.

Criada: Hay que darlo.

Novia: Ya me he comprometido.

Criada: Te voy a poner la corona.

Novia: (*Se sienta.*) Date prisa, que ya deben ir llegando.

Criada: Ya llevarán lo menos dos horas de camino.

Novia: ¿Cuánto hay de aquí a la iglesia?

Criada: Cinco leguas por el arroyo, que por el camino hay el doble.

(*La novia se levanta y la criada se entusiasma al verla.*)

Despierte la novia
la mañana de la boda.
¡Que los ríos del mundo
lleven tu corona!

Maid: But, darling! A wedding, what is it? That's what it is, and nothing else. Is it sweets? Is it bouquets of flowers? No. It's a shining bed—and a man and a woman.

Bride: That shouldn't be said.

Maid: That's another matter. But it's happy!

Bride: Or bitter.

Maid: I'm going to pin the orange blossoms from here to here, so that the crown shows on your hair. (*She holds a sprig of blossoms to her head.*)

Bride: (*Gazing in the mirror.*) Give it to me. (*She takes the sprig, looks at it, and lets her head fall despondently.*)

Maid: What is this?

Bride: Let me alone.

Maid: This is not the time to be sad. (*Lively.*) Give me back the orange blossoms. (*The bride tosses the sprig.*) Darling! What punishment are you looking for—throwing your crown on the floor! Lift up your head. Don't you want to be married? Say so. You can still change your mind. (*She stands up.*)

Bride: Just some clouds. A bad feeling inside, who doesn't have it?

Maid: Do you love your fiancé?

Bride: I love him.

Maid: Yes, I'm sure you do.

Bride: But this is such a big step.

Maid: You must take it.

Bride: I gave my word.

Maid: I'll put your crown on.

Bride: (*She sits down.*) Hurry, they'll be arriving.

Maid: They've been on the road at least two hours.

Bride: How far is it from here to the church?

Maid: A dozen miles along the creek, twice as far on the road.

(*The bride gets up and the maid looks at her happily.*)

> May the bride awake
> the morning of her wedding.
> May the rivers of the world
> wear your crown!

Novia: (*Sonriente.*) Vamos.

Criada: (*La besa entusiasmada y baila alrededor.*)

> Que despierte
> con el ramo verde
> del laurel florido.
> ¡Que despierte
> por el tronco y la rama
> de los laureles!

(*Se oyen unos aldabonazos.*)

Novia: ¡Abre! Deben ser los primeros convidados. (*Entra. La Criada abre sorprendida.*)

Criada: ¿Tú?

Leonardo: Yo. Buenos días.

Criada: ¡El primero!

Leonardo: ¿No me han convidado?

Criada: Sí.

Leonardo: Por eso vengo.

Criada: ¿Y tu mujer?

Leonardo: Yo vine a caballo. Ella se acerca por el camino.

Criada: ¿No te has encontrado a nadie?

Leonardo: Los pasé con el caballo.

Criada: Vas a matar al animal con tanta carrera.

Leonardo: ¡Cuando se muera, muerto está! (*Pausa.*)

Criada: Siéntate. Todavía no se ha levantado nadie.

Leonardo: ¿Y la novia?

Criada: Ahora mismo la voy a vestir.

Leonardo: ¡La novia! ¡Estará contenta!

Criada: (*Variando la conversación.*) ¿Y el niño?

Leonardo: ¿Cuál?

Criada: Tu hijo.

Leonardo: (*Recordando como soñoliento.*) ¡Ah!

Criada: ¿Lo traen?

Leonardo: No.

(*Pausa. Voces cantando muy lejos.*)

Bride: (*Smiling.*) Oh, come on.

Maid: (*Kissing her excitedly and dancing around her.*)

> May she awake
> with the green bouquet
> of flowering laurel.
> May she awake
> for the trunk and bough
> of the laurel trees!

(*The door knocker bangs.*)

Bride: Open up! These must be the first guests. (*She goes out. The maid opens the door, and looks surprised.*)

Maid: You?

Leonardo: Me. Good morning.

Maid: Here first!

Leonardo: Wasn't I invited?

Maid: Yes.

Leonardo: And so I came.

Maid: And your wife?

Leonardo: I came on horseback. She's coming by the road.

Maid: Did you meet anyone?

Leonardo: I passed them riding.

Maid: You'll kill that horse if you run it so hard.

Leonardo: When he dies, he'll be dead! (*Pause.*)

Maid: Have a seat. No one is up yet.

Leonardo: And the bride?

Maid: I'm going to dress her now.

Leonardo: The bride! She must be happy.

Maid: (*Changing the subject.*) And the little boy?

Leonardo: Which?

Maid: Your child.

Leonardo: (*Remembering as though in a dream.*) Ah.

Maid: Are they bringing him?

Leonardo: No.

(*Pause. Voices singing far away.*)

Voces:

> ¡Despierte la novia
> la mañana de la boda!

Leonardo:

> Despierte la novia
> la mañana de la boda.

Criada: Es la gente. Viene lejos todavía.

Leonardo: (*Levantándose.*) ¿La novia llevará una corona grande, no? No debía ser tan grande. Un poco más pequeña le sentaría mejor. ¿Y trajo ya el novio el azahar que se tiene que poner en el pecho?

Novia: (*Apareciendo todavía en enaguas y con la corona de azahar puesto.*) Lo trajo.

Criada: (*Fuerte.*) No salgas así.

Novia: ¿Qué mas da? (*Seria.*) ¿Por qué preguntas si trajeron el azahar? ¿Llevas intención?

Leonardo: Ninguna. ¿Qué intención iba a tener? (*Acercándose.*) Tú, que me conoces, sabes que no la llevo. Dímelo. ¿Quién he sido yo para ti? Abre y refresca tu recuerdo. Pero dos bueyes y una mala choza son casi nada. Ésa es la espina.

Novia: ¿A qué vienes?

Leonardo: A ver tu casamiento.

Novia: ¡También yo vi el tuyo!

Leonardo: Amarrado por ti, hecho con tus dos manos. A mí me pueden matar, pero no me pueden escupir. Y la plata, que brilla tanto, escupe algunas veces.

Novia: ¡Mentira!

Leonardo: No quiero hablar, porque soy hombre de sangre y no quiero que todos estos cerros oigan mis voces.

Novia: Las mías serían más fuertes.

Criada: Estas palabras no pueden seguir. Tú no tienes que hablar de lo pasado. (*La criada mira a las puertas presa de inquietud.*)

Novia: Tiene razón. Yo no debo hablarte siquiera. Pero se me calienta el alma de que vengas a verme y atisbar mi boda y preguntes con intención por el azahar. Vete y espera a tu mujer en la puerta.

Voices:

> May the bride awake
> the morning of her wedding!

Leonardo:

> May the bride awake
> the morning of her wedding.

Maid: Those are the guests. They're still far off.

Leonardo: (*Rising.*) The bride will wear a big crown, won't she? It shouldn't be all that big. A little smaller would suit her better. And did the groom bring the corsage to pin on her chest?

Bride: (*She appears in petticoats, wearing the crown of orange blossoms.*) He brought it.

Maid: (*Forceful.*) Don't come out like that.

Bride: What difference does it make? (*Solemn.*) Why do you ask if he brought the corsage? Is there a reason?

Leonardo: No reason. What reason would I have? (*Coming nearer.*) You know me, and you know I don't have one. Tell me. What have I been to you? Open your memory, remember. But a pair of oxen and a hut are nothing. That's what hurts.

Bride: Why have you come?

Leonardo: To see your wedding.

Bride: I saw your wedding, too.

Leonardo: Your two hands tied the knot. They can kill me, but they can't spit on me. Money shines—but it sometimes also spits.

Bride: A lie!

Leonardo: I don't want to talk, because I'm hotheaded, and I don't want these hills to hear me shouting.

Bride: My shouts would be louder!

Maid: These words must not be said. You must not speak about the past. (*She looks at the doors worriedly.*)

Bride: You're right. I should not even speak. But it burns up my soul that you would come to see me and spy on my wedding and ask me about the corsage, as though it meant something to you. Go and wait for your wife at the door.

Leonardo: ¿Es que tú y yo no podemos hablar?

Criada: (*Con rabia.*) No; no podéis hablar.

Leonardo: Después de mi casamiento he pensado noche y día de quién era la culpa, y cada vez que pienso sale una culpa nueva que se come a la otra; ¡pero siempre hay culpa!

Novia: Un hombre con su caballo sabe mucho y puede mucho para poder estrujar a una muchacha metida en un desierto. Pero yo tengo orgullo. Por eso me caso. Y me encerraré con mi marido, a quien tengo que querer por encima de todo.

Leonardo: El orgullo no te servirá de nada. (*Se acerca.*)

Novia: ¡No te acerques!

Leonardo: Callar y quemarse es el castigo más grande que nos podemos echar encima. ¿De qué me sirvió a mí el orgullo y el no mirarte y el dejarte despierta noches y noches? ¡De nada! ¡Sirvió para echarme fuego encima! Porque tú crees que el tiempo cura y que las paredes tapan, y no es verdad, no es verdad. ¡Cuando las cosas llegan a los centros, no hay quien las arranque!

Novia: (*Temblando.*) No puedo oírte. No puedo oír tu voz. Es como si me bebiera una botella de anís y me durmiera en una colcha de rosas. Y me arrastra, y sé que me ahogo, pero voy detrás.

Criada: (*Cogiendo a Leonardo por las solapas.*) ¡Debes irte ahora mismo!

Leonardo: Es la última vez que voy a hablar con ella. No temas nada.

Novia: Y sé que estoy loca y sé que tengo el pecho podrido de aguantar, y aquí estoy quieta por oírlo, por verlo menear los brazos.

Leonardo: No me quedo tranquilo si no te digo estas cosas. Yo me casé. Cásate tú ahora.

Criada: (*A Leonardo.*) ¡Y se casa!

Voces: (*Cantando más cerca.*)

> Despierte la novia
> la mañana de la boda.

Novia:

> ¡Despierte la novia!

(*Sale corriendo a su cuarto.*)

Leonardo: You and I can't speak?

Maid: (*Angry.*) No, you can't speak.

Leonardo: Ever since my wedding, I've thought night and day about who was to blame, and every time I think about it there's a new blame that swallows the first one; but there's still always blame!

Bride: A man on his horse knows a lot and can do a lot to trap a girl stuck out in the desert. But I have pride. So I'm marrying. And I will shut myself in with my husband—who I will have to love more than anyone else.

Leonardo: Pride won't save you. (*He approaches her.*)

Bride: Don't come near me!

Leonardo: Burning up silently is the worst punishment we can lay on ourselves. What good did pride do me, not seeing you and leaving you awake night after night? No good! All I did was burn up! You think time cures all and that the walls will hold you in, and it's not true—not true. When things get into the heart, there is nobody who can get them out.

Bride: (*Trembling.*) I can't listen to you. I can't hear your voice. It's as though I drank a bottle of anisette and fell asleep on a bed of roses. And it drags me along and I know I'm drowning, but I follow anyway.

Maid: (*Taking Leonardo by the lapels.*) You must go now!

Leonardo: This is the last time I will speak with her. Don't worry.

Bride: I know I am mad and I know that my heart is rotten from longing, and all I want is to listen to him, and watch him move his arms.

Leonardo: I won't have peace if I don't say these things. I got married. Now you marry.

Maid: (*To Leonardo.*) And she's marrying!

Voices: (*Singing, closer now.*)

> May the bride awake
> the morning of her wedding.

Bride:

> May the bride awake.

> (*She exits, running into her room.*)

Criada: Ya está aquí la gente. (*A Leonardo.*) No te vuelvas a acercar a ella.

Leonardo: Descuida.

(*Sale por la izquierda. Empieza a clarear el día.*)

Muchacha 1ª: (*Entrando.*)
>Despierte la novia
>la mañana de la boda;
>ruede la ronda
>y en cada balcón una corona.

Voces:
>¡Despierte la novia!

Criada: (*Moviendo algazara.*)
>Que despierte
>con el ramo verde
>del amor florido.
>¡Que despierte
>por el tronco y la rama
>de los laureles!

Muchacha 2ª: (*Entrando.*)
>Que despierte
>con el largo pelo,
>camisa de nieve,
>botas de charol y plata
>y jazmines en la frente.

Criada:
>¡Ay, pastora,
>que la luna asoma!

Maid: The guests are arriving. (*To Leonardo.*) Don't come near her again.

Leonardo: Don't worry.

(*He exits left. The day begins to dawn.*)

First girl: (*Entering.*)

> May the bride awake
> the morning of her wedding.
> Let the revels begin.
> On all the balconies
> a crown—

Voices:

> May the bride awake.

Maid: (*Making merry.*)

> May she awake
> with the green bouquet
> of flowering love.
> May she awake
> for the trunk and bough
> of the laurel trees!

Second girl: (*Entering.*)

> May she awake
> with her long hair
> and her blouse of snow
> and her shiny black boots
> trimmed in silver—
> jasmine petals
> on her brow.

Maid:

> Ay shepherdess,
> the moon is rising!

Muchacha 1ª:

> ¡Ay, galán,
> deja tu sombrero por el olivar!

Mozo 1°: (*Entrando con el sombrero en alto.*)

> Despierte la novia
> que por los campos viene
> rodando la boda,
> con bandeja de dalias
> y panes de gloria.

Voces:

> ¡Despierte la novia!

Muchacha 2ª:

> La novia
> se ha puesto su blanca corona,
> y el novio
> se la prende con lazos de oro.

Criada:

> Por el toronjil
> la novia no puede dormir.

Muchacha 3ª: (*Entrando.*)

> Por el naranjel
> el novio le ofrece cuchara y mantel.

> (*Entran los tres convidados.*)

Mozo 1:

> ¡Despierta, paloma!
> El alba despeja
> campanas de sombra.

First girl:

> Ay lover boy,
> leave your hat in the olive groves!

First boy: (*Entering with hat held high.*)

> May the bride awake,
> for they come through the fields
> dancing round and round,
> trays laden with dahlias
> and loaves of sweet bread.

Voices:

> May the bride awake!

Second girl:

> The bride
> dons the white crown,
> the groom ties it on
> with gold ribbons.

Maid:

> The bride can't sleep
> under the grapefruit tree.

Third girl:

> Under the orange tree
> the groom gives her a spoon
> and a tablecloth.

(*Three guests enter.*)

First boy:

> Awake, dove—
> the dawn scatters
> bells of shadow.

Convidado:

La novia, la blanca novia,
hoy doncella,
mañana señora.

Muchacha 1ª:

Baja, morena,
arrastrando tu cola de seda.

Convidado:

Baja, morenita,
que llueve rocío la mañana fría.

Mozo 1º:

Despertad, señora, despertad,
porque viene el aire lloviendo azahar.

Criada:

Un árbol quiero bordarle
lleno de cintas granates
y en cada cinta un amor
con vivas alrededor.

Voces:

Despierte la novia.

Mozo 1º:

¡La mañana de la boda!

Convidado:

La mañana de la boda
qué galana vas a estar;
pareces, flor de los montes,
la mujer de un capitán.

Guest:

> The bride, the white bride,
> today a girl,
> tomorrow a wife.

First girl:

> Go down, girl with dark hair,
> dragging your silky gown.

Guest:

> Go down, girl with dark eyes,
> the cold morning rains down dew.

First boy:

> Awake, wife, awake—
> here comes the wind
> raining orange blossoms.

Maid:

> I want to embroider a tree
> with garnet ribbons,
> love on each ribbon
> and hurrahs all around.

Voices:

> May the bride awake!

First boy:

> The morning of the wedding!

Guest:

> The morning of the wedding
> how lovely you will be,
> like the captain's lady
> and a meadow flower.

Padre: (*Entrando.*)

    La mujer de un capitán
    se lleva el novio.
    ¡Ya viene con sus bueyes por el tesoro!

Muchacha 3ª:

    El novio
    parece la flor del oro.
    Cuando camina,
    a sus plantas se agrupan las clavelinas.

Criada:

    ¡Ay mi niña dichosa!

Mozo 2º:

    Que despierte la novia.

Criada:

    ¡Ay mi galana!

Muchacha 1ª:

    La boda está llamando
    por las ventanas.

Muchacha 2ª:

    Que salga la novia.

Muchacha 1ª:

    ¡Que salga, que salga!

Criada:

    ¡Que toque y repiquen
    las campanas!

Father: (*Entering.*)

> The groom
> takes the captain's lady.
> He's coming on his oxen
> for the treasure!

Third girl:

> The groom
> looks like the golden flower.
> When he walks
> carnations cling
> to the soles of his feet.

Maid:

> Oh my happy girl!

Second boy:

> May the bride awake.

Maid:

> Ay my beauty!

First girl:

> The wedding beckons
> at the windows.

Second girl:

> May the bride come out!

First girl:

> Come out! Come out!

Maid:

> May the bells ring
> and ring again.

Mozo 1°:

> ¡Que viene aquí! ¡Que sale ya!

Criada:

> ¡Como un toro, la boda
> levantándose está!

(Aparece la novia. Lleva un traje negro mil novecientos, con caderas y larga cola rodeada de gasas plisadas y encajes duros. Sobre el peinado de visera lleva la corona de azahar. Suenan las guitarras. Las muchachas besan a la novia.)

Muchacha 3ª: ¿Qué esencia te echaste en el pelo?
Novia: (*Riendo.*) Ninguna.
Muchacha 2ª: (*Mirando el traje.*) La tela es de lo que no hay.
Mozo 1°: ¡Aquí está el novio!
Novio: ¡Salud!
Muchacha 1ª: (*Poniéndole una flor en la oreja.*)

> El novio
> parece la flor de oro.

Muchacha 2ª:

> ¡Aires de sosiego
> le manan los ojos!

(El novio se dirige al lado de la novia.)

Novia: ¿Por qué te pusiste esos zapatos?
Novio: Son más alegres que los negros.
Mujer de Leonardo: (*Entrando y besando a la novia.*) ¡Salud!

(Hablan todas con algazara.)

First boy:

> In she comes,
> out she goes!

Maid:

> The wedding
> heats up
> like a bull.

(The bride appears. She's wearing a nineteenth-century black gown with full hips and a long train covered in pleated gauze and stiff lace. In her hair she wears the crown of orange blossoms. Guitars play. The girls kiss the bride.)

Third girl: What perfume did you put in your hair?
Bride: (*Laughing.*) None.
Second girl: (*Looking at the dress.*) The finest cloth.
First boy: Here's the groom!
Groom: Health to you!
First girl: (*Putting a flower behind his ear.*)

> The groom
> looks like the golden flower.

Second girl:

> Bliss flows
> from his eyes!

(The groom goes to stand beside the bride.)

Bride: Why are you wearing those shoes?
Groom: They're more festive than the black shoes.
Leonardo's wife: (*Entering and kissing the bride.*) Health to you!

(The women chatter together joyfully.)

Leonardo: (*Entrando como quien cumple un deber.*)
La mañana de casada
la corona te ponemos.

Mujer:

¡Para que el campo se alegre
con el agua de tu pelo!

Madre: (*Al padre.*) ¿También están ésos aquí?
Padre: Son familia. ¡Hoy es día de perdones!
Madre: Me aguanto, pero no perdono.
Novio: ¡Con la corona da alegría mirarte!
Novia: ¡Vámonos pronto a la iglesia!
Novio: ¿Tienes prisa?
Novia: Sí. Estoy deseando ser tu mujer y quedarme sola contigo, y no oír más voz que la tuya.
Novio: ¡Eso quiero yo!
Novia. Y no ver más que tus ojos. Y que me abrazarás tan fuerte, que aunque me llamara mi madre, que está muerta, no me pudiera despegar de ti.
Novio: Yo tengo fuerza en los brazos. Te voy a abrazar cuarenta años seguidos.
Novia: (*Dramática, cogiéndole del brazo.*) ¡Siempre!
Padre: ¡Vamos pronto! ¡A coger las caballerías y los carros! Que ya ha salido el sol.
Madre: ¡Que llevéis cuidado! No sea que tengamos malahora.

(*Se abre el gran portón del fondo. Empiezan a salir.*)

Criada: (*Llorando.*)

Al salir de tu casa,
blanca doncella,
acuérdate que sales
como una estrella . . .

Leonardo: (*Entering as though dutifully.*)
>
> On the morning of the wedding
> we dress you in a crown.

Wife:

> May the fields rejoice
> in the water of your hair.

Mother: (*To the father.*) Are they here too?

Father: They are family. Today is the day of forgiveness!

Mother: I'll bear it, but I won't forgive.

Groom: I'm happy to see you in your crown!

Bride: Let's go straight to the church!

Groom: Are you in a hurry?

Bride: Yes, I long to be your wife and to be alone with you, and hear only your voice and no other.

Groom: That's what I want!

Bride: And see your eyes only. And you'll hold me so tight that even if my mother—my dead mother—called to me, I could not pull away from you.

Groom: I have strong arms. I will hold you for forty years, one after the other.

Bride: (*Dramatic, taking him by the arm.*) Forever!

Father: Let's go soon! Let's get the horses and carts! The sun has come up.

Mother: Take care, may nothing go wrong.

> (*The big door at the back of the stage opens. They begin to go out.*)

Maid: (*Crying.*)

> When you go from your home,
> pure white girl,
> know that you shine like a star . . .

Muchacha 1ª:

> Limpia de cuerpo y ropa
> al salir de tu casa para la boda.

(Van saliendo.)

Muchacha 2ª:

> ¡Ya sales de tu casa
> para la iglesia!

Criada:

> ¡El aire pone flores
> por las arenas!

Muchacha 3ª:

> ¡Ay la blanca niña!

Criada:

> Aire oscuro el encaje de su mantilla.

(Salen. Se oyen guitarras, palillos y panderetas. Quedan solos Leonardo y su mujer.)

Mujer: Vamos.
Leonardo: ¿Adónde?
Mujer: A la iglesia. Pero no vas en el caballo. Vienes conmigo.
Leonardo: ¿En el carro?
Mujer: ¿Hay otra cosa?
Leonardo: Yo no soy hombre para ir en carro.
Mujer: Y yo no soy mujer para ir sin su marido en un casamiento. ¡Que no puedo más!
Leonardo: ¡Ni yo tampoco!
Mujer: ¿Por qué me miras así? Tienes una espina en cada ojo.
Leonardo: ¡Vamos!

First girl:

> Clean in body and clothing
> when you go from your home
> for the wedding.

(They go out.)

Second girl:

> You're leaving your home
> and going to the church!

Maid:

> The wind strews
> flowers in the sand!

Third girl:

> Ay the pure-white girl!

Maid:

> Dark in her black lace mantilla.

(They go out. Guitars, castanets and tambourines are heard playing. Leonardo and his wife remain alone.)

Wife: Let's go.
Leonardo: Where?
Wife: To the church. But not on your horse, you're coming with me.
Leonardo: In the cart?
Wife: Is there another way?
Leonardo: I'm not a man for riding in carts.
Wife: I'm not a woman that goes to a wedding without her husband. I can't stand any more of this.
Leonardo: Nor can I!
Wife: Why do you look at me like that! With a thorn in each eye.
Leonardo: Let's go!

Mujer: No sé lo que pasa. Pero pienso y no quiero pensar. Una cosa sé. Yo ya estoy despachada. Pero tengo un hijo. Y otro que viene. Vamos andando. El mismo sino tuvo mi madre. Pero de aquí no me muevo.

(*Voces fuera.*)

Voces:

¡Al salir de tu casa
para la iglesia,
acuérdate que sales
como una estrella!

Mujer: (*Llorando.*)

¡Acuérdate que sales
como una estrella!

Así salí yo de mi casa también. Que me cabía todo el campo en la boca.
Leonardo: (*Levantándose.*) Vamos.
Mujer: ¡Pero conmigo!
Leonardo: Sí. (*Pausa.*) ¡Echa a andar! (*Salen.*)

Voces:

Al salir de tu casa
para la iglesia
acuérdate que sales
como una estrella.

TELÓN LENTO

Wife: I don't know what's happening. I think and I don't want to think. One thing I know. I've already been cast off. But I've got a child, and another on the way. Let's go. The same fate as my mother. But I'm not giving in.

(*Voices from outside.*)

Voices:

> When you go from your home
> to the church,
> know that you shine
> like a star!

Wife: (*Crying.*)

> Know that you shine
> like a star!

I went from my home like that. With the world in my hands.
Leonardo: (*Standing up.*) Let's go.
Wife: With you!
Leonardo: Yes. (*Pause.*) Start walking! (*They go out.*)

Voices:

> When you go from your home
> to the church,
> know that you shine
> like a star.

SLOW CURTAIN

Acto segundo

CUADRO II

Exterior de la cueva de la novia. Entonación en blancos grises y azules fríos. Grandes chumberas. Tonos sombríos y plateados. Panoramas de mesetas color barquillo, todo endurecido como paisaje de cerámica popular.

Criada: (*Arreglando en una mesa copas y bandejas.*)
> Giraba,
> giraba la rueda
> y el agua pasaba,
> porque llega la boda
> que se aparten las ramas
> y la luna se adorne
> por su blanca baranda.

(*En voz alta.*)
> ¡Pon los manteles!

(*En voz patética.*)
> Cantaban,
> cantaban los novios
> y el agua pasaba.
> Porque llega la boda
> que relumbre la escarcha
> y se llenen de miel
> las almendras amargas.

(*En voz alta.*)
> ¡Prepara el vino!

Act Two

SCENE TWO

Outside the bride's cave room. Color scheme in gray whites and cold blues. Tall prickly pears. Solemn, silvery hues. Scenery: mesetas the color of wafers, like a landscape in terra cotta.

Maid: (*Arranging goblets and trays on a table.*)

>Spun—
>the wheel spun,
>and the water flowed,
>for the wedding day comes
>and may the branches part
>and the moon festoon
>the white railing.

(*In a loud voice.*)

>Lay cloths on the tables!

(*In a tender voice.*)

>Sang—
>the bride and groom sang,
>and the water flowed,
>for the wedding day comes
>and may the frost shine,
>and lace the bitter almonds
>with honey.

(*In a loud voice.*)

>Prepare the wine!

(*En voz poética.*)

Galana.
Galana de la tierra,
mira cómo el agua pasa.
Porque llega tu boda
recógete las faldas
y bajo el ala del novio
nunca salgas de tu casa.
Porque el novio es un palomo
con todo el pecho de brasa
y espera el campo el rumor
de la sangre derramada.
Giraba,
giraba la rueda
y el agua pasaba.
¡Porque llega tu boda,
deja que relumbre el agua!

Madre: (*Entrando.*) ¡Por fin!

Padre: ¿Somos los primeros?

Criada: No. Hace rato llegó Leonardo con su mujer. Corrieron como demonios. La mujer llegó muerta de miedo. Hicieron el camino como si hubieran venido a caballo.

Padre: Ése busca la desgracia. No tiene buena sangre.

Madre: ¿Qué sangre va a tener? La de toda su familia. Mana de su bisabuelo, que empezó matando y sigue en toda la mala ralea, manejadores de cuchillos y gente de falsa sonrisa.

Padre: ¡Vamos a dejarlo!

Criada: ¿Cómo lo va a dejar?

Madre: Me duele hasta la punta de las venas. En la frente de todos ellos yo no veo más que la mano con que mataron a lo que era mío. ¿Tú me ves a mí? ¿No te parezco loca? Pues es loca de no haber gritado todo lo que mi pecho necesita. Tengo en mi pecho un grito siempre puesto de pie a quien tengo que castigar y meter entre los mantos. Pero se llevan a los muertos y hay que callar. Luego la gente critica. (*Se quita el manto.*)

Padre: Hoy no es día de que te acuerdes de esas cosas.

(*In a poetic voice.*)

> Beauty—
> beauty of the land,
> see how the water flows.
> Your wedding has come
> so lift up your skirts
> and under the wings of the groom
> never step from your home.
> For the groom is a dove
> with a burning breast
> and the land longs for the sound
> of spilled blood.
> Spun—
> the wheel spun
> and the water flowed.
> Your wedding has come
> so let the water shine—

Mother: (*Entering.*) At last!

Father: Are we the first to come?

Maid: No. Leonardo and his wife came a while ago. They were running like demons—as fast as horses. His wife looked scared to death.

Father: That man wants trouble. He has bad blood.

Mother: What blood could he have? All the family has it. It flows from the great-grandfather, who began the killing, and that whole clan has got it—along with knives and false smiles.

Father: Let's let it go.

Maid: How can she let it go!

Mother: It aches in my veins. All I see in their faces is the hand that killed what was mine. Do you see me? Do I seem mad? It was mad not to have screamed all that my heart longed to scream. Right here in my chest there's a scream ready to rise against all those I must punish and lay in shrouds. But they carry away the dead and you have to be silent. And then people talk. (*She takes off her cloak.*)

Father: Today is not the day to remember this.

Madre: Cuando sale la conversación, tengo que hablar. Y hoy más. Porque hoy me quedo sola en mi casa.

Padre: En espera de estar acompañada.

Madre: Ésa es mi ilusión: los nietos. (*Se sientan.*)

Padre: Yo quiero que tengan muchos. Esta tierra necesita brazos que no sean pagados. Hay que sostener una batalla con las malas hierbas, con los cardos, con los pedruscos que salen no se sabe dónde. Y estos brazos tienen que ser de los dueños, que castiguen y que dominen, que hagan brotar las simientes. Se necesitan muchos hijos.

Madre: ¡Y alguna hija! ¡Los varones son del viento! Tienen por fuerza que manejar armas. Las niñas no salen jamás a la calle.

Padre: (*Alegre.*) Yo creo que tendrán de todo.

Madre: Mi hijo la cubrirá bien. Es de buena simiente. Su padre pudo haber tenido conmigo muchos hijos.

Padre: Lo que yo quisiera es que esto fuera cosa de un día. Que en seguida tuvieran dos o tres hombres.

Madre: Pero no es así. Se tarda mucho. Por eso es tan terrible ver la sangre de una derramada por el suelo. Una fuente que corre un minuto y a nosotros nos ha costado años. Cuando yo llegué a ver a mi hijo, estaba tumbado en mitad de la calle. Me mojé las manos de sangre y me las lamí con la lengua. Porque era mía. Tú no sabes lo que es eso. En una custodia de cristal y topacios pondría yo la tierra empapada por ella.

Padre: Ahora tienes que esperar. Mi hija es ancha y tu hijo es fuerte.

Madre: Así espero. (*Se levantan.*)

Padre: Prepara las bandejas de trigo.

Criada: Están preparadas.

Mujer: (*De Leonardo, entrando.*) ¡Que sea para bien!

Madre: Gracias.

Leonardo: ¿Va a haber fiesta?

Padre: Poca. Le gente no puede entretenerse.

Criada: ¡Ya están aquí!

(*Van entrando invitados en alegres grupos. Entran los novios cogidos del brazo. Sale Leonardo.*)

Mother: When they talk about it, I have to speak. Today more than ever. Today I will be alone in my house.

Father: Waiting for company.

Mother: This is my hope, grandchildren. (*They sit.*)

Father: I want them to have many. This land needs strong hands that are not hired—owners' hands—that can beat and tame the land and make the seeds grow. Hands that can fight weeds and thistle—and the stones that are everywhere you look. There must be many sons.

Mother: And a daughter! Boys are like the wind! They carry knives, you can't stop them. Girls never go out in the street.

Father: (*Happily.*) I believe they will have many of each.

Mother: My son will cover her well. He has good seed. His father could have made me many sons.

Father: I wish it were done in a day. I want two or three men, right now.

Mother: That's not how it works. Seeing your own blood spilled in the dirt is—terrible. It takes years to make, and then flows out in a minute. When I saw my son lying in the middle of the street, I wet my hands with his blood and I licked them with my tongue. It was my blood. You don't know what this means. I wanted to put that blood-soaked dirt into an urn made of crystal and topaz.

Father: Now you have to wait. My daughter has broad hips and your son is strong.

Mother: That's my hope. (*They stand up.*)

Father: Ready the trays of wheat.

Maid: They are ready.

Leonardo's wife: (*Entering.*) All the best!

Mother: Thank you.

Leonardo: Will there be a celebration?

Father: Not long. People can't stay long.

Maid: Here they are!

(*Guests enter in happy groups. The bride and groom enter arm in arm. Leonardo exits.*)

Novio: En ninguna boda se vio tanta gente.

Novia: (*Sombría.*) En ninguna.

Padre: Fue lucida.

Madre: Ramas enteras de familias han venido.

Novio: Gente que no salía de su casa.

Madre: Tu padre sembró mucho y ahora lo recoges tú.

Novio: Hubo primos míos que yo ya no conocía.

Madre: Toda la gente de la costa.

Novio: (*Alegre.*) Se espantaban de los caballos. (*Hablan.*)

Madre: (*A la novia.*) ¿Qué piensas?

Novia: No pienso en nada.

Madre: Las bendiciones pesan mucho.

(*Se oyen guitarras.*)

Novia: Como plomo.

Madre: (*Fuerte.*) Pero no han de pesar. Ligera como paloma debes ser.

Novia: ¿Se queda usted aquí esta noche?

Madre: No. Mi casa está sola.

Novia: ¡Debía usted quedarse!

Padre: (*A la madre.*) Mira el baile que tienen formado. Bailes de allá de la orilla del mar.

(*Sale Leonardo y se sienta. Su mujer detrás de él en actitud rígida.*)

Madre: Son los primos de mi marido. Duros como piedras para la danza.

Padre: Me alegra al verlos. ¡Qué cambio para esta casa! (*Se va.*)

Novio: (*A la novia.*) ¿Te gustó el azahar?

Novia: (*Mirándole fija.*) Sí.

Novio: Es todo de cera. Dura siempre. Me hubiera gustado que llevaras en todo el vestido.

Novia: No hace falta.

(*Mutis Leonardo por la derecha.*)

Groom: No wedding has had more guests.

Bride: (*Sullen.*) None.

Father: It was splendid.

Mother: Whole branches of families have come.

Groom: Folks who never go out.

Mother: Your father sowed and now you will reap.

Groom: Cousins I had never met.

Mother: All the cousins from the coast.

Groom: (*Happily.*) They were afraid of the horses. (*They go on talking.*)

Mother: (*To the bride.*) What are you thinking about?

Bride: About nothing.

Mother: Blessings are heavy.

(*Guitars are heard playing.*)

Bride: As lead.

Mother: (*Forceful.*) They shouldn't be heavy. You should be light as a dove.

Bride: Will you stay here tonight?

Mother: No, my house is lonely without me.

Bride: You should stay.

Father: (*To the mother.*) Look how they dance. Dances from down by the sea.

(*Leonardo enters and sits down. His wife stands behind him, rigidly.*)

Mother: Those are my husband's cousins. Hard as stone when they dance.

Father: I'm happy to see them. They grace this house! (*He exits.*)

Groom: (*To the bride.*) Did you like the corsage?

Bride: (*Staring hard at him.*) Yes.

Groom: It's made of wax, it will last forever. I wish you had them all over your dress.

Bride: No need for that.

(*Leonardo exits right, without speaking.*)

Muchacha 1ª: Vamos a quitarte los alfileres.

Novia: (*Al novio.*) Ahora vuelvo.

Mujer: ¡Que seas feliz con mi prima!

Novio: Tengo seguridad.

Mujer: Aquí los dos; sin salir nunca y a levantar la casa. ¡Ojalá yo viviera también así de lejos!

Novio: ¿Por qué no compráis tierras? El monte es barato y los hijos se crían mejor.

Mujer: No tenemos dinero. ¡Y con el camino que llevamos!

Novio: Tu marido es un buen trabajador.

Mujer: Sí, pero le gusta volar demasiado. Ir de una cosa a otra. No es hombre tranquilo.

Criada: ¿No tomáis nada? Te voy a envolver unos roscos de vino para tu madre, que a ella le gustan mucho.

Novio: Ponle tres docenas.

Mujer: No, no. Con media tiene bastante.

Novio: Un día es un día.

Mujer: (*A la criada.*) ¿Y Leonardo?

Criada: No lo vi.

Novio: Debe estar con la gente.

Mujer: ¡Voy a ver! (*Se va.*)

Criada: Aquello está hermoso.

Novio: ¿Y tú no bailas?

Criada: No hay quien me saque.

(*Pasan al fondo dos muchachas; durante todo este acto el fondo será un animado cruce de figuras.*)

Novio: (*Alegre.*) Eso se llama no entender. Las viejas frescas como tú bailan mejor que las jóvenes.

Criada: Pero ¿vas a echarme requiebros, niño? ¡Qué familia la tuya! ¡Machos entre los machos! Siendo niña vi la boda de tu abuelo. ¡Qué figura! Parecía como si se casara un monte.

Novio: Yo tengo menos estatura.

Criada: Pero el mismo brillo en los ojos. ¿Y la niña?

Novio: Quitándose la toca.

First girl: Let's take her pins.

Bride: (*To the groom.*) I'll be back.

Wife: I hope you'll be happy with my cousin.

Groom: I'm sure I will be.

Wife: Here you'll stay, the two of you, making a home. I wish I lived far out here!

Groom: Why don't you buy some land? The hills are cheap; it's better for raising children.

Wife: We have no money. And the way things are going . . .

Groom: Your husband is a good worker.

Wife: Yes, but he flits around too much. From one thing to another. He's not steady.

Maid: Don't you want something to eat or drink? I'll wrap up some wine cakes for your mother—she likes them so much.

Groom: Give her three dozen.

Wife: No, no. A half is plenty.

Groom: A day is a day.

Wife: (*To the maid.*) Have you seen Leonardo?

Maid: I haven't seen him.

Groom: He must be with the others.

Wife: I'll go see! (*She goes out.*)

Maid: It's a fine party.

Groom: Don't you dance?

Maid: There's no one to ask me.

> (*Two girls pass at the back of the stage; throughout this scene, figures will step lively across the back of the stage.*)

Groom: (*Gaily.*) They don't know that hearty ladies like you dance better than the girls.

Maid: Are you flirting with me, young man? What a family you have! Men among men. When I was young I saw your granddad's wedding. What a figure he cut! As though a mountain were about to be married.

Groom: I'm not that tall.

Maid: Same shine in your eyes. Where's my darling girl?

Groom: Taking off her crown.

Criada: ¡Ah! Mira. Para la media noche, como no dormiréis, os he preparado jamón, y unas copas grandes de vino antiguo. En la parte baja de la alacena. Por si lo necesitáis.

Novio: (*Sonriente.*) No como a media noche.

Criada: (*Con malicia.*) Si tú no, la novia. (*Se va.*)

Mozo 1º: (*Entrando.*) ¡Tienes que beber con nosotros!

Novio: Estoy esperando a la novia.

Mozo 2º: ¡Ya la tendrás en la madrugada!

Mozo 1º: ¡Que es cuando más gusta!

Mozo 2º: Un momento.

Novio: Vamos.

> (*Salen. Se oye gran algaʒara. Sale la novia. Por el lado opuesto salen dos muchachas corriendo a encontrarla.*)

Muchacha 1ª: ¿A quién diste el primer alfiler, a mí, o a ésta?

Novio: No me acuerdo.

Muchacha 1ª: A mí me lo diste aquí.

Muchacha 2ª: A mí delante del altar.

Novia: (*Inquieta y con una gran lucha interior.*) No sé nada.

Muchacha 1ª: Es que yo quisiera que tú . . .

Novia: (*Interrumpiendo.*) Ni me importa. Tengo mucho que pensar.

Muchacha 2ª: Perdona.

> (*Leonardo cruʒa el fondo.*)

Novia: (*Ve a Leonardo.*) Y estos momentos son agitados.

Muchacha 1ª: ¡Nosotras no sabemos nada!

Novia: Ya lo sabréis cuando os llegue la hora. Estos pasos son pasos que cuestan mucho.

Muchacha 1ª: ¿Te ha disgustado?

Novia: No. Perdonad vosotras.

Muchacha 2ª: ¿De qué? Pero los dos alfileres sirven para casarse, ¿verdad?

Novia: Los dos.

Muchacha 1ª: Ahora que una se casa antes que otra.

Novia: ¿Tantas ganas tenéis?

Maid: Ah. Since you won't be asleep at midnight, I put out some ham for you, and some big cups of aged wine. In the lower part of the pantry, in case you want it.

Groom: (*Smiling.*) I don't dine at midnight.

Maid: (*Naughtily.*) If you won't, maybe the bride will. (*She goes out.*)

First boy: (*Entering.*) Come and drink with us!

Groom: I'm waiting for the bride.

Second boy: She'll be yours before dawn.

First boy: The best hours of the night!

Second boy: Say no more.

Groom: Let's go.

> (*They exit. Loud revelry is heard. The bride appears. From the other side of the stage, two girls come running toward her.*)

First girl: Who did you give the first pin to—her or me?

Bride: I don't remember.

First girl: You gave it to me—right here.

Second girl: You gave it to me—in front of the altar.

Bride: (*Anxious, and in great inner turmoil.*) I don't know.

First girl: I wanted you to . . .

Bride: (*Cutting her off.*) I'm not interested, I have to think.

Second girl: Pardon me.

> (*Leonardo passes at the back of the stage.*)

Bride: (*Seeing Leonardo.*) These moments are hard.

First girl: We don't know about that!

Bride: You'll know when your time comes. These are hard steps to take.

First girl: Aren't you glad?

Bride: Yes, pardon me.

Second girl: What for? But both pins are for marrying, isn't that right?

Bride: Yes, both.

First girl: But one of us will marry first.

Bride: Are you in such a hurry?

Muchacha 2ª: (*Vergonzosa.*) Sí.

Novia: ¿Para qué?

Muchacha 1ª: Pues . . . (*Abrazando a la segunda.*)

> (*Echan a correr las dos. Llega el novio y muy despacio abraza a la novia por detrás.*)

Novia: (*Con gran sobresalto.*) ¡Quita!

Novio: ¿Te asustas de mí?

Novia: ¡Ay! ¿Eras tú?

Novio: ¿Quién iba a ser? (*Pausa.*) Tu padre o yo.

Novia: ¡Es verdad!

Novio: Ahora que tu padre te hubiera abrazado más blando.

Novia: (*Sombría.*) ¡Claro!

Novio: (*La abraza fuertemente de modo un poco brusco.*) Porque es viejo.

Novia: (*Seca.*) ¡Déjame!

Novio: ¿Por qué? (*La deja.*)

Novia: Pues . . . la gente. Pueden vernos.

> (*Vuelve a cruzar el fondo la criada, que no mira a los novios.*)

Novio: ¿Y qué? Ya es sagrado.

Novia: Sí, pero déjame . . . Luego.

Novio: ¿Qué tienes? ¡Estás como asustada!

Novia: No tengo nada. No te vayas.

> (*Sale la mujer de Leonardo.*)

Mujer: No quiero interrumpir . . .

Novio: Dime.

Mujer: ¿Pasó por aquí mi marido?

Novio: No.

Mujer: Es que no lo encuentro, y el caballo está tampoco en el establo.

Novio: (*Alegre.*) Debe estar dándole una carrera.

Second girl: (*Bashful.*) Yes.
Bride: Why?
First girl: Well . . . (*Hugging the second girl.*)

> (*They run off. The groom arrives and slowly puts his arms around the bride from behind.*)

Bride: (*Startled.*) Stop!
Groom: Do I scare you?
Bride: Ay! Was that you?
Groom: Who would it be? (*Pausing.*) Either your father or me.
Bride: True.
Groom: Your father would not hug you so tightly.
Bride: (*Sullen.*) True!
Groom: Because he's an old man. (*He hugs her tightly and somewhat brusquely.*)
Bride: (*Sharp.*) Let me go!
Groom: Why? (*He lets her go.*)
Bride: The . . . guests. They might see us.

> (*The maid crosses at the back of the stage without looking at the couple.*)

Groom: So what? It's sacred now.
Bride: Yes, but let me go . . . Later.
Groom: What's the matter? You seem scared.
Bride: Nothing. Don't go.

> (*Leonardo's wife appears.*)

Wife: I don't want to interrupt . . .
Groom: What is it?
Wife: Did my husband come this way?
Groom: No.
Wife: I can't find him and the horse isn't in the stable.
Groom: (*Gaily.*) He must've taken him out for a run.

(Se va la mujer inquieta. Sale la criada.)

Criada: ¿No andáis satisfechos de tanto saludo?

Novio: Ya estoy deseando que esto acabe. La novia está un poco cansada.

Criada: ¿Qué es eso, niña?

Novia: ¡Tengo como un golpe en las sienes!

Criada: Una novia de estos montes debe ser fuerte. *(Al novio.)* Tú eres el único que la puedes curar, porque tuya es.

(Sale corriendo.)

Novio: *(Abrazándola.)* Vamos un rato al baile. *(La besa.)*

Novia: *(Angustiada.)* No. Quisiera echarme en la cama un poco.

Novio: Yo te haré compañía.

Novia: ¡Nunca! ¿Con toda la gente aquí? ¿Qué dirían? Déjame sosegar un momento.

Novio: ¡Lo que quieras! ¡Pero no estés así por la noche!

Novia: *(En la puerta.)* A la noche estaré mejor.

Novio: ¡Que es lo que yo quiero!

(Aparece la madre.)

Madre: Hijo.

Novio: ¿Dónde anda usted?

Madre: En todo ese ruido. ¿Estás contento?

Novio: Sí.

Madre: ¿Y tu mujer?

Novio: Descansa un poco. ¡Mal día para las novias!

Madre: ¿Mal día? El único bueno. Para mí fue como una herencia. *(Entra la criada y se dirige al cuarto de la novia.)* Es la roturación de las tierras, la plantación de árboles nuevos.

Novio: ¿Usted se va a ir?

Madre: Sí. Yo tengo que estar en mi casa.

Novio: Sola.

Madre: Sola no. Que tengo la cabeza llena de cosas y de hombres y de luchas.

(The wife goes out, anxiously. The maid enters.)

Maid: Aren't you two happy from so many blessings?

Groom: I'm wishing this would end. The bride is tired.

Maid: What is it, darling girl?

Bride: My temples are pounding!

Maid: A bride from these hills must be strong. (*To the groom.*) You're
the only one who can cure her, she's yours.

(She runs out.)

Groom: (*Embracing her.*) Let's go dance. (*He kisses her.*)

Bride: (*Anguished.*) No—I want to lie down for a while.

Groom: I will keep you company.

Bride: No! With all these guests here? What will they say? Let me rest
a moment.

Groom: If you like. I hope you're not this way tonight!

Bride: (*At the door.*) I will be better tonight.

Groom: That's what I want!

(The mother appears.)

Mother: Son.

Groom: Where have you been?

Mother: In all that revelry. Are you happy?

Groom: Yes.

Mother: And your wife?

Groom: She's resting for a moment. A bad day for brides!

Mother: A bad day? The only good day. For me it was a great blessing.
(*The maid enters and walks toward the bride's room.*) The plowing
of fields, the planting of trees.

Groom: Are you going home?

Mother: Yes, I need to be home.

Groom: Alone.

Mother: Alone, no. My head is full of thoughts and men and fights.

Novio: Pero luchas que ya no son luchas.

(*Sale la criada rápidamente; desaparece corriendo por el fondo.*)

Madre: Mientras una vive, lucha.

Novio: ¡Siempre la obedezco!

Madre: Con tu mujer procura estar cariñoso, y si la notas infatuada o arisca, hazle una caricia que le produzca un poco de daño, un abrazo fuerte, un mordisco y luego un beso suave. Que ella no pueda disgustarse, pero que sienta que tú eres el macho, el amo, el que mandas. Así aprendí de tu padre. Y como no lo tienes, tengo que ser yo la que te enseñe estas fortalezas.

Novio: Yo siempre haré lo que usted mande.

Padre: (*Entrando.*) ¿Y mi hija?

Novio: Está dentro.

Muchacha 1ª: ¡Vengan los novios, que vamos a bailar la rueda!

Mozo 1º: (*Al novio.*) Tú la vas a dirigir.

Padre: (*Saliendo.*) ¡Aquí no está!

Novio: ¿No?

Padre: Debe haber subido a la baranda.

Novio: ¡Voy a ver! (*Entra.*)

(*Se oye algazara y guitarras.*)

Muchacha 1ª: ¡Ya han empezado! (*Sale.*)

Novio: (*Saliendo.*) No está.

Madre: (*Inquieta.*) ¿No?

Padre: ¿Y adónde pudo haber ido?

Criada: (*Entrando.*) ¿Y la niña, dónde está?

Madre: (*Seria.*) No lo sabemos.

(*Sale el novio. Entran tres invitados.*)

Padre: (*Dramático.*) Pero, ¿no está en el baile?

Criada: En el baile no está.

Padre: (*Con arranque.*) Hay mucha gente. ¡Mirad!

Groom: But fights that are no longer fights.

(*The maid runs out rapidly, and disappears at the back of the stage.*)

Mother: While we're alive, we fight.

Groom: I will always do as you say.

Mother: Try to be loving to your wife, and if she's haughty or won't let you touch her, give her a pat that hurts a little, a hard hug, a bite, and then a soft kiss. Not to make her angry, but to show her that you're the man, the master, the one who commands. I learned this from your father. And since he's not here for you, I have to teach you how to be strong.

Groom: I will always do as you say.

Father: (*Entering.*) Have you seen my daughter?

Groom: She's in her room.

First girl: Bring the bride and groom out, we'll dance the round.

First boy: (*To the groom.*) You'll lead.

Father: (*Looking in her room.*) She's not in here.

Groom: She's not there?

Father: She must have climbed over the railing.

Groom: I'll go look! (*He goes into her room.*)

(*Guitars are heard, and sounds of revelry.*)

First girl: The round has begun! (*She exits.*)

Groom: (*Returning.*) She's not there.

Mother: (*Anxious.*) She's not there?

Father: Where could she have gone?

Maid: (*Entering.*) Where is she?

Mother: (*Grave.*) We don't know.

(*The groom goes out. Three guests enter.*)

Father: (*Dramatic.*) She's not dancing?

Maid: She's not dancing.

Father: (*Vehement.*) There's a crowd. Look for her!

Criada: ¡Ya he mirado!

Padre: (*Trágico.*) ¿Pues dónde está?

Novio: (*Entrando.*) Nada. En ningún sitio.

Madre: (*Al padre.*) ¿Qué es esto? ¿Dónde está tu hija?

(*Entra la mujer de Leonardo.*)

Mujer: ¡Han huido! ¡Han huido! Ella y Leonardo. En el caballo. ¡Iban abrazados, como una exhalación!

Padre: ¡No es verdad! ¡Mi hija, no!

Madre: ¡Tu hija, sí! Planta de mala madre y él, también él. ¡Pero ya es la mujer de mi hijo!

Novio: (*Entrando.*) ¡Vamos detrás! ¿Quién tiene un caballo?

Madre: ¿Quién tiene un caballo ahora mismo, quién tiene un caballo?, que le daré todo lo que tengo, mis ojos y hasta mi lengua . . .

Voz: Aquí hay uno.

Madre: (*Al hijo.*) ¡Anda! ¡Detrás! (*Sale con dos mozos.*) No. No vayas. Esa gente mata pronto y bien . . . ; ¡pero sí, corre, y yo detrás!

Padre: No será ella. Quizá se ha tirado al aljibe.

Madre: Al agua se tiran las honradas, las limpias; ¡ésa, no! Pero ya es mujer de mi hijo. Dos bandos. Aquí hay dos bandos. (*Entran todos.*) Mi familia y la tuya. Salid todos de aquí. Limpiarse el polvo de los zapatos. Vamos a ayudar a mi hijo. (*La gente se separa en dos grupos.*) Porque tiene gente; que son sus primos del mar y todos los que llegan de tierra adentro. ¡Fuera de aquí! Por todos los caminos. Ha llegado otra vez la hora de la sangre. Dos bandos. Tú con el tuyo y yo con el mío. ¡Atrás! ¡Atrás!

TELÓN

Maid: I looked.

Father: (*Tragic.*) So where is she?

Groom: (*Entering.*) Nowhere.

Mother: (*To the father.*) What is this? Where is your daughter?

(*Leonardo's wife enters.*)

Wife: They ran away! They ran away! She went with Leonardo. On the horse. They left holding each other—like a whirlwind.

Father: It can't be true. My daughter—no!

Mother: Your daughter—yes! Spawn of a bad mother, and him—him too. But now she's my son's wife!

Groom: (*Entering.*) We'll go after them! Who has a horse?

Mother: Who has a horse, quick—who has a horse? I'll give him all I've got, my eyes and my tongue . . .

Voice: Here's a horse.

Mother: (*To her son.*) Go after them! (*He exits with two boys.*) No. Don't go. These people kill fast, and sure . . . But yes, hurry, I'll follow behind.

Father: It can't be her. Maybe she threw herself in the cistern.

Mother: Clean, honorable girls throw themselves in water. That girl, no! But now she's my son's wife. Two camps. Now there are two camps. (*All enter.*) My family and yours. We're all going. Wipe the dust off your shoes. We're going to help my son. (*The people part into two groups.*) All his people are here: cousins from the sea, and all the cousins from inland. Out of here! On all the roads! The hour of blood has come again. Two camps. You with yours and me with mine. Go after them!

CURTAIN

Acto tercero

CUADRO PRIMERO

Bosque. Es de noche. Grandes troncos húmedos. Ambiente oscuro. Se oyen dos violines.

(Salen tres leñadores.)

Leñador 1°: ¿Y los han encontrado?

Leñador 2°: No. Pero los buscan por todas partes.

Leñador 3°: Ya darán con ellos.

Leñador 2°: ¡Chissss!

Leñador 3°: ¿Qué?

Leñador 2°: Parece que se acercan por todos los caminos a la vez.

Leñador 1°: Cuando salga la luna los verán.

Leñador 2°: Debían dejarlos.

Leñador 1°: El mundo es grande. Todos pueden vivir en él.

Leñador 3°: Pero los matarán.

Leñador 2°: Hay que seguir la inclinación; han hecho bien en huir.

Leñador 1°: Se estaban engañando uno a otro y al fin la sangre pudo más.

Leñador 3°: ¡La sangre!

Leñador 1°: Hay que seguir el camino de la sangre.

Leñador 2°: Pero sangre que ve la luz se la bebe la tierra.

Leñador 1°: ¿Y qué? Vale más ser muerto desangrado que vivo con ella podrida.

Leñador 3°: Callar.

Leñador 1°: ¿Qué? ¿Oyes algo?

Leñador 3°: Oigo los grillos, las ranas, el acecho de la noche.

Leñador 1°: Pero el caballo no se siente.

Leñador 3°: No.

Act Three

SCENE ONE

Forest. Night. Great damp tree trunks. Dark ambience. Two violins are heard playing.

(*Three woodcutters appear.*)

First woodcutter: Did they find them?

Second woodcutter: No, but they're looking everywhere.

Third woodcutter: They'll find them soon.

Second woodcutter: Shhh . . .

Third woodcutter: What?

Second woodcutter: They seem to be arriving on all roads at once.

First woodcutter: When the moon comes out they'll see them.

Second woodcutter: They should leave them alone.

First woodcutter: The world is big. There's room for everyone.

Third woodcutter: But they'll kill them.

Second woodcutter: We need to follow our desires: they were right to run.

First woodcutter: They weren't telling the truth to each other, and in the end, the blood won out.

Third woodcutter: The blood!

First woodcutter: We have to go the way of the blood.

Second woodcutter: But blood that sees the light is soaked up by the ground.

First woodcutter: And so? Better to be dead and bloodless than alive with rotten blood.

Third woodcutter: Hush.

First woodcutter: Why? Do you hear something?

Third woodcutter: I hear the crickets, the frogs, and the night, watching.

First woodcutter: But you can't hear the horse.

Third woodcutter: No.

Leñador 1º: Ahora la estará queriendo.

Leñador 2º: El cuerpo de ella era para él y el cuerpo de él para ella.

Leñador 3º: Los buscan y los matarán.

Leñador 1º: Pero ya habrán mezclado sus sangres y serán como dos cántaros vacíos, como dos arroyos secos.

Leñador 2º: Hay muchas nubes y será fácil que la luna no salga.

Leñador 3º: El novio los encontrará con luna o sin luna. Yo lo vi salir. Como una estrella furiosa. La cara color ceniza. Expresaba el sino de su casta.

Leñador 1º: Su casta de muertos en mitad de la calle.

Leñador 2º: ¡Eso es!

Leñador 3º: ¿Crees que lograrían romper el cerco?

Leñador 2º: Es difícil. Hay cuchillos y escopetas a diez leguas a la redonda.

Leñador 3º: Él lleva un buen caballo.

Leñador 2º: Pero lleva una mujer.

Leñador 1º: Ya estamos cerca.

Leñador 2º: Un árbol de cuarenta ramas. Lo cortaremos pronto.

Leñador 3º: Ahora sale la luna. Vamos a darnos prisa.

(Por la izquierda surge una claridad.)

Leñador 1º:

> ¡Ay luna que sales!
> Luna de las hojas grandes.

Leñador 2º:

> ¡Llena de jazmines la sangre!

Leñador 1º:

> ¡Ay luna sola!
> ¡Luna de las verdes hojas!

Leñador 2º:

> Plata en la cara de la novia.

First woodcutter: He's loving her now.

Second woodcutter: Her body was for him and his for her.

Third woodcutter: They will find them and kill them.

First woodcutter: But by now their blood is mixed together, and they're like two empty jugs, like two dry creeks.

Second woodcutter: There are many clouds and the moon may not come out.

Third woodcutter: The groom will find them, moon or no moon. I saw him on his way—a furious star. His face the color of ashes—showing the fate of his clan.

First woodcutter: His clan—men dead in the middle of the street.

Second woodcutter: Yes.

Third woodcutter: Do you think they can get away?

Second woodcutter: It's hard to do. There are knives and shotguns for thirty miles around.

Third woodcutter: He has a good horse.

Second woodcutter: But he's carrying a woman.

First woodcutter: We're near now.

Second woodcutter: A tree with forty branches. We'll cut it down soon.

Third woodcutter: The moon is coming out. We should hurry.

(A glow rises from the left.)

First woodcutter:

> Ay moon, arising!
> Moon with great leaves.

Second woodcutter:

> Jasmine petals in the blood.

First woodcutter:

> Ay moon alone!
> Moon with green leaves.

Second woodcutter:

> Silver on the face of the bride.

Leñador 3°:

> ¡Ay luna mala!
> Deja para el amor la oscura rama.

Leñador 1°:

> ¡Ay triste luna!
> ¡Deja para el amor la rama oscura!

(*Salen. Por la claridad de la izquierda aparece la Luna.*
La Luna es un leñador joven con la cara blanca. La escena
adquiere un vivo resplandor azul.)

Luna:

> Cisne redondo en el río,
> ojo de las catedrales,
> alba fingida en las hojas
> soy; ¡no podrán escaparse!
> ¿Quién se oculta? ¿Quién solloza
> por la maleza del valle?
> La luna deja un cuchillo
> abandonado en el aire,
> que siendo acecho de plomo
> quiere ser dolor de sangre.
> ¡Dejadme entrar! ¡Vengo helada
> por paredes y cristales!
> ¡Abrir tejados y pechos
> donde pueda calentarme!
> ¡Tengo frío! Mis cenizas
> de soñolientos metales,
> buscan la cresta del fuego
> por los montes y las calles.
> Pero me lleva la nieve
> sobre su espalda de jaspe,
> y me anega, dura y fría,
> el agua de los estanques.
> Pues esta noche tendrán

Third woodcutter:

>   Ay, bad moon!
>   Leave the dark branch for love.

First woodcutter:

>   Ay, sad moon!
>   Leave the branch dark for love.

> (*They exit. In the glow at the left, the Moon appears. Moon is a young woodcutter, with a white face. The stage begins to gleam vividly.*)

Moon:

>   Round swan on the river,
>   eye of the cathedrals,
>   I am dawn in the leaves,
>   they will not escape!
>   Who hides? Who sobs
>   in the leafy valley?
>   The moon leaves a knife
>   waiting on the wind—
>   its leaden blade wants
>   to be the ache of blood.
>   Let me in! I'm so cold
>   from slipping along
>   the windows and walls.
>   Open roofs and hearts
>   so that I can warm up!
>   I'm so cold! My ashes
>   made of sleeping metals
>   search for the crest of fire
>   on the hills and streets.
>   But the snow carries me
>   on its jasper back
>   and the pond water
>   floods me—cold and hard.
>   Tonight my cheeks

mis mejillas roja sangre,
y los juncos agrupados
en los anchos pies del aire.
¡No haya sombra ni emboscada,
que no puedan escaparse!
¡Que quiero entrar en un pecho
para poder calentarme!
¡Un corazón para mí!
¡Caliente!, que se derrame
por los montes de mi pecho;
dejadme entrar, ¡ay, dejadme!

(A las ramas.)

No quiero sombras. Mis rayos
han de entrar en todas partes,
y haya en los troncos oscuros
un rumor de claridades,
para que esta noche tengan
mis mejillas dulce sangre,
y los juncos agrupados
en los anchos pies del aire.
¿Quién se oculta? ¡Afuera digo!
¡No! ¡No podrán escaparse!
Yo haré lucir al caballo
una fiebre de diamante.

(Desaparece entre los troncos, y vuelve la escena a su luz oscura. Sale una anciana totalmente cubierta por tenues paños verdeoscuro. Lleva los pies descalzos. Apenas si se le verá el rostro entre los pliegues.)

Mendiga:

Esa luna se va, y ellos se acercan.
De aquí no pasan. El rumor del río
apagará con el rumor de troncos

will be blood red,
and the reeds will cluster
in the wide feet of the wind.
There's no shadow,
no place to lie in wait—
they will not escape!
Let me climb into a heart
and heat myself up.
A heart for me!
Hot, let it spill down
the hills of my chest.
Let me in! Ay, let me!

(*To the branches.*)

I want no shadows—my shine
must enter everywhere—
and may my rays rustle
among the dark trunks,
and may my cheeks tonight
fill with sweet blood,
and the reeds cluster
in the wide feet of the wind.
Who's hiding? Out! I say.
No, they will not escape.
I'll make the horse shine
in a fever of diamonds.

(*Moon disappears among the tree trunks and the stage
dims again. An old woman appears, covered from head to
foot in fluttery dark-green rags. She is barefoot. Her face
is barely visible among the folds.*)

Beggar:

The moon goes and they come.
Beyond here they will not pass.
The murmuring river and the rustling trees

el desgarrado vuelo de los gritos.
Aquí ha de ser, y pronto. Estoy cansada.
Abren los cofres, y los blancos hilos
aguardan por el suelo de la alcoba
cuerpos pesados con el cuello herido.
No se despierte un pájaro y la brisa
recogiendo en su falda los gemidos,
huya con ellos por las negras copas
o los entierre por el blando limo.

(*Impaciente.*)

¡Esa luna, esa luna!

(*Aparece la Luna. Vuelve la luz azul intensa.*)

Luna: Ya se acercan. Unos por la cañada y el otro por el río. Voy a alumbrar las piedras. ¿Qué necesitas?
Mendiga: Nada.
Luna: El aire va llegando duro, con doble filo.
Mendiga: Ilumina el chaleco y aparta los botones, que después las navajas ya saben el camino.
Luna:
Pero que tarden mucho en morir.
Que la sangre
me ponga entre los dedos su delicado silbo.
¡Mira que ya mis valles de ceniza despiertan
en ansia de esta fuente de chorro estremecido!

Mendiga: No dejemos que pasen el arroyo. ¡Silencio!
Luna: ¡Allí vienen!

(*Se va. Queda la escena oscura.*)

Mendiga: De prisa. ¡Mucha luz! ¿Me has oído? ¡No pueden escaparse!

(*Entran el novio y mozo 1°. La mendiga se sienta y se tapa con el manto.*)

will muffle the torn flight of screams.
Here it must be and soon. I am tired.
They open the coffins and the white cloths
will be waiting on the floor of the chamber
for the heavy bodies with their throats cut.
May no bird wake, and may the wind,
gathering the screams up in its skirt,
flee with them through the black crowns of the trees
or bury them under the soft mud.

(*Impatient.*)

That moon, that moon!

(*Moon appears, accompanied by an intense blue glow.*)

Moon: Nearer they come. Some through the gully, some by the river. I will shine on the stones. What do you need?

Beggar: Nothing.

Moon: The wind is coming on hard, with a double blade.

Beggar: Shine on his vest and undo the buttons so the blades will know their way.

Moon:
But may they die slowly. May the blood
hiss sweetly between my fingers.
See how my ashen valleys wake with desire
for the source of the trembling flow.

Beggar: Don't let them pass the creek! Hush!

Moon: Here they come!

(*Moon exits. The stage is dark.*)

Beggar: Hurry! More light. Do you hear me? They won't escape!

(*The groom and the first boy enter. The beggar sits down and wraps herself in her cloak.*)

Novio: Por aquí.

Mozo 1º: No los encontrarás.

Novio: (*Enérgico.*) ¡Sí, los encontraré!

Mozo 1º: Creo que se han ido por otra vereda.

Novio: No. Yo sentí hace un momento el galope.

Mozo 1º: Sería otro caballo.

Novio: (*Dramático.*) Oye. No hay más que un caballo en el mundo, y es éste. ¿Te has enterado? Si me sigues, sígueme sin hablar.

Mozo 1º: Es que quisiera . . .

Novio: Calla. Estoy seguro de encontrármelos aquí. ¿Ves este brazo? Pues no es mi brazo. Es el brazo de mi hermano y el de mi padre y el de toda mi familia que está muerta. Y tiene tanto poderío, que puede arrancar este árbol de raíz si quiere. Y vamos pronto, que siento los dientes de todos los míos clavados aquí de una manera que se me hace imposible respirar tranquilo.

Mendiga: (*Quejándose.*) ¡Ay!

Mozo 1º: ¿Has oído?

Novio: Vete por ahí y da la vuelta.

Mozo 1º: Esto es una caza.

Novio: Una caza. La más grande que se puede hacer.

(*Se va el mozo. El novio se dirige rápidamente hacia la izquierda y tropieza con la mendiga, la muerte.*)

Mendiga: (*Quejándose.*) ¡Ay!

Novio: ¿Qué quieres?

Mendiga: Tengo frío.

Novio: ¿Adónde te diriges?

Mendiga: (*Siempre quejándose como una mendiga.*) Allá lejos . . .

Novio: ¿De dónde vienes?

Mendiga: De allí . . . , de muy lejos.

Novio: ¿Viste un hombre y una mujer que corrían montados en un caballo?

Mendiga: (*Despertándose.*) Espera . . . (*Lo mira.*) Hermoso galán. (*Se levanta.*) Pero mucho más hermoso si estuviera dormido.

Novio: Dime, contesta, ¿los viste?

Groom: This way.

First boy: You won't find them!

Groom: (*Vehement.*) Yes, I will find them!

First boy: I think they've gone down another path.

Groom: No. I heard hoofbeats a moment ago.

First boy: It could be another horse.

Groom: (*Dramatic.*) There's no other horse in the world, do you hear me? If you want to come with me, come but don't speak.

First boy: I wanted to . . .

Groom: Quiet! I'm sure I'll find them here. Do you see this arm? It is not my arm. It is the arm of my brother and my father and all my dead family. It is so strong it can rip out that tree by the roots, if it wants. Let's go, I feel all their teeth clenched so hard I can barely breathe.

Beggar: (*Moaning.*) Ay!

First boy: Did you hear that?

Groom: Go that way and look around.

First boy: This is a hunt.

Groom: A hunt, the greatest hunt of all.

(*The boy goes out. The groom turns quickly to the left and stumbles into the beggar, Death.*)

Beggar: (*Moaning.*) Ay!

Groom: What do you want?

Beggar: I'm cold.

Groom: Where are you going?

Beggar: (*Still moaning like a beggar.*) Far away . . .

Groom: Where are you from?

Beggar: Out there . . . far away.

Groom: Did you see a man and a woman on horseback, riding fast?

Beggar: (*Awaking.*) Wait . . . (*She looks at him.*) Handsome. (*She stands up.*) But you would be more handsome if you were asleep.

Groom: Tell me, answer me, did you see them?

Mendiga: Espera . . . ¡Qué espaldas más anchas! ¿Cómo no te gusta estar tendido sobre ellas y no andar sobre las plantas de los pies, que son tan chicas?

Novio: (*Zamarreándola.*) ¡Te digo si los viste! ¿Han pasado por aquí?

Mendiga: (*Enérgica.*) No han pasado; pero están saliendo de la colina. ¿No los oyes?

Novio: No.

Mendiga: ¿Tú no conoces el camino?

Novio: ¡Iré sea como sea!

Mendiga: Te acompañaré. Conozco esta tierra.

Novio: (*Impaciente.*) ¡Pero vamos! ¿Por dónde?

Mendiga: (*Dramática.*) ¡Por allí!

> (*Salen rápidos. Se oyen lejanos dos violines que expresan el bosque. Vuelven los leñadores. Llevan las hachas al hombro. Pasan lentos entre los troncos.*)

Leñador 1°:

> ¡Ay muerte que sales!
> Muerte de las hojas grandes.

Leñador 2°:

> ¡No abras el chorro de la sangre!

Leñador 1°:

> ¡Ay muerte sola!
> Muerte de las secas hojas.

Leñador 3°:

> ¡No cubras de flores la boda!

Leñador 2°:

> ¡Ay triste muerte!
> Deja para el amor la rama verde.

Beggar: Wait . . . Such wide shoulders! Wouldn't you like to be leaning on them, instead of walking on the soles of your feet, which are so narrow.

Groom: (*Shaking her.*) I asked if you saw them! Did they come this way?

Beggar: (*Vehement.*) No, but they're coming down the hill. Don't you hear them?

Groom: No.

Beggar: Don't you know the way?

Groom: I will find it however I can.

Beggar: I will go with you. I know this place.

Groom: (*Impatient.*) Let's go then! Which way?

Beggar: (*Dramatic.*) This way.

> (*They go out quickly. Two violins are heard playing, as the voice of the forest. The woodcutters appear again, with axes on their shoulders. They pass slowly among the trees.*)

First woodcutter:

> Ay death, arising.
> Death of great leaves.

Second woodcutter:

> Don't let the blood run out!

First woodcutter:

> Ay lonely death!
> Death of dry leaves.

Third woodcutter:

> Do not bury the wedding in flowers.

Second woodcutter:

> Ay sad death!
> Leave the green branch for love.

Leñador 1°:

> ¡Ay muerte mala!
> ¡Deja para el amor la verde rama!

> (*Van saliendo mientras hablan. Aparecen Leonardo y la novia.*)

Leonardo:

> ¡Calla!

Novia:

> Desde aquí yo me iré sola.
> ¡Vete! Quiero que te vuelvas.

Leonardo:

> ¡Calla, digo!

Novia:

> Con los dientes, con las manos, como puedas,
> quita de mi cuello honrado
> el metal de esta cadena,
> dejándome arrinconada
> allá en mi casa de tierra.
> Y si no quieres matarme
> como a víbora pequeña,
> pon en mis manos de novia
> el cañón de la escopeta.
> ¡Ay, qué lamento, qué fuego
> me sube por la cabeza!
> ¡Qué vidrios se me clavan en la lengua!

Leonardo:

> Ya dimos el paso; ¡calla!,
> porque nos persiguen cerca
> y te he de llevar conmigo.

First woodcutter:

> Ay bad death!
> Leave the branch green for love.

(They go out talking. Leonardo and the bride enter.)

Leonardo:

> Quiet!

Bride:

> I'll go on alone.
> Go! I want you to go back!

Leonardo:

> Hush, I said.

Bride:

> With your teeth,
> with your hands,
> lift the metal of this chain
> off my honorable throat,
> leave me abandoned
> in my house of dirt.
> If you don't want to kill me
> like a small snake,
> put the butt of a gun
> in my hands—the hands of a bride—
> Ay, what grief, what fire
> rise in my head.
> What slivers of glass pierce my tongue!

Leonardo:

> It's done now, hush!
> They are close behind
> and I have to take you with me.

Novia:

>
> ¡Pero ha de ser a la fuerza!

Leonardo:

>
> ¿A la fuerza? ¿Quién bajó
> primero las escaleras?

Novia:

>
> Yo las bajé.

Leonardo:

>
> ¿Quién le puso
> al caballo bridas nuevas?

Novia:

>
> Yo misma. Verdad.

Leonardo:

>
> ¿Y qué manos
> me calzaron las espuelas?

Novia:

>
> Estas manos, que son tuyas,
> pero que al verte quisieran
> quebrar las ramas azules
> y el murmullo de tus venas.
> ¡Te quiero! ¡Te quiero! ¡Aparta!
> Que se matarte pudiera,
> te pondría una mortaja
> con los filos de violetas.
> ¡Ay, qué lamento, qué fuego
> me sube por la cabeza!

Leonardo:

>
> ¡Qué vidrios se me clavan en la lengua!
> Porque yo quise olvidar
> y puse un muro de piedra

Bride:

Only by force!

Leonardo:

By force? Who ran down the steps first?

Bride:

I ran down them.

Leonardo:

Who put new reins on the horse?

Bride:

I did, this is true.

Leonardo:

What hands put my feet in the spurs?

Bride:

These hands that are yours,
but when they see you they want
to break the blue branches
and the murmur of your veins.
I love you! I love you! Leave me!
If I could kill you I would wrap you
in a shroud of sharp violets.
Ay what grief, what fire
rise in my head!

Leonardo:

What slivers of glass pierce my tongue!
I wanted to forget
and I put a wall of stone

entre tu casa y la mía.
Es verdad. ¿No lo recuerdas?
Y cuando te vi de lejos
me eché en los ojos arena.
Pero montaba a caballo
y el caballo iba a tu puerta.
Con alfileres de plata
mi sangre se puso negra,
y el sueño me fue llenando
las carnes de mala hierba.
Que yo no tengo la culpa,
que la culpa es de la tierra
y de ese olor que te sale
de los pechos y las trenzas.

Novia:

¡Ay qué sinrazón! No quiero
contigo cama ni cena,
y no hay minuto del día
que estar contigo no quiera,
porque me arrastras y voy,
y me dices que me vuelva
y te sigo por el aire
como una brizna de hierba.
He dejado a un hombre duro
y a toda su descendencia
en la mitad de la boda
y con la corona puesta.
Para ti será el castigo
y no quiero que lo sea.
¡Déjame sola! ¡Huye tú!
No hay nadie que te defienda.

Leonardo:

Pájaros de la mañana
por los árboles se quiebran.
La noche se está muriendo

between your house and mine.
This is true. Don't you remember?
When I saw you from afar
I threw sand in my eyes.
But I climbed on my horse
and it went to your door.
The silver wedding pins
turned my blood black
and the dream filled my body
with evil weeds.
I am not to blame,
the blame lies in the land,
and in the smell that rises
from your breasts and your braids.

Bride:

Ay what nonsense! With you
I never wanted supper or a bed
and there's no minute in a day
I don't want to be with you,
for you drag me and I go,
and you tell me to come back,
and I chase you through the air
like a blade of grass.
I left a strong hard man
and all his clan
in the middle of the wedding
with the crown on my head.
You will be punished,
this is not what I want.
Leave me alone! Go alone!
For you, no one will stand up.

Leonardo:

Birds of the morning
break in the trees.
The night is dying

en el filo de la piedra.
Vamos al rincón oscuro,
donde yo siempre te quiera,
que no me importa la gente
ni el veneno que nos echa.

(La abraza fuertemente.)

Novia:

Y yo dormiré a tus pies
para guardar lo que sueñas.
Desnuda, mirando al campo,

(Dramática.)

como si fuera una perra,
¡porque eso soy! Que te miro
y tu hermosura me quema.

Leonardo:

Se abrasa lumbre con lumbre.
La misma llama pequeña
mata dos espigas juntas.
¡Vamos!

(La arrastra.)

Novia:

¿Adónde me llevas?

Leonardo:

Adonde no puedan ir
estos hombres que nos cercan.
¡Donde yo pueda mirarte!

on the blade of a stone.
Let's go to a dark corner
where I'll love you forever
and people won't matter
or the poison they spread.

(He holds her tightly.)

Bride:

I will sleep at your feet
and watch over your dreams.
Naked, gazing at the fields

(Dramatic.)

like a watch dog—
That's what I am! I watch you
and your beauty burns me.

Leonardo:

One flame joins another.
The same small flame
burns two spikes of wheat.
Let's go.

(He pulls her.)

Bride:

Where are you taking me?

Leonardo:

Where the men following us
can't come.
Where I can look at you!

Novia: (*Sarcástica.*)

> Llévame de feria en feria,
> dolor de mujer honrada,
> a que las gentes me vean
> con las sábanas de boda
> al aire, como banderas.

Leonardo:

> También yo quiero dejarte
> si pienso como se piensa.
> Pero voy donde tú vas.
> Tú también. Da un paso. Prueba.
> Clavos de luna nos funden
> mi cintura y tus caderas.

> (*Toda esta escena es violenta, llena de gran sensualidad.*)

Novia:

> ¿Oyes?

Leonardo:

> Viene gente.

Novia:

> ¡Huye!
> Es justo que yo aquí muera
> con los pies dentro del agua,
> espinas en la cabeza.
> Y que me lloren las hojas,
> mujer perdida y doncella.

Leonardo:

> Cállate. Ya suben.

Novia:

> ¡Vete!

Bride: (*Sarcastic.*)

> Lead me from fair to fair,
> an honorable woman's shame,
> so all of them can see me
> with my wedding sheets
> flapping in the wind like flags.

Leonardo:

> I would want to leave you too
> if I thought what they think.
> But I'll go where you go.
> You too, go on—try.
> Moon nails join us together,
> my waist and your hips.

(*This whole scene is violent and strongly sensual.*)

Bride:

> Do you hear them?

Leonardo:

> They're coming.

Bride:

> Run!
> It's right for me to die here
> with my feet in the water
> and thorns on my head.
> Let the leaves cry for me,
> lost wife—and still a girl.

Leonardo:

> Hush! They're coming up the hill.

Bride:

> Go!

Leonardo:

> Silencio. Que no nos sientan.
> Tú delante. ¡Vamos, digo!

> (*Vacila la novia.*)

Novia:

> ¡Los dos juntos!

Leonardo: (*Abrazándola.*)

> ¡Cómo quieras!
> Si nos separan, será
> porque esté muerto.

Novia:

> Y yo muerta.

> (*Salen abrazados.*)

(*Aparece la Luna muy despacio. La escena adquiere una fuerte luz azul. Se oyen los dos violines. Bruscamente se oyen dos largos gritos desgarrados, y se corta la música de los violines. Al segundo grito aparece la mendiga y queda de espaldas. Abre el manto y queda en el centro como un gran pájaro de alas inmensas. La Luna se detiene. El telón baja en medio de un silencio absoluto.*)

TELÓN

Leonardo:

Quiet. They will hear us.
You first. I said, let's go.

(*The bride hesitates.*)

Bride:

Both, together.

Leonardo: (*Holding her.*)

As you want.
Until my death
do us part.

Bride:

Or my death.

(*They go out holding each other.*)

(*Moon enters very slowly. The stage fills with strong blue light. The two violins are heard playing. Suddenly there are two long wild screams and the music stops. After the second scream, the beggar appears and stands with her back to the audience. She opens her cloak, standing in the center of the stage, like an immense bird with great wings. Moon stops still. The curtain drops in utter silence.*)

CURTAIN

Acto tercero

Habitación blanca con arcos y gruesos muros. A la derecha y a la izquierda escaleras blancas. Gran arco al fondo y pared del mismo color. El suelo será también de un blanco reluciente. Esta habitación simple tendrá un sentido monumental de iglesia. No habrá ni un gris, ni una sombra, ni siquiera lo preciso para la perspectiva.

> (*Dos muchachas vestidas de azul oscuro están devanando una madeja roja.*)

Muchacha 1ª:

> Madeja, madeja,
> ¿qué quieres hacer?

Muchacha 2ª:

> Jazmín de vestido,
> cristal de papel.
> Nacer a las cuatro,
> morir a las diez.
> Ser hilo de lana,
> cadena a tus pies
> y nudo que apriete
> amargo laurel.

Niña: (*Cantando.*)

> ¿Fuisteis a la boda?

Muchacha 1ª:

> No.

Act Three

LAST SCENE

White room with arches and thick walls. To the right and left, white stair-cases. Ample arch at the back and a wall in the same color. The floor will also be shining white. This simple room will have the monumental feeling of a church. There will be no grays, no shadows, not even enough to show perspective.

> (*Two girls wearing dark blue are winding a ball of red yarn.*)

First girl:

> Yarn, yarn,
> what will you do?

Second girl:

> Dress of jasmine,
> paper and glass,
> be born at four
> and die at ten.
> Be a length of yarn,
> chain 'round your feet
> and the knot that ties
> the bitter laurel.

Little girl: (*Singing.*)

> Were you at the wedding?

First girl:

> No.

Niña:

>¡Tampoco fui yo!
>¿Qué pasaría
>por los tallos de las viñas?
>¿Qué pasaría
>por el ramo de la oliva?
>¿Qué pasó
>¿que nadie volvió?
>¿Fuisteis a la boda?

Muchacha 2ª:

>Hemos dicho que no.

Niña: (*Yéndose.*)

>¡Tampoco fui yo!

Muchacha 2ª:

>Madeja, madeja,
>¿qué quieres cantar?

Muchacha 1ª:

>Heridas de cera,
>dolor de arrayán.
>Dormir la mañana,
>de noche velar.

Niña: (*En la puerta.*)

>El hilo tropieza
>con el pedernal.
>Los montes azules
>lo dejan pasar.
>Corre, corre, corre,
>y al fin llegará
>a poner cuchillo
>y a quitar el pan.

(*Se va.*)

Little girl:

> I wasn't either!
> What happened
> near the vinestalks?
> What happened
> near the olive branch?
> Why did no one
> come back?
> Were you at the wedding?

Second girl:

> We said we weren't.

Little girl: (*Turning to go.*)

> I wasn't either!

Second girl:

> Yarn, yarn,
> what will you sing?

First girl:

> Wounds of wax,
> pain of myrtle.
> Sleep in the morning,
> stay up all night.

Little girl: (*In the doorway.*)

> The yarn
> snags on the flint.
> The blue hills
> let it pass.
> Pull, pull, pull,
> and in the end
> he'll stick in the knife
> and take out the bread.

(*She goes out.*)

Muchacha 2ª:

>Madeja, madeja,
>¿qué quieres decir?

Muchacha 1ª:

>Amante sin habla.
>Novio carmesí.
>Por la orilla muda
>tendidos los vi.

>>>*(Se detiene mirando la madeja.)*

Niña: (*Asomándose a la puerta.*)

>Corre, corre, corre,
>el hilo hasta aquí.
>Cubiertos de barro
>los siento venir.
>¡Cuerpos estirados,
>paños de marfil!

>>>*(Se va.)*

(Aparecen la mujer y la suegra de Leonardo. Llegan angustiadas.)

Muchacha 1ª:

>¿Vienen ya?

Suegra: (*Agria.*)

>No sabemos.

Muchacha 2ª:

>¿Qué contáis de la boda?

Muchacha 1ª:

>Dime.

Second girl:

> Yarn, yarn,
> what will you say?

First girl:

> Lover with no voice,
> groom blood-red.
> On the riverbank
> I saw them lying dead.

> *(She pauses, looking at the ball of yarn.)*

Little girl: *(Appearing in the doorway.)*

> Pull, pull, pull
> the yarn—
> I hear them coming
> caked in mud.
> Bodies stiff
> in ivory cloths!

> *(She goes out.)*

> *(Leonardo's wife and mother-in-law appear, looking anguished.)*

First girl:

> Are they coming?

Mother-in-law: *(Bitter.)*

> We don't know.

Second girl:

> What happened at the wedding?

First girl:

> Tell me.

Suegra: (*Seca.*)
	Nada.

Mujer:
	Quiero volver para saberlo todo.

Suegra: (*Enérgica.*)
	Tú, a tu casa.
	Valiente y sola en tu casa.
	A envejecer y a llorar.
	Pero la puerta cerrada.
	Nunca. Ni muerto ni vivo.
	Clavaremos las ventanas.
	Y vengan lluvias y noches
	sobre las hierbas amargas.

Mujer:
	¿Qué habrá pasado?

Suegra:
	No importa.
	Échate un velo en la cara.
	Tus hijos son hijos tuyos
	nada más. Sobre la cama
	pon una cruz de ceniza
	donde estuvo su almohada.

	(*Salen.*)

Mendiga: (*A la puerta.*)
	Un pedazo de pan, muchachas.

Niña:
	¡Vete!

	(*Las muchachas se agrupan.*)

Mother-in-law: (*Dry.*)
>Nothing.

Wife:
>I want to go back and see what happened.

Mother-in-law: (*Vigorously.*)
>You—to your house.
>Brave and alone in your house.
>You will weep and grow old.
>With the door shut. Never.
>No man dead or alive.
>We'll nail the windows shut.
>May the rain fall
>and the night fall
>into the bitter grass.

Wife:
>But what happened?

Mother-in-law:
>What does it matter.
>Put on a veil.
>Your children are your children,
>that is all. On your bed,
>mark a cross of ash
>where his pillow lay.

>>>>(*They exit.*)

Beggar: (*At the door.*)
>Some bread, girls.

Little girl:
>Go away!

>>>(*The girls gather around.*)

Mendiga:

    ¿Por qué?

Niña:

    Porque tú gimes: vete.

Muchacha 1ª:

    ¡Niña!

Mendiga:

    ¡Pude pedir tus ojos! Una nube
    de pájaros me sigue; ¿quieres uno?

Niña:

    ¡Yo me quiero marchar!

Muchacha 2ª: (*A la mendiga.*)
    ¡No le hagas caso!

Muchacha 1ª:

    ¿Vienes por el camino del arroyo?

Mendiga:

    ¡Por allí vine!

Muchacha 1ª: (*Tímida.*)
    ¿Puedo preguntarte?

Mendiga:

    Yo los vi; pronto llegan: dos torrentes
    quietos al fin entre las piedras grandes,
    dos hombres en las patas del caballo.
    Muertos en la hermosura de la noche.

                (*Con delectación.*)

Beggar:

>Why?

Little girl:

>Because you are whining. Go away!

First girl:

>Hush.

Beggar:

>I could have asked for your eyes!
>A cloud of birds is following me.
>Do you want one?

Little girl:

>I want to go home!

Second girl: (*To the beggar.*)

>Don't mind her!

First girl:

>Did you take the path along the creek?

Beggar:

>I came that way.

First girl: (*Shy.*)

>May I ask a question?

Beggar:

>I saw them; they're coming soon. Two torrents,
>lying still at last among the great stones,
>two men on the hooves of a horse.
>Dead in the beauty of the night.

>(*Taking pleasure.*)

Muertos, sí, muertos.

Muchacha 1ª:

¡Calla, vieja, calla!

Mendiga:

Flores rotas los ojos, y sus dientes
dos puñados de nieve endurecida.
Los dos cayeron, y la novia vuelve
teñida en sangre falda y cabellera.
Cubiertos con dos mantas ellos vienen
sobre los hombros de los mozos altos.
Así fue; nada más. Era lo justo.
Sobre la flor del oro, sucia arena.

(*Se va. Las muchachas inclinan las cabezas y rítmicamente van saliendo.*)

Muchacha 1ª:

Sucia arena.

Muchacha 2ª:

Sobre la flor del oro.

Niña:

Sobre la flor del oro
traen a los muertos del arroyo.
Morenito el uno,
morenito el otro.
¡Qué ruiseñor de sombra, vuela y gime
sobre la flor del oro!

(*Se va. Queda la escena sola. Aparece la madre con una vecina. La vecina viene llorando.*)

Madre: Calla.
Vecina: No puedo.

Dead, yes, dead.

First girl:

Hush, old woman, hush!

Beggar:

Their eyes are shattered flowers and their teeth
two fistfuls of hard snow. Both have fallen
and the bride is coming home, her skirt
and her hair stained with blood. They come
under two cloths, on the shoulders of tall boys.
This happened, that is all. It is as it should be.
Dirty sand on the golden flower.

(*She exits. The girls lower their heads and exit swaying
rhythmically.*)

First girl:

Dirty sand.

Second girl:

On the golden flower.

Little girl:

They bring the dead
up from the creek
on the golden flower.
One with dark hair and dark eyes,
the other dark hair and dark eyes.
What nightingale of shadow moans and flies
over the golden flower!

(*She exits. The stage is vacant. The mother and a neigh-
bor appear. The neighbor is crying.*)

Mother: Hush.
Neighbor: I can't.

Madre: Calla, he dicho. (*En la puerta.*) ¿No hay nadie aquí? (*Se lleva las manos a la frente.*) Debía contestarme mi hijo. Pero mi hijo es ya un brazado de flores secas. Mi hijo es ya una voz oscura detrás de los montes. (*Con rabia a la vecina.*) ¿Te quieres callar? No quiero llantos en esta casa. Vuestras lágrimas son lágrimas de los ojos nada más, y las mías vendrán cuando yo esté sola, de las plantas de mis pies, de mis raíces, y serán más ardientes que la sangre.

Vecina: Vente a mi casa; no te quedes aquí.

Madre: Aquí, aquí quiero estar. Y tranquila. Ya todos están muertos. A media noche dormiré, dormiré sin que ya me aterren le escopeta o el cuchillo. Otras madres se asomarán a las ventanas, azotadas por la lluvia, para ver el rostro de sus hijos. Yo no. Yo haré con mi sueño una fría paloma de marfil que lleve camelias de escarcha sobre el camposanto. Pero no; camposanto no, camposanto no: lecho de tierra, cama que los cobija y que los mece por el cielo. (*Entra una mujer de negro que se dirige a la derecha y allí se arrodilla. A la vecina.*) Quítate las manos de la cara. Hemos de pasar días terribles. No quiero ver a nadie. La Tierra y yo. Mi llanto y yo. Y estas cuatro paredes. ¡Ay! ¡Ay! (*Se sienta transida.*)

Vecina: Ten caridad de ti misma.

Madre: (*Echándose el pelo hacia atrás.*) He de estar serena. (*Se sienta.*) Porque vendrán las vecinas y no quiero que me vean tan pobre. ¡Tan pobre! Una mujer que no tiene un hijo siquiera que poderse llevar a los labios.

(*Aparece la novia. Viene sin azahar y con un manto negro.*)

Vecina: (*Viendo a la novia, con rabia.*) ¿Dónde vas?

Novia: Aquí vengo.

Madre: (*A la vecina.*) ¿Quién es?

Vecina: ¿No la reconoces?

Madre: Por eso pregunto quién es. Porque tengo que no reconocerla, para no clavarle mis dientes en el cuello. ¡Víbora! (*Se dirige hacia la novia con ademán fulminante; se detiene. A la vecina.*) ¿La ves? Está ahí, y está llorando, y yo quieta sin arrancarle los ojos. No me entiendo. ¿Será que yo no quería a mi hijo? Pero ¿y su honra? ¿Dónde está su honra?

(*Golpea a la novia. Ésta cae al suelo.*)

Mother: Hush, I said. (*At the door.*) Is anyone home? (*She lifts her hands to her brow.*) My son should have answered me. But now my son is an armful of withered flowers. My son is a dark voice beyond the hills. (*Angrily, to the neighbor.*) Will you hush! I don't want crying in this house. Your tears come only from your eyes. And mine will come when I'm alone, up from the soles of my feet, from my roots, and they will be hotter than blood.

Neighbor: Come to my house, don't stay here.

Mother: Here. I want to stay here. Alone. Now they're all dead. At midnight I'll sleep, I'll sleep and never again be afraid of the knife or the gun. Other mothers will go to their windows battered by rain, and watch for the faces of their sons. Not me, no. Out of my dreams I will make a cold ivory dove carrying camellias of frost to the graveyard. But no graveyard—no. No graveyard—no. Bed of dirt that will cover them, bed that will cradle them in the sky. (*A woman comes in wearing black, turns to the right, and kneels. To the neighbor.*) Take your hands off your face. There are terrible days to come. I want to see no one. The dirt and me. My sobbing and me. And the four walls. Ay! Ay! (*She sits down, stricken.*)

Neighbor: Be kind to yourself.

Mother: (*Tossing her hair back.*) I have to be calm. (*She sits.*) The neighbors will come and I don't want them to see how poor I am. So poor! A woman without even a son to press to her lips.

> (*The bride appears, without her corsage and wearing a black cloak.*)

Neighbor: (*Seeing the bride. Angrily.*) Where are you going?

Bride: I'm coming here.

Mother: (*To the neighbor.*) Who is it?

Neighbor: Don't you know her?

Mother: That's why I'm asking who she is. I can't know her or I will sink my teeth into her throat. Snake! (*She walks toward the bride with a gesture of fury and stops. To the neighbor.*) Do you see her? Here she is, crying, and here I am—and I'm not tearing out her eyes. I don't understand myself. Didn't I love my son. And his honor? Where is his honor?

> (*She smacks the bride, who falls to the ground.*)

Vecina: ¡Por Dios! (*Trata de separarlas.*)

Novia: (*A la vecina.*) Déjala; he venido para que me mate y que me lleven con ellos. (*A la madre.*) Pero no con las manos; con garfios de alambre, con una hoz, y con fuerza, hasta que se rompa en mis huesos. ¡Déjala! Que quiero que sepa soy limpia, que estaré loca, pero que me pueden enterrar sin que ningún hombre se haya mirado en la blancura de mis pechos.

Madre: Calla, calla; ¿qué me importa eso a mí?

Novia: ¡Porque yo me fui con el otro, me fui! (*Con angustia.*) Tú también te hubieras ido. Yo era una mujer quemada, llena de llagas por dentro y por fuera, y tu hijo era un poquito de agua de la que yo esperaba hijos, tierra, salud; pero el otro era un río oscuro, lleno de ramas que acercaba a mí el rumor de los juncos y su cantar entre dientes. Y yo corría con tu hijo que era como un niñito de agua fría y el otro me mandaba cientos de pájaros que me impedían el andar y que dejaban escarcha sobre mis heridas de pobre mujer marchita, de muchacha acariciada por el fuego. Yo no quería, ¡óyelo bien!; yo no quería. ¡Tu hijo era mi fin y yo no lo he engañado, pero el brazo del otro me arrastró como un golpe de mar, como la cabezada de un mulo, y me hubiera arrastrado siempre, siempre, siempre, aunque hubiera sido vieja y todos los hijos de tu hijo me hubiesen agarrado de los cabellos!

(*Entra una vecina.*)

Madre: Ella no tiene la culpa, ¡ni yo! (*Sarcástica.*) ¿Quién la tiene, pues? ¡Floja, delicada, mujer de mal dormir, es quien tira una corona de azahar para buscar un pedazo de cama calentado por otra mujer!

Novia: ¡Calla, calla! Véngate de mí; ¡aquí estoy! Mira que mi cuello es blando; te costará menos trabajo que segar una dalia de tu huerto. Pero ¡eso no! Honrada, honrada como una niña recién nacida. Y fuerte para demostrártelo. Enciende la lumbre. Vamos a meter las manos; tú, por tu hijo, yo, por mi cuerpo. Las retirarás antes tú.

(*Entra otra vecina.*)

Neighbor: Please God, no. (*She tries to part them.*)

Bride: (*To the neighbor.*) Let her, I came so that she would kill me and send me away with them. (*To the mother.*) But not with your hands! With a hook, with a sickle—hit me hard till it breaks in my bones. Let her! I want her to know I'm clean, and I may be mad; and they can bury me—but no man has seen the whiteness of my breasts.

Mother: Quiet, what can that matter to me?

Bride: I went with the other man, I went with him! (*Anguished.*) You would have gone too. I was on fire inside, all wounds inside and out, and your son was a trickle of water who would give me children and land and health. But the other was a dark river full of branches, bringing me the sound of the rushes and singing through his teeth. And I was with your son who was like a little boy, a little cold water; and the other sent me flocks of birds that hampered my feet when I walked and spread frost on my wounds. The wounds of a little withered woman, a girl stroked by fire. I didn't want it, hear me say it! I didn't want it. Your son was my purpose and I didn't deceive him. But the other man's arm was like the sea, dragging at me, a mule yanking its head, and he would have yanked at me always always always—I could have been an old woman, and the sons of your son would have held me back by the hair.

(*A neighbor enters.*)

Mother: She's not to blame and I'm not to blame. (*Sarcastic.*) Who is, then? Weak sleepless woman tosses away a crown of orange blossoms for the corner of a bed warmed by another woman!

Bride: Hush, hush! Take revenge! Here I am! Look how soft my throat is; it will be easier to cut than the stem of a dahlia. But no! Honorable—honorable as a newborn girl. I can show you how strong I am. Light the fire. Let's put our hands in the flames, you for your son, me for my body. You'll take yours out first.

(*Another neighbor enters.*)

Madre: Pero ¿qué me importa a mí tu honradez? ¿Qué me importa tu muerte? ¿Qué me importa a mí nada de nada? Benditos sean los trigos, porque mis hijos están debajo de ellos; bendita sea la lluvia, porque moja la cara de los muertos. Bendito sea Dios, que nos tiende juntos para descansar.

(*Entra otra vecina.*)

Novia: Déjame llorar contigo.
Madre: Llora. Pero en la puerta.

(*Entra la niña. La novia queda en la puerta. La madre, en el centro de la escena.*)

Mujer: (*Entrando y dirigiéndose a la izquierda.*)
Era hermoso jinete,
y ahora montón de nieve.
Corrió ferias y montes
y brazos de mujeres.
Ahora, musgo de noche
le corona la frente.

Madre:

Girasol de tu madre,
espejo de la tierra.
Que te pongan al pecho
cruz de amargas adelfas;
sábana que te cubra
de reluciente seda,
y el agua forme un llanto
entre tus manos quietas.

Mujer:

¡Ay, que cuatro muchachos
llegan con hombros cansados!

Mother: But what does your honor matter to me! Your death, what does it matter to me? What nothing can matter to me! Blessed is the wheat, because my sons are beneath it; blessed is the rain, because it wets the faces of the dead. Blessed is God, who lays us together in rest.

(*Another neighbor enters.*)

Bride: Let me cry with you.
Mother: Cry, but at the door.

(*The little girl enters. The bride is standing at the door. The mother at center stage.*)

Wife: (*Entering and turning to the left.*)
        He was a handsome rider.
        Now a drift of snow.
        He rode through the fairs
        and over the hills and
        into the arms of women.
        Now the moss of night
        crowns his brow.

Mother:

        Sunflower of your mother,
        mirror of the dirt.
        May they lay a cross
        of bitter oleander on your chest,
        may the sheet cover you
        with shining silk,
        may the water sob
        between your quiet hands.

Wife:

        Ay, four boys are arriving
        with their shoulders tired out.

Novia:

> ¡Ay, que cuatro galanes
> traen a la muerte por el aire!

Madre:

> Vecinas.

Niña: (*En la puerta.*)

> Ya los traen.

Madre:

> Es lo mismo.
> La cruz, la cruz.

Mujeres:

> Dulces clavos,
> dulce cruz,
> dulce nombre
> de Jesús.

Novia:

> Que la cruz ampare a muertos y a vivos.

Madre:

> Vecinas: con un cuchillo,
> con un cuchillito,
> en un día señalado, entre las dos y las tres,
> se mataron los dos hombres del amor.
> Con un cuchillo,
> con un cuchillito
> que apenas cabe en la mano,
> pero que penetra fino
> por las carnes asombradas,
> y que se para en el sitio
> donde tiembla enmarañada
> la oscura raíz del grito.
> Y esto es un cuchillo,

Bride:

Ay, four handsome boys
carry death through the air.

Mother:

Neighbors.

Little Girl: (*At the door.*)

They're bringing them now.

Mother:

It's the same as ever.
The cross, the cross.

Women:

Sweet nails,
sweet cross,
sweet name of Jesus.

Bride:

May the cross shield the living and the dead.

Mother:

Neighbors: with a knife,
with a little knife,
on a given night, between two and three o'clock,
two men killed each other for love.
With a knife,
with a little knife
that barely fits in the hand,
but cuts neat
into the startled skin
and stops at the tangled
dark root of the scream.
And this is a knife,

un cuchillito
que apenas cabe en la mano;
pez sin escamas ni río,
para que un día señalado, entre las dos y las tres,
con este cuchillo
se queden dos hombres duros
con los labios amarillos.
Y apenas cabe en la mano,
pero que penetra frío
por las carnes asombradas
y allí se para, en el sitio
donde tiembla enmarañada
la oscura raíz del grito.

(Las vecinas, arrodilladas en el suelo, lloran.)

TELÓN

a little knife
that barely fits in the hand,
a fish with no scales and no river,
so that on a given night, between two and three o'clock,
this knife
leaves two hard men
with yellow lips.
It barely fits in the hand,
but cuts neat
into the startled skin
and stops at the trembling
dark root of the scream.

(*The neighbors are kneeling on the ground, crying.*)

CURTAIN

Note on the Composition of Poet in Spain

Lorca wrote his poems mostly in sequences, and in sets of sequences. "Poems," which opens this book, is not one of Lorca's sequences or titles. It is my title for an assemblage or montage of poems that I chose from the young work. Two poems are from the early Book of Poems; many from Suites; more from Songs; three were never part of a completed sequence.

Suites, which Lorca wrote in his early twenties, is a big grab bag made up of many sequences of short, narrow poems. Since the full Suites was not published until almost forty years after the poet's death, we don't know whether he would have published these poems, or in what shape or form. In among them are some small gems. After shuffling, sorting and revising, he eventually set them aside and moved on to write Poem of the Cante Jondo, a more fully achieved work that was not published until he was in his early thirties. Next, he ransacked Suites to create his second published book of poems, Songs, which is also a set of sequences of mostly short and often narrow poems.

Following Lorca's lead, I've done my own sorting and ransacking. I've chosen the poems I like best—taking freely from any of the sequences, and giving them a new order.

From Suites, I've retained only one full sequence, a short three-part suite called "Capriccios"; and two parts of a three-part suite called "Three Sunsets." From Songs, I've kept three full sequences, including the intriguingly experimental triptych, "Three Portraits with Shadow," which uses a different typography to represent the three shadows.

For Poem of the Cante Jondo, I've used the flamenco core—the part that reenacts types of cante jondo as words, while describing the culture of the gypsies. These are the four cante sequences, and the three brief sequences that follow.

I've given all other poem sequences in full and in the chronological order of their composition: Gypsy Ballads, The Tamarit Diwan, Lament for Ignacio Sánchez Mejías and Dark Love Sonnets. The play Blood Wedding—written close in time to The Tamarit Diwan—is given pride of place at the close of the book.

In the introduction, I explain the reason that I did not include Poet in New York or other poems of Lorca's avant-garde middle period.

The writings of Lorca—poems and plays—were published some under the poet's watch, some long after he was no longer with us. Since the titles don't always match those of the books in which they first appeared, and most of the books don't have publications in English with titles that match the original Spanish ones, I've chosen to handle them typographically as "works" in a classical sense, whether a set of eleven sonnets that can't fill a book, Dark Love Sonnets; a set of sequences that make a thick volume, Suites; or a play, Blood Wedding. All titles in English are therefore given in roman type, rather than italicized.

I've used Miguel García-Posada's four-volume *Obras completas* as my source text because it's my edition—the one I read. I picked up a copy of volume i, *Poesía*, in Madrid, the year it was published, and later got hold of the full set. I noticed while preparing my Spanish text that this editor followed Lorca's first editions and manuscripts devotedly, respecting his punctuation and other unusual nuances of style. Mario Hernández's edition of *Bodas de sangre* has also been helpful.

I came across both the love poem "[That blond from Albacete]" and the fragment of a dark love sonnet "[Oh hotel bed oh this sweet bed]" in an article in the Mexican newspaper *La Jornada* not long after the death of Lorca's sweetheart Juan Ramírez de Lucas. In the section on provenance that follows, there is a list of six poems published here, as far as I know, for the first time in English; it includes these two love poems.

The title of this book was suggested to me by Laura García-Lorca in a conversation we had over breakfast at the Residencia de Estudiantes. I was toying with "Poet of Spain," and she came back with "Poet *in* Spain."

Provenance of "Poems"

from Book of Poems

Trees · Árboles
Another Dream · Otro sueño

from Suites[*]

Space in the Clock · Claro de reloj
Caught · Cautiva
Songset · Puesta de canción
Fifth Page · Quinta página
All · Total
Forest of Clocks · Selva de los relojes
Curve · Curva
Western Sky · Poniente
First and Last Meditation · Meditación primera y última
[One . . . two . . . and three] · [Una . . . dos . . . y tres]
Sphinx Hour · La hora esfinge
Pan · Pan
Woodcutter · Leñador
from Three Sunsets · *de* Tres crepúsculos
Half Moon · Media luna
Delirium · Delirio
[And his eyes were] · [Y sus ojos tuvieron]—entitled "Epitaph for a
   Bird" in earlier editions
Lemon Grove · Limonar
Horizon · Horizonte
Siren · Sirena
[The mown field] · [El campo segado]
Alone · Solitario
From Here · [Desde aquí]

* "Space in the Clock" and "Caught" appeared in First Songs.

from Songs

Little Madrigal · Madrigalillo
[Narcissus] · [Narciso]
[On the green sky] · [Sobre el cielo verde]
Song of November and April · Canción de noviembre y abril
[Water where do you go] · [¿Agua, dónde vas?]
March Orchard · Huerto de marzo

Other poems

Song of the Little Death · Canción de la muerte pequeña
Omega · Omega
[To find a kiss of yours] · [Por encontrar un beso tuyo]

Poems published here for the first time in English

Siren · Sirena
[To find a kiss of yours] · [Por encontrar un beso tuyo]
[The mown field] · [El campo segado]
Another Dream · Otro sueño
[Oh hotel bed oh this sweet bed] · [¡Oh cama del hotel! ¡oh dulce cama!]
[That blond from Albacete] · [Aquel rubio de Albacete]

Notes to the Introduction

xvii "All that has black sounds has duende": Federico García Lorca, "Juego y teoría del duende," *Obras completas*, vol. 3, *Prosa*; this talk, translated into English by Christopher Maurer as "Play and Theory of the Duende," appears in *In Search of Duende* (New Directions, 1998).

xviii Dalí's criticism of his madly successful Gypsy Ballads: Christopher Maurer, *Sebastian's Arrows: Letters and Mementos of Salvador Dalí and Federico García Lorca* (Swan Isle Press, 2005).

xix expressed by Federico's sister Isabel in her memoir: Isabel García Lorca, *Recuerdos míos* (Tusquets Editores, 2002).

xxi a man attested that he had buried Lorca: Ian Gibson, *Federico García Lorca: A Life* (Faber & Faber, 1989).

xxi letter of inquiry from a French writer: Marcelle Auclair, author of *Enfances et mort de García Lorca* (Seuil, 1968).

xxi a police report was written: "Los documentos sobre la muerte de Lorca," Cadena Ser (cadenaser.com, Madrid), April 22, 2015.

xxi one writer suggested that some of the men: Miguel Caballero Pérez, *Las trece últimas horas en la vida de García Lorca* (La Esfera De Los Libros, 2011).

xxii distinguished art historian Juan Ramírez de Lucas: "El amor oscuro de García Lorca," *El País Cultura* (cultura.elpais.com, Madrid), May 9, 2012.

xxii read them to Pablo Neruda while soaking in a bathtub: Luis María Anson, "Lorca, Ramírez de Lucas, Rapún," *El Imparcial* (elimparcial.es, Madrid), June 28, 2015.

xxii roamed the countryside, listening to gypsy cantaores: Nelson A. Orringer, *Lorca in Tune with Falla* (University of Toronto Press, 2014).

xxii In it he proposed that cante jondo (deep song): "Arquitectura del cante jondo," in *Obras completas*, vol. 3, *Prosa;* an earlier talk on which this one is based has been translated into English by Christopher Maurer as "Deep Song," in *In Search of Duende*. Some of

Lorca's speculations about the evolution of cante jondo were later refuted by historians.

xxiv in his opus on haiku: Robert Hass, *The Essential Haiku: Versions of Basho, Buson & Issa* (Ecco Press, 1994).

xxx a talk he gave about Spanish lullabies: "Canciones de cuna españolas," in *Obras completas,* vol. 3, *Prosa.*

xxxiv tells us that the Arabic word *ghaẓal*: Peter Cole, *The Dream of the Poem: Hebrew Poetry from Muslim and Christian Spain, 950–1492* (Princeton University Press, 2007).

xxxv One commentator suggested that this hummingbird: Mario Hernández, introduction to *Diván del Tamarit, Llanto por Ignacio Sánchez Mejías, Sonetos* (Alianza Editorial, 1981).

xxxviii mourned their absence: Vicente Aleixandre, "Federico," *Hora de España,* no. 7 (1937), reprinted as the epilogue to Lorca, *Obras completas.*

xxxviii*n* not published in Francoist Spain until 1954: Federico García Lorca, *Obras completas* (Aguilar, 1954). And see: Arturo del Hoyo, "Un poeta reunido," *ABC Hemeroteca,* August 17, 1986.

xlv time-shifting is a convention of the traditional: W. S. Merwin, in the introduction to his *Spanish Ballads* (Doubleday Anchor, 1961).

xlvii*n* Neruda and others have said: Mario Hernández, "Jardin deshecho: los 'sonetos' de García Lorca," *El Crotalón,* vol. 1 (1984), and Pablo Neruda, *Para nacer he nacido* (Seix Barral, 1978).

xlix father collected all the manuscripts he could find: Isabel M. Reverte, "Lorca: la historia oculta de los sonetos de amor," *ABC Cultura* (ABC.es, Madrid), May 22, 2015.

xlix Francisco had, at his desk in New York: Hernández, "Jardin deshecho."

xlix in a Spanish-language literary review: Federico García Lorca, "Obras inéditas," *Revista Hispánica Moderna* 6, nos. 3–4 (July–Oct. 1940).

l reached Francisco folded into a letter: Hernández, "Jardin deshecho."

l*n* an edition of Lorca's poems in English: Federico García Lorca, *Selected Poems*, with preface by Francisco García Lorca (New Directions, 1955).

li in the widely read Madrid newspaper *ABC*: Federico García Lorca, "Sonetos de amor," *ABC Sabado Cultural*, no. 164, March 17, 1984.

li Many years afterward: Reverte, "Lorca: la historia oculta."

li*n* a hispanist and literary activist: Daniel Eisenberg, "Reaction to the Publication of the *Sonetos del amor oscuro*," *Bulletin of Hispanic Studies* 65 (1988).

li*n* the sonnets appeared in French: Federico García Lorca, *Oeuvre complète*, vol. 1, edited by André Belamich (La Pléiade, Gallimard, 1981).

lii Among the piles of manuscripts was a folder: Hernández, "Jardin deshecho."

lii Manolo tells us in his memoir: Manuel Fernández-Montesinos, *Lo que en nosotros vive* (Tusquets Editores, 2003).

lii all amorous love sought secrecy and shadow: Francisco Ayala, "Los réprobos," *ABC*, April 3, 1984: *"Muy verdad es que todo amor, y no sólo el homosexual, es amor oscuro; todo amor busca el secreto, la sombra . . ."*

lii the love described in the poems was universal: André Belamich, *"Esos sonetos son maravillosos y expresan sentimientos amorosos universales,"* quoted by Silvia Llopis in "Fin de una leyenda: La familia de García Lorca se decide a publicar los sonetos del amor oscuro," *Cambio 16* (April 2, 1984).

Bibliography

SOURCE TEXT

Obras completas. Edited by Miguel García-Posada. Galaxia Gutenberg. 1997. (With minor typographical and editorial corrections.) vol. 1, *Poesía*, vol. 2, *Teatro*, vol. 3, *Prosa*, and vol. 4, *Primeros escritos*.

ESSENTIAL EARLIER EDITIONS IN ENGLISH

Collected Poems. Edited by Christopher Maurer. Farrar, Straus & Giroux, 1991; revised, 2002. *Selected Verse*, 1994; revised, 2004.
Selected Poems. Edited by Francisco García Lorca and Donald Allen. New Directions, 1955; reissued with an introduction by W. S. Merwin, 1995.

MAJOR POETIC WORKS PUBLISHED DURING LIFETIME

Impressions and Landscapes · *Impresiones y viajes,* 1918
Book of Poems · *Libro de poemas,* 1921
Songs · *Canciones 1921–1924,* 1927
Gypsy Ballads · *Primer romancero gitano,* 1928
Poem of the Cante Jondo · *Poema del cante jondo,* 1931
Lament for Ignacio Sánchez Mejías · *Llanto por Ignacio Sánchez Mejías,* 1935
First Songs · *Primeras canciones,* 1936

MAJOR POETIC WORKS PUBLISHED POSTHUMOUSLY

Poet in New York · *Un poeta en Nueva York,* 1940 in New York and Mexico
The Tamarit Diwan · *Diván del Tamarit,* 1940 in New York and Argentina
Dark Love Sonnets · *Los sonetos del amor oscuro,* 1981 in France, 1984 in Spain
Suites · *Suites,* 1983 in Spain

Major Plays Produced During Lifetime

Mariana Pineda · *Mariana Pineda*
Blood Wedding · *Bodas de sangre*
Yerma · *Yerma*

Major Plays Produced Posthumously

The House of Bernarda Alba · *La casa de Bernarda Alba*
The Public · *El público*

About the Life and Work in English

García Lorca, Francisco. *In the Green Morning: Memories of Federico.* Translated by Christopher Maurer. 1986.
Gibson, Ian. *The Assassination of Federico García Lorca.* 1983.
Gibson, Ian. *Federico García Lorca.* 1989.
Hirsch, Edward. *The Demon and the Angel: Searching for the Source of Artistic Inspiration.* 2003.
Stainton, Leslie. *Lorca: A Dream of Life.* 1999.

About the Life and Work in Spanish

Cernuda, Luis. "Federico García Lorca (Recuerdo [Remembrance]) (1938)." *Obra completa.* Vol. 3, *Prosa II,* 1993.
Conejero, Alberto. *La piedra negra* (The black stone), a play. 2014.
García Lorca, Isabel. *Recuerdos míos* (My memories). 2002.
Gibson, Ian. *Lorca y el mundo gay* (Lorca and the gay world). 2007.
Hernández, Mario. Introductions to his editions of *Diván del Tamarit, Llanto por Ignacio Sánchez Mejías, Sonetos; Canciones 1921–1924;* and *Romancero gitano,* all 1981; *Poema del cante jondo,* 1982; and *Bodas de sangre,* 1984.

About Prosody and Music

García Gómez, Emilio. *Poemas arábigoandaluces.* 1930. *Las jarchas romances de la serie árabe en su marco.* 1965.
Navarro Tomás, Tomás. *Métrica española.* 1966.
Orringer, Nelson F. *Lorca in Tune with Falla.* 2014.

Acknowledgments

I am indebted to the work of Leslie Stainton, Christopher Maurer, Ian Gibson, Miguel García-Posada, Mario Hernández, Francisco García Lorca, and all the translators of Lorca who have come before me—in particular W. S. Merwin, who once told me that the subjects of poetry are love and death.

I want to thank Deborah Garrison, the late Mark Strand, Edward Hirsch, Luis Muñoz, Cyrus Cassells, Richard Zenith and Maricruz Bilbao for their counsel and encouragement.

Infinite thanks to Rigel Garcia de la Cabada, my first reader.

Special thanks, as well, to Laura García-Lorca for her warmth and insight, and for sharing her family history with me.

Special thanks to Leslie Stainton for her wonderful help with biographical matters.

Thanks to Dennis Nurkse for his generous and careful reading of the introduction.

Thanks to the archivists of the Fundación Federico García Lorca, Rosa María Illán and Sonia González, for their expert help with manuscripts, and to the librarians of the Biblioteca de la Residencia de Estudiantes, Alfredo Valverde and Javier Arias Bal, for their assistance with early editions.

Thanks as well to the staff of the Residencia de Estudiantes, which hosted me while I worked in the archive and library; above all to Pilar Manso.

Particular thanks to Ian Beilin, research librarian at Columbia University Libraries, for his invaluable assistance in procuring hard-to-find texts.

Thanks to Ryan Szpiech, Denis McCauley and Piers Amodia for their help in understanding Arabic and Persian literary forms.

Thanks to Sergio Sánchez-Monge Escardó, Pilar Serrano and María Elena Cuenca Rodríguez, for their help in understanding the forms and rhythms of cante jondo.

Thanks to Aranxta Romero and Isabel Anglada Rodríguez for their help with textual nuances.

Thanks to Linda Ollerenshaw and Marina di Piero for hosting me while I translated Blood Wedding.

Grateful acknowledgment to the magazines and reviews that first published some of these poems in their pages:

Agni: "Bells for the Dead" and "[The mown field]"
Antioch Review: "Ballad of the Black Sorrow," "The Gypsy Nun" and "Martyrdom of Santa Olalla"
Arkansas International: "Burla of Don Pedro on Horseback," "Hunter," "Little Madrigal," "March Orchard," "They Cut Down Three Trees," "Trees" and "[Water where do you go]"
Harvard Review: "The Guitar" and "Landscape"
Tinhouse: "The Marked Man"
Poem-A-Day: "[To find a kiss of yours]"
Poetry: "Ballad of the Moon Moon," "Of the Dark Doves" and "Two Evening Moons"
Poetry Northwest: "Curve," "Forest of Clocks," "Space in the Clock" and "Woodcutter"
Southwest Review: "Little Song of the Boy Who Wasn't Born," "Poem of the Fair" and "Window Nocturnes"

And to *Hopkins Review,* for publishing Act One, SCENE TWO and Act Three, SCENE ONE of Blood Wedding

Index of Titles in Spanish

Index of Titles in English

A NOTE ON THE TYPE

This book was sent in Fournier, a typeface named for Pierre Simon Fournier *le jeune* (1712–1768), a celebrated French type designer. He was the author of the important *Manuel typographique* (1764–1766), in which he attempted to work out a system standardizing type measurement in points, a system that is still in use internationally.

Fournier's type is considered transitional in that it drew its inspiration from the old style yet was ingeniously innovational, providing for an elegant, legible appearance. In 1925 his type was revived by the Monotype Corporation of London.

Composed by North Market Street Graphics, Lancaster, Pennsylvania
Printed and bound by Berryville Graphics, Berryville, Virginia
Designed by Peter A. Andersen